FROM THE FOREST TO THE SEA

The management of common pool resources and publicly owned areas is fraught with difficulty. This book explores the long, complex, and frequently contentious history of public lands management in the United States in order to draw lessons for the emerging field of marine spatial planning (MSP).

The author first establishes that these two seemingly different settings are in fact remarkably similar, drawing on established theories of policy analysis. The work then examines the management of U.S. National Forests over the past 120 years, including three place-based case studies, to discover recurring themes. The analysis shows how different management approaches evolved over time in response to changing laws and cultural norms, producing outcomes favored by different constituencies. This history also reveals the ambiguities and contradictions inherent in multiple-use management of any public space. Next, the book analyzes recent efforts to advance MSP, both in the U.S. and globally, showing how they mirror past experiences in National Forest management, including similar disagreements among stakeholders.

In conclusion the author suggests how those within ocean-related sectors—government, academia, industry, and environmental groups—might achieve their individual and collective goals more effectively based on lessons from the public lands setting.

Morgan Gopnik is an Environmental Policy Consultant based in Washington, D.C., USA, with over 20 years of professional experience in ocean policy. Recent clients include the Gordon and Betty Moore Foundation, the American Petroleum Institute, NOAA's Coastal Services Center, the Foundation for Ocean Renewables, and the Nicholas Institute for Environmental Policy Solutions at Duke University, North Carolina, among others. She was previously the Director of the Ocean Studies Board at the National Academy of Sciences and Senior Adviser to the U.S. Commission on Ocean Policy. Dr. Gopnik holds a PhD from Duke University.

"Morgan Gopnik presents an engaging analysis and balanced view of the tensions that challenge the practice of marine spatial planning, while drawing compelling parallels to the resolution of similarly contentious issues in the realm of public lands management. *From the Forest to the Sea* illustrates the importance of drawing on past lessons to inform a more rational and durable approach to managing our ocean resource for the future. An important and timely work."

Deerin Babb-Brott, Senior Partner, SeaPlan, USA and former Director of the White House National Ocean Council

"Morgan Gopnik brings her unique and diverse perspectives to the slippery issue of ocean ecosystem management. Although marine spatial planning is new, she shows that we can rely on a century's experience in public lands management to probe the abyss. Gopnik argues that sustainability, for marine ecosystems and the communities that depend upon them, requires broad engagement and dialog rather than pernicious advocacy. Gopnik's vision suggests a possible win–win for oceans and marine economies that we should all take very seriously—if we truly want a brighter future for the ocean."

Larry Crowder, Science Director, Center for Ocean Solutions, Professor of Biology, Hopkins Marine Station and Senior Fellow, Stanford Woods Institute for the Environment

"Morgan Gopnik takes her readers on a voyage through the 100-year history of US public lands management, focusing on forest management, pointing out insights and lessons that can be used by a growing community interested in effectively managing the multiple uses of another public resource—the ocean space of nations. A must read for everyone in the international marine planning community."

Charles Ehler, consultant to UNESCO's Marine Spatial Management Initiative and former senior executive at the National Oceanic and Atmospheric Administration

"A growing number of states and regions in the United States are utilizing marine spatial planning as a tool to manage their coastal and offshore waters. As decision-makers, businesses, and community stakeholders work together to find holistic solutions for sustainable ocean use and a healthy ecosystem, Morgan Gopnik's research provides an insightful tour of what has gone before. Ocean planning may be relatively new in the United States, but planning for sustainable use of public resources is not, and the lessons learned in over a century of public land management provide valuable advice for planning in our oceans."

Sandra T. Whitehouse, Senior Policy Advisor to Ocean Conservancy, USA.

FROM THE FOREST TO THE SEA

Public lands management and marine spatial planning

Morgan Gopnik

Routledge
Taylor & Francis Group
LONDON AND NEW YORK
earthscan
from Routledge

First published 2015
by Routledge

2 Park Square, Milton Park, Abingdon, Oxfordshire OX14 4RN
711 Third Avenue, New York, NY 10017

Routledge is an imprint of the Taylor & Francis Group, an informa business

First issued in paperback 2017

British Library Cataloguing-in-Publication Data
A catalogue record for this book is available from the British Library

Library of Congress Cataloging-in-Publication Data
Gopnik, Morgan, author.
From the forest to the sea : public lands management and marine spatial planning / Morgan Gopnik.
pages cm
1. Public lands–United States–Management–History. 2. Forest policy–United States–History. 3. Marine spatial planning. I. Title.
HD216.G67 2014
352.570973–dc23
2014015371

ISBN: 978-1-138-01442-8 (hbk)
ISBN: 978-0-8153-9534-8 (pbk)

Typeset in Baskerville
by GreenGate Publishing Services, Tonbridge, Kent

CONTENTS

FIGURES

TABLES

BOXES

PREFACE

I have spent most of my professional career thinking about environmental policy issues, particularly those related to ocean and coastal management, in positions at the National Academy of Sciences, environmental advocacy groups, federal agencies, and the U.S. Commission on Ocean Policy. But the idea of looking seriously at the similarities between land and ocean management first took root during the National Academy of Sciences' Roger Revelle Lecture, presented by Dr. Michael Orbach in 2003. In that thought-provoking talk, Orbach concluded that "ocean space and resources are not significantly different from the terrestrial and atmospheric in terms of functionally appropriate governance institutions."

Around the same time, I developed an interest in the emerging concept of marine spatial planning (MSP), strengthened by attendance at a UNESCO MSP workshop held in 2005 and the fact that a number of people I respect and admire, including Larry Crowder, Fanny Douvere, Charles Ehler, Barry Gold, Elliott Norse and others, were actively promoting MSP as an innovative approach for achieving more holistic, integrated, and effective ocean management.

These two streams of interest came together while doing research for a report to the Gordon and Betty Moore Foundation (Gopnik 2008), during which I first delved into the history of public lands management in the U.S. and was surprised to see how the debates, conflicts, players, and trends often mirrored what I knew of the ocean policy story. I decided that nothing short of an in-depth doctoral dissertation could do the subject justice, and headed back to school after a twenty-year career. Over the next four years, with financial support from Duke University and intellectual support from many friends and colleagues, I immersed myself in the intertwined study of public lands management (as it has played out for over 100 years) and marine spatial planning (as it is just being conceptualized and implemented around the world), which forms the basis of this book. Along the way, I took several fascinating and enlightening detours, learning about theories of policy analysis, the limitations of policy transfer, the potential for structured dialogue to overcome conflict, and the dangers of rationalist hubris. This book presents both the process and results of my research and reveals my emerging understanding of the challenges inherent in managing publicly owned resources. At the end of the book—keenly aware that there are no simple answers—I make some suggestions about how elected and appointed officials, agency staff, environmental organizations, industry, and academia might approach ocean management in a way that better reflects a variety of interests, advances understanding, and achieves sustainable and productive ocean ecosystems.

Those concerned directly with improving ocean and coastal management, particularly in the U.S., can use this book to gain valuable insights into the world of their forest management peers. The book should also prove stimulating and useful to the international ocean policy community, resource managers in other settings, academic faculties and students working to better understand the theory and practice of resource management, and anyone interested in how nations go about making decisions concerning the use, allocation, and long-term preservation of natural resources.

I could not have completed this project without the help of many others. First, I owe my thanks to the scores of people who shared their time and insights with me over the course of this study, from high-level officials in government, industry, and civil society to ordinary citizens who care about their land and ocean patrimony. Their words make this document come alive. Professionally, I am grateful to Mike Orbach, who first inspired my interest in the subject and guided my subsequent exploration; Larry Crowder, an early supporter and consistent cheerleader for my efforts; Xavier Basurto, who opened my eyes to the world of rigorous policy analysis; and Josh Eagle, my first guide to the previously unfamiliar world of public lands management. I am also indebted to Andrew Thaler, a friend and colleague, who took the time to read the final manuscript, provided insightful suggestions, and gave me the confidence to believe that others would be interested in what I had to say.

On a personal note, my two incomparable parents and five extraordinary brothers and sisters shaped me from my earliest years. I am continually gratified by their loyalty, encouragement, and insights. A wider circle of dear friends consistently challenges, amuses, and sustains me. But the three people who undoubtedly sacrificed the most during the completion of this book are my husband, Tom, and two sons, Adrian and Trevor. Without their love and support, none of it would have been possible.

ACRONYMS

ACF	Advocacy Coalition Framework
ADR	Alternate Dispute Resolution
BLM	Bureau of Land Management
CEQ	Council on Environmental Quality
CMSP	coastal and marine spatial planning (a variant of MSP)
EBM	ecosystem-based management
ECR	Environmental Conflict Resolution
EEZ	exclusive economic zone
EIS	environmental impact statement
ENGO	environmental non-governmental organization
ESA	Endangered Species Act
FACA	Federal Advisory Committee Act
FEMAT	Forest Ecosystem Management Assessment Team
FOIA	Freedom of Information Act
FWS	Fish and Wildlife Service
GLO	General Land Office
IAD	Institutional Analysis and Design
LME	large marine ecosystem
LPE	local public economy
MMBF	million board feet
MSFCMA	Magnuson-Stevens Fishery Conservation and Management Act
MSP	marine (or maritime) spatial planning
MUSY	Multiple-Use Sustained Yield Act
NEPA	National Environmental Policy Act
NFMA	National Forest Management Act
NGO	non-governmental organization
NMFS	National Marine Fisheries Service
NOAA	National Oceanic and Atmospheric Administration
NOC	National Ocean Council
NOP	National Ocean Policy
NOPP	National Oceanographic Partnership Program
NRC	National Research Council

OCSLA	Outer Continental Shelf Lands Act
PTD	public trust doctrine
RARE	Roadless Area Review and Evaluation
RCW	Red-cockaded Woodpecker
RFA	Recreational Fishing Alliance
RPA	Forest and Rangelands Renewable Resources Planning Act
RPB	Regional Planning Body
TSP	terrestrial spatial planning
U.N.	United Nations
UNCLOS	U.N. Convention (or Conference) on the Law of the Sea
UNESCO	United Nations Educational, Scientific and Cultural Organization
USCOP	U.S. Commission on Ocean Policy
USDA	U.S. Department of Agriculture

1

INTRODUCTION

From "untamable" to regulated seas

Although ocean waters cover over 70 percent of the Earth's surface, the governance and management of this space is in its infancy compared to that on land. For most of recorded history, people have viewed the ocean as "wild, unruly, and untamable" (Steinberg 2001), considering it "a source of inexhaustible resources, the use of which need not be restricted" (Orbach 2003). Gradually, as technology advanced and oceans became more accessible, people began to occupy this space and exploit its resources to ever greater extents. This in turn led to expanding efforts by nations to control access to ocean space and the use of its resources (Russ and Zeller 2003). By the middle of the 20th century, ocean waters were home to intensive nearshore recreational activities, large international fishing operations, ever-deeper offshore oil extraction, and a tangle of commercial and military ship routes, while ocean management remained relatively weak and Balkanized by sector.

Through the end of the millennium, single-issue ocean laws and programs multiplied while the scientific study of marine ecosystems became more sophisticated. Problems such as declining fish stocks, the loss of large predators, changes in marine biodiversity, marine debris, endangered species, coastal habitat loss, hypoxic "dead zones," and ocean acidification became increasingly evident, as documented in multiplying scientific publications (e.g., NRC 1990; Gray 1997; Pauly et al. 1998; and Rabalais and Turner 2013, among many others) and disseminated to broader audiences in reports from highly regarded sources such as the Millennium Ecosystem Assessment (2005, Chs. 18 and 19) and the U.S. Commission on Ocean Policy (USCOP 2004a). Explanations for the declines in ocean health pointed to human behavior as the major culprit, highlighting the impacts of overfishing, coastal development, point and non-point source pollution, and climate change. In response, spokespeople, activists, and new organizations emerged to publicize and combat these problems, using time-tested advocacy tools such as media campaigns, grassroots organizing, political lobbying, lawsuits, and public education.

The solutions proposed varied from tighter regulation and better enforcement (e.g., Graham and Reilly 2011), to market mechanisms (e.g., Wilen 2000), community-based management (e.g., Jentoft 2000), marine protected areas (e.g., NRC 2001), and more. Marine ecosystem-based management (EBM), defined in a consensus statement as "an integrated approach to management that considers the entire ecosystem, including humans" (COMPASS 2005), has been frequently advanced as a more effective approach for managing complex and highly interconnected marine ecosystems (e.g., McLeod and Leslie 2009). However, despite several attempts to articulate the necessary elements of EBM, widely disparate programs have been labeled as such, including the California Marine Life Protection Act process, the Great Barrier Reef re-zoning project, the U.S. National Marine Sanctuaries Program, and other efforts that share little more than their commitment to being more holistic than traditional management (Arkema et al. 2006). An ambitious, collaborative project recently analyzed marine EBM efforts around the world,[1] summarizing many of their common features and suggesting lessons learned, although it is likely to take some time for these lessons to be confirmed and to make their way into practice.

A different approach: marine spatial planning[2]

One approach that was advanced sporadically over the years, but gained little traction, suggested that comprehensive, multiple-use planning of ocean space would help in coping with the complexities of marine ecosystems and human uses (see Young and Fricke 1975; Knecht and Kitsos 1984; Juda and Burroughs 1990). Almost forty years ago, Young and Fricke wrote:

> Sea use planning, we believe, is a necessary intellectual tool ... to seize hold of some of the problems that so far have been too slippery ... Because of the multiplicity of competitive, and potentially damaging uses, sea use now needs to be ordered and controlled ... in the interests of the community as a whole.

The writings of these authors seem prescient in light of recent developments.

By the start of the 21st century, the call for planning in the marine environment—which has gone by many names in its brief life, including ocean zoning, ocean planning, maritime spatial planning, sea-use planning, area-based ocean management, and marine spatial planning (MSP)—was being actively taken up in a number of countries (Rothwell and VanderZwaag 2006; Douvere and Ehler 2009). The most widely cited definition of MSP describes it as "a public process of analyzing and allocating the spatial and temporal distribution of human activities in marine areas to achieve ecological, economic, and social objectives" (Ehler and Douvere 2009), but the term has been used to describe a wide range of management activities in the ocean, from siting marine protected areas to regional fisheries management, that fail to meet all those criteria. A more general definition is offered in a report to the United Nations' Global Environment Facility: "MSP is a framework which provides a means for improving decision-making as it relates to the use of marine resources and space. It is based on principles of the ecosystem approach and ecosystem-based management" (GEF 2012).

Although Australia had undertaken spatial planning of the Great Barrier Reef Marine Park for decades—and many MSP proponents point to their approach as a model—that effort was driven primarily by a marine conservation mission rather than being propelled by an integrated, multiple-use perspective. Experiments and pilot projects in "true" MSP were conducted in the early 2000s in Ireland, Belgium, and Canada. One study of the genesis of MSP (Merrie and Olsson 2014) found that a relatively small group of individuals, embedded in formal and informal networks, were key to framing MSP as a solution and promoting its spread around the world. The process started with a National Center for Ecological Analysis and Synthesis Working Group that met four times in 2005 and 2006 and published an influential article in *Science* magazine (Crowder et al. 2006). That article summarized growing concerns about marine ecosystems worldwide and stated the authors' belief that "marine spatial planning with comprehensive ocean zoning can help address these problems." In November of that year, with partial funding from the California-based Gordon and Betty Moore Foundation,[3] the United Nations Educational, Scientific and Cultural Organization (UNESCO) hosted the first international meeting devoted to the developing theory and practice of MSP. The forty-nine attendees included academics and practitioners from seventeen countries, including twelve Americans, and the resulting workshop report is considered by many to have put MSP on the map (Ehler and Douvere 2007). Dozens of countries around the world are currently engaged in some version of MSP, as discussed further in Chapter 8.

In the U.S. the adoption of MSP moved more slowly. In 2004, after three years of public hearings, research, and deliberations, a blue-ribbon commission issued a report (USCOP 2004a) that highlighted the need for greater agency coordination and regional flexibility in U.S. ocean management. In particular, Recommendation 6.2 stated that "Congress … should establish a balanced, ecosystem-based offshore management regime that sets forth guiding principles for the coordination of offshore activities." At the time of the USCOP's deliberations, the relatively new term "marine spatial planning" was not well established in U.S. policy circles and does not appear anywhere in the final report. Nevertheless, Recommendation 6.2, and the reasoning behind it, foreshadowed events to come.

In early 2007, an informal poll was conducted at a meeting of U.S. ocean policy experts hosted by the Ocean Conservancy in Washington, D.C. Predictions for when MSP might be implemented in the U.S. ranged from eight to twenty years, with an average of around twelve years.[4] Participants saw few economic drivers and little political support for such an approach to be adopted in the U.S. at that time. Yet only two years later, in 2009, Massachusetts had prepared an Ocean Plan for its waters, Rhode Island and Oregon had similar plans underway, and a Presidential Memorandum had directed an interagency taskforce to develop a national "framework for effective coastal and marine spatial planning" (White House 2009). To top off this eventful year, the December 2009 issue of *Scientific American* included MSP as one of its twenty "World Changing Ideas." As of this writing, active steps are being taken in Washington, D.C. and nine regions around the country to launch marine planning efforts, looking largely to MSP implementation in Europe and elsewhere for justification, guidance, and models. This is a remarkable pace for embracing a significant new policy direction—in ocean management or any other area—based on little track record and scant national dialogue.

Looking critically at marine spatial planning

Not everyone has embraced MSP as a desirable next step in ocean management. Some ocean industry sectors, particularly offshore oil and gas and international shipping, worry that MSP "could create uncertainty and harm economic activity" and that "the policy is being developed without adequate congressional engagement and consideration of the views of ocean, coastal, Great Lakes, and inland user groups, including commercial and recreational interests" (NOPC 2012). A series of workshops organized by Duke University's Nicholas Institute for Environmental Policy Solutions brought together a broad array of ocean users who expressed similar concerns, albeit with greater optimism that they might be overcome (Gopnik et al. 2012). The U.S. House of Representatives' Natural Resources Committee has held a number of hearings highly critical of this new direction in ocean policy,[5] and released a number of disparaging—and not entirely accurate—factsheets and press releases deploring its adoption (e.g., House Resources Committee 2011). Groups representing fishermen decry efforts that might reduce their access to ocean waters (e.g., RFA 2009; CCA 2012), and a conservative website ominously speculates that: "CMSP has the potential for the greatest encroachment on private property rights we have ever faced in this nation ... CMSP has the potential for turning over control of commercial and recreational fishing to the United Nations" (*Beaufort Observer* 2012).

Even groups that are generally supportive of MSP worry that their constituencies' concerns may not be given sufficient weight. For example, public comments on a proposed federal framework for MSP reveal that environmental advocates believe that ecosystem protection, including the siting of additional marine protected areas, should trump economic goals, while renewable energy advocates worry that any new planning process might interfere with their ongoing efforts to obtain permits for offshore facilities. But beyond such sector-specific concerns, more fundamental questions arise:

- *Is MSP being oversold as the overarching solution to ocean governance problems?* Public policy scholars warn against the "perverse and extensive use of policy panaceas in misguided efforts to make ... human-environment systems sustainable" and "the danger of blueprint approaches to the governance of tough social-ecological problems" (Ostrom 2007). Ostrom recommends instead adopting a more analytic, diagnostic approach, whereby each situation is treated as a unique combination of human and ecological variables necessitating uniquely designed solutions. Already, some observers have suggested that the focus on MSP is stealing attention away from more specific problems and more targeted solutions (e.g., Spalding 2011).
- *Might MSP be undermined by the common pitfalls of centralized, technocratic approaches?* James Scott's landmark studies of projects as diverse as Prussian forestry, Soviet collective farms, and the design of Brazil's capital city, Brasilia, provide ample lessons about the perils of large, centralized, "scientific" government projects that fail to perceive or allow for human psychology and pre-existing social patterns (Scott 1998). These cautionary tales raise concerns about whether rapid, nationwide implementation of MSP based on a federal framework might override existing, functional policy systems and decrease management experimentation at local and regional scales.
- *Can experience with MSP implementation in other countries serve as a valid model for U.S. practice?* As MSP moves forward in the U.S., managers have primarily relied on lessons learned in other countries. However, a substantial body of research, coming largely out of the international development community, has explored the limitations associated with transferring seemingly successful policy approaches from one country to another (e.g., Rose 1991; Bennett and Howlett 1992; Dolowitz and Marsh 1996; de Jong et al. 2002). Existing "guides" to MSP, based on experiences in Europe, Canada, Australia, and elsewhere (e.g., Ehler and Douvere 2009), may not be fully applicable in the very different U.S. context where there is a history of strong private property rights and individual freedoms, and substantial mistrust of government programs, federal mandates, and the very notion of central planning.

To reconcile the promise and potential pitfalls of MSP and achieve a realistic assessment of its likely outcomes, MSP needs to be examined in a critical light, using the available tools and accumulated wisdom of policy analysts and natural resource governance scholars, informed by appropriate historical perspective. Unfortunately, much of the current thinking and writing on ocean policy, notably including the two recent commission reports (Pew Oceans Commission 2003 and USCOP 2004a), does not provide such links between theory and practice (Duff 2004). In fact, Kidd and Ellis observe that MSP's "core concepts and assumptions ... have not been subject to rigorous intellectual debate" (Kidd and Ellis 2012).

Exploring marine spatial planning through a different lens

Proponents of MSP frequently explain it to new audiences using analogies to the more familiar and widespread practice of urban land-use planning (e.g., Tyldesley and Hunt 2003; Gopnik 2008; Agardy 2010). Although this has proved helpful in conveying the general concept to lay audiences, the analogy is fundamentally flawed. Land-use plans guide the use of property—largely privately owned—in densely populated areas to achieve certain economic and quality-of-life goals typically determined through a political process. These conditions are far different from those in the ocean. Within 200 miles of shore, with few exceptions, the unpopulated ocean and its resources are already considered a *public good*, to be managed by national governments for the welfare of their citizens (Turnipseed et al. 2010). Thus, a more promising avenue might be to compare ocean planning and management to that undertaken for other common-pool resources—such as public land and certain government services—that have been more thoroughly studied. As explained by Duff (2004): "Ocean areas are *public* space. As a result, the more apt models that ought to be considered in assessing ocean space/resource management issues are those models that have been employed to manage other *public* areas and resources" (emphasis added).

The purpose of this book and the research on which it is based is to place ocean management, and MSP particularly, within the broader context of research and practice in fields such as policy analysis, common-pool resource theory, institutional analysis, planning and design, community engagement, and conflict resolution, and to look at the history of U.S. public lands management as a promising comparative model. In preliminary interviews, individuals who had experience in only one of land or ocean management were very resistant to the idea that the two systems might be compared. They focused, instead, on elements that seemed different and foreign to them, hardly able to imagine what a landscape of mountains, streams, and forests, with its associated communities of loggers, hikers, and hunters, might have in common with beaches, coral reefs, and wide-open waters plied by surfers, boaters, fishermen, and container ships. However, a handful of individuals who had substantial experience in both settings jumped at the suggestion of similarities, eager to discuss the overlaps they had observed. As reported by one staff-member at an ocean advocacy group who had previously worked for many years on forest policy: "As soon as I started working on ocean issues, I saw the similarities. But I've become reluctant to say anything, because my ocean colleagues can't see it."

At the heart of this inquiry lie three questions:

1 Are U.S. public lands and U.S.-controlled ocean space (i.e., the exclusive economic zone [EEZ]) sufficiently similar, based on the variables deemed important by policy analysts, that successes and failures in one arena might be relevant to the other?
2 If so, has over 100 years of active public land management in the U.S. produced any lessons that might inform the more recently developing field of ocean management, particularly with respect to multiple-use planning and management?
3 *If* the settings are similar in meaningful ways, and *if* lessons can be distilled from public lands management, how might these be translated to inform the current drive for more integrated ocean management, particularly through the tool of marine spatial planning?

Embedded in these broad questions is a suite of subsidiary theoretical and practical inquiries, such as: What kinds of similarities (or differences) are likely to make policy comparisons meaningful? What is the meaning of policy "success" and "failure" and, thus, what constitutes a "lesson"? Is there any agreement about what approaches have worked best on land? Can success be translated from one policy context to another? Fortunately, there is a substantial body of ongoing research in each of these areas on which to draw.

The analysis presented in this book does not follow one overarching theoretical framework or political perspective on resource management. Instead, it looks to a wide range of scholars, disciplines, analytic approaches, and policy theories—many of which were developed within different academic traditions and exhibit little recognition of the others—in order to extract whatever knowledge and insights seem helpful for answering the questions at hand. This tactic is succinctly endorsed in one influential study of multiorganizational systems where the author unapologetically admits to "borrowing freely from whatever theories seemed most useful for understanding the problem" (Chisholm 1989).

Guide to this book

This book is organized to follow the trajectory of my thinking and research on these subjects. Chapter 2 lays the groundwork by providing an overview of the history of federally managed spaces on land and in the ocean. It outlines the transition in the ocean from "freedom of the seas," to declaration of EEZs and development of ocean laws and agencies. It then reviews the genesis of U.S. public lands and the agencies that oversee them. The National Forests, with their diverse ecosystems and multiple-use mandate, emerge as the most apt analogy for management challenges in the EEZ. In an effort to improve on previous ad-hoc comparisons of terrestrial and ocean systems, Chapter 3 develops a more structured study approach based on the theoretical literature on natural resource governance and public policy. I pinpoint the variables considered most critical to understanding a given policy situation, and thus most likely to support or negate the validity of land–ocean comparisons. The set of variables thus identified helps guide the remainder of the study.

Chapter 4 takes us back into the woods, offering an in-depth look at the extensive historical and theoretical literature on U.S. National Forests, with a focus on the evolution of forest management approaches in the 20th century, the forces that drove them, and the outcomes that resulted. Because most readers of this work are assumed to come from the ocean policy community and may know little about forest management, this history is presented in some detail. Chapters 5 and 6 supplement this account with the results of two National Forest case studies, one in Oregon and one in coastal North Carolina. Based on site visits, conversations with professionals and community members in those locations, formal interviews with key decision-makers, and analyses of official government documents, these case studies add nuance and a human voice to the overview of forest history. Chapter 7 summarizes the key findings from the exploration of forest management history, identifying themes and potential "lessons" that might be applicable to the ocean setting.

Chapter 8 brings us back to the ocean, looking at recent MSP developments around the world, particularly current U.S. efforts to implement its new National Ocean Policy (NOP), to see how they compare to the lessons set out in Chapter 7. Recommendations are made about how ocean managers might learn from the past to advance their understanding of policy implications and better achieve their goals. Finally, the book closes with an unabashedly optimistic vision of how each participant in the ocean community—broadly defined to include elected officials, agency staff, advocacy organizations, maritime industries, funders, academia, and the interested public—might fulfill their individual responsibilities while helping to realize collective aspirations for sustainable and productive ocean ecosystems.

Notes

1 See Marine Ecosystem-based Management in Practice, Ecosystem Management Initiative, University of Michigan School of Natural Resources and Environment. Accessed September 17, 2013 at http://webservices.itcs.umich.edu/drupal/mebm.

2 The terminology used to describe ocean planning has been quite inconsistent over time, and from place to place. The most common usage around the world and in the academic literature currently seems to be marine spatial planning, or MSP, and I adopt that usage throughout this book.

3 The private Gordon and Betty Moore Foundation, a U.S.-based philanthropy, has played a significant role in advancing the adoption of marine spatial planning. Based on information posted on the Foundation's website (www.moore.org), it provided over $74 million in grant funding to support MSP from 2006 through 2013.

4 Meeting notes on file with the author.

5 U.S. House Resources Committee Oversight Hearings on "The President's New National Ocean Policy—A Plan for Further Restrictions on Ocean, Coastal and Inland Activities," October 4, 2011 and October 26, 2011; Oversight Hearing on "Empty Hooks: The National Ocean Policy is the Latest Threat to Access for Recreational and Commercial Fishermen," March 22, 2012; Oversight Field Hearing on "Alaska's Sovereignty in Peril: The National Ocean Policy's Goal to Federalize Alaska," April 3, 2012.

2

PUBLIC LAND/PUBLIC OCEAN

To kick off this exploration of whether and how oceans and forests may be similar, I begin by describing the jurisdictional, administrative, and management features of these two spaces, within the U.S. context. Understanding how these areas have traditionally been viewed and how they have evolved over time is critical to deciding whether it will be valid or useful to compare their governance institutions. Fortunately, an enormous amount of documentation and scholarship exists to address these questions, and I draw on it extensively in the following discussion.

Comparing two federally controlled spaces

The U.S. is a vast country, exceeded in area only by Russia, approximately the same size as China and Canada, and more than twice as large as all European Union countries combined. It includes 3.6 million square miles of land and exerts various forms of authority over another 4.5 million square miles of open water in the Great Lakes and the ocean. Of the total land area, 62 percent is privately owned, the federal government owns approximately 27 percent, and the remaining 11 percent is under the control of Indian tribes and state and local governments.[1] In the ocean, there is local control at the coastline, and state governments control nearshore waters, but the federal government has jurisdiction over the far larger EEZ, extending from the boundary of state waters out to 200 miles from shore. It is significant that the terminology of "control" and "jurisdiction" over ocean areas differs from the concept of "ownership" on land. At this time, based on shared traditions, national laws, and international treaties, there is no private ownership of ocean territory (USCOP 2004b), as will be discussed further below.

This chapter explores two areas controlled primarily by the U.S. federal government, the EEZ and the public lands,[2] briefly outlining their genesis and modern-day features, noting their differences, and identifying some ways in which they are remarkably similar.

The U.S. exclusive economic zone

A brief history

For thousands of years, the global ocean was thought of as a vast expanse, unconquerable, fearsome, and inexhaustible.[3] From time to time, countries attempted to assert authority or ownership over ocean space, but these self-declared and unenforceable claims were mostly ignored by other nations wishing to ply the ocean for trade and military purposes. A 1608 treatise arguing for "Freedom of the Seas"[4] set out the guiding principle for maritime activities for the next 300 years, with repercussions for ocean management to this day. In its most general articulation, the Freedom of the Seas doctrine allowed ships of all nations to traverse ocean waters without hindrance, although its current incarnation, based on language in the U.N. Convention on the Law of the Sea (UNCLOS), is more complex (USCOP 2004b).

Over the same time period, there was general agreement that nations had a special interest in, and could exert a greater degree of control over, their coastal waters—assumed in the 17th and 18th centuries to be waters within reach of a cannon-shot from land, or around three miles. In 1793, shortly after declaring its newfound independence, the U.S. declared full sovereignty over the area within three miles of its shores, claiming powers equivalent to its control over land-based territory. (See Table 2.1 for a timeline of significant U.S. ocean management-related events.) Other coastal nations followed suit, establishing widespread acceptance of a three-mile Territorial Sea. For over 100 years, politicians, ocean scientists, and legal scholars continued to debate the appropriate level of control and ownership over ocean space, some rejecting restrictions even within three miles and others arguing that the zone of national control should be expanded, primarily to allow greater influence over fisheries resources. In 1898, a French scholar wrote, presciently, that there might be "one limit for the prohibition of hostile engagements, one limit for customs, one limit for fishing, one limit for jurisdiction; and even within the same group ... the limits may still vary" (quoted in Juda 1996).

By the turn of the 20th century, there was a growing recognition that the bright-line distinction between fully sovereign territorial seas and fully free high seas was insufficient to deal with the complexities of ocean management (Wenk 1972). This reality was accentuated by the profusion of new ocean uses, including trans-ocean cables, subsea mineral and fossil fuel extraction, and increasingly large-scale offshore fishing, as well as the growing realization that ocean waters and resources were being harmed by human activities. Different kinds of protections, liberties, and controls would be needed to promote national security, commerce, resource use, and conservation above, in, and beneath ocean waters. Decades of international meetings, expert committees, and draft treaties followed, but no agreement was concluded.

Table 2.1 Timeline of major U.S. ocean management-related events

Date	*Event*
1793	U.S. assertion of sovereignty over a 3-mile Territorial Sea
1945	Truman Proclamations on the Continental Shelf (U.S. control over outer continental shelf resources) and on Fisheries (U.S. ability to create fishery "conservation zones" outside territorial waters)
1953	Submerged Lands Act and Outer Continental Shelf Lands Act (OCSLA) passed; codified the Truman Proclamation on the Continental Shelf
1958	First UNCLOS
1969	Stratton Commission releases "Our Nation and the Sea"; National Environmental Policy Act (NEPA) and Endangered Species Act (ESA) passed
1970	National Oceanic and Atmospheric Administration (NOAA) created
1972	Coastal Zone Management Act, Marine Mammal Protection Act, Marine Sanctuaries Act, and Clean Water Act passed
1976	Magnuson Act asserts U.S. control over fisheries resources out to 200 miles
1978	OCSLA Amendments passed requiring detailed process for offshore oil and gas leasing
1982	UNCLOS adopted and opened for nation-state ratification
1983	U.S. claims 200-mile EEZ, in keeping with UNCLOS provisions
1988	U.S. claims 12-mile Territorial Sea, in keeping with UNCLOS provisions
1997	National Oceanographic Partnership Program (NOPP) creates first cabinet-level, interagency ocean group, the National Ocean Research Leadership Council
1999	U.S. claims 12–24-mile Contiguous Zone, in keeping with UNCLOS provisions
2004	USCOP report released; Pres. Bush establishes cabinet-level, interagency Committee on Ocean Policy
2010	Pres. Obama issues Executive Order establishing an NOP, creating a cabinet-level, interagency National Ocean Council (NOC), and calling for MSP in nine designated regions

Source: Compiled by author from various sources.

The growing U.S. and global dependence on oil during and immediately after World War II, combined with the surge in increasingly mechanized factory-fishing, helped break this logjam. In 1945, President Truman issued Proclamation 2667 asserting U.S. "jurisdiction and control" over the resources on and below its continental shelf, considered to be "an extension of the land mass of the coastal nation and thus naturally appurtenant to it." Mindful of U.S. military and commercial desires to maintain access to *other* nations' waters, the Proclamation did *not* claim sovereignty over the ocean space extending above the seafloor. On the contrary, it emphasized that "the character as high seas of the waters above the continental shelf, and the right to free and unimpeded navigation, are in no way thus affected." Truman's second Proclamation, on fisheries, treaded a similarly fine line, declaring a U.S. right to create fishery conservation zones without attempting to prohibit foreign fishing outside territorial waters.

These unilateral declarations by the U.S. precipitated a variety of competing claims by other nations and the U.N. quickly recognized that this hodgepodge of conflicting assertions was not conducive to world order. In 1958, the U.N. General Assembly convened UNCLOS I, which established committees to address five issues: the territorial sea, the continental shelf, an overall regime for the high seas, high seas fishing and living resources, and ocean access for land-locked countries. Subsequent conferences, convened in 1960 (UNCLOS II) and 1973 (UNCLOS III), considered these and additional issues brought forth by member states. Finally, in 1982, UNCLOS was completed and opened for ratification by U.N. member states. In brief, the Convention changed international ocean law in several ways: it allowed greater national control over some areas, including an expanded 12-mile territorial sea, a 12–24-mile contiguous zone, and a 12–200-mile EEZ;[5] it institutionalized the generally accepted freedom of innocent passage through territorial waters; it instructed nations to "protect and preserve" and "prevent, reduce, and control pollution of" the marine environment; and it promoted greater international coordination regarding the ocean, including cooperation in managing marine mammals and migratory fish species, U.N.-based dispute resolution mechanisms, environmental standard setting, and a declaration that seabed resources outside any EEZ constitute "the common heritage of mankind." Although the U.S. has still not acceded to UNCLOS for complex internal political reasons, many of its provisions have been enshrined in U.S. law and successive administrations have indicated their intentions to adhere to its provisions (USCOP 2004b).

While these international negotiations played out, disputes were also raging concerning U.S. state and federal authorities over coastal waters (Salcido 2007). As a result of the overlapping political and legal processes described above, waters surrounding U.S. territory are now classified into several zones, as outlined below and illustrated in Figure 2.1, although Salcido (2007) reminds us that "the borders we have constructed offshore are merely a legal fiction: they are not consistent with ecosystem management, nor do they have any binding power over wildlife." The blurriness of these lines will be discussed further in later chapters.

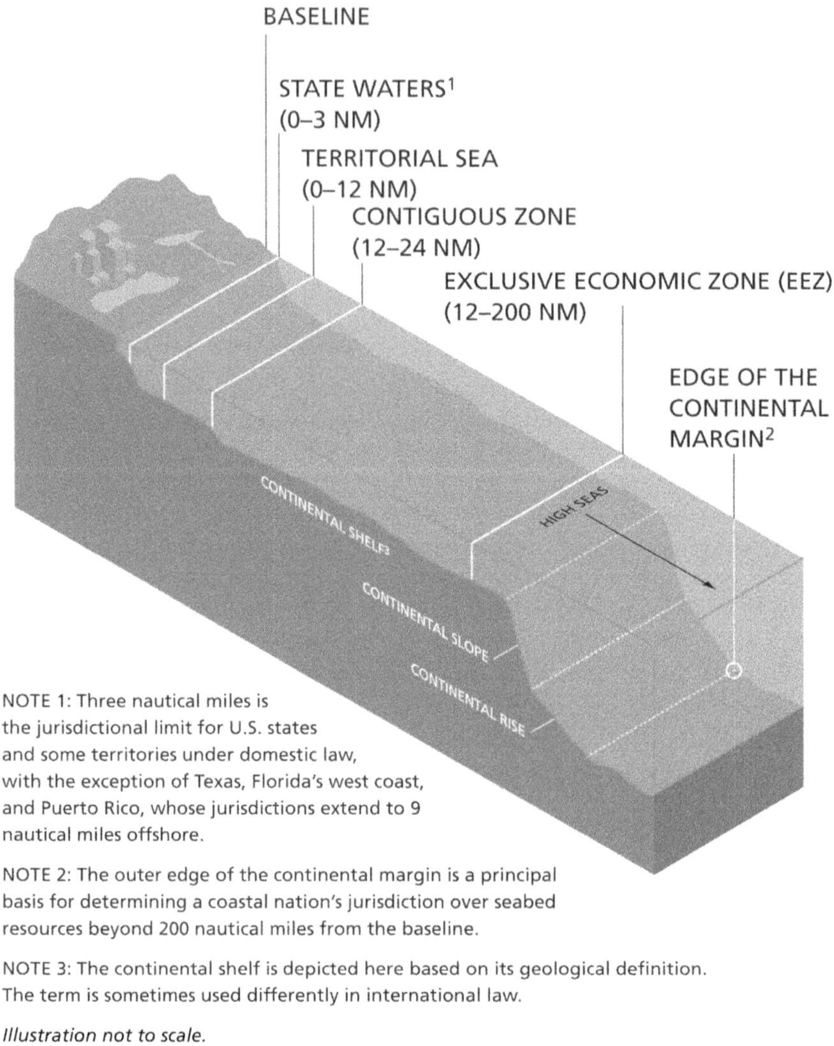

Figure 2.1 U.S. ocean jurisdictions

Source: USCOP 2004a.

State waters: 0–3 (or 9) miles

States hold proprietary rights over waters out to three miles from shore (nine miles from the Gulf Coast of Florida, Puerto Rico, and Texas) including the authority to manage natural resources throughout the water column and in the seabed, but the federal government retains its authorities over navigation, electrical power generation, national defense, and international affairs in this zone.

Territorial sea: 0–12 miles

For the purposes of international law, the U.S. government has sovereignty over the air space, water column, seabed, and subsea area out to 12 miles from its shores, with limited provisions for "innocent passage" of foreign vessels. This does not override State authorities within three miles.

Contiguous zone: 12–24 miles

In this area, the U.S. can ensure adherence to customs, fiscal, immigration, and pollution laws that apply within its territorial sea.

Exclusive economic zone (EEZ): 12–200 miles

In the EEZ, the U.S. claims sovereign rights over living and non-living resources throughout the water column and on and beneath the seafloor, and rights to other economic benefits derived in that area, such as wind or wave energy. The federal government also has jurisdiction over structures and environmental protection in the EEZ. However, the U.S. cannot control the passage of airborne, surface, or subsurface foreign vessels or the laying of seafloor cables and pipelines in the EEZ.

Extended continental shelf: 200 miles to the edge of the continental margin

According to UNCLOS, if a nation believes that its continental shelf (defined as the seafloor and subsoil of the continental shelf, slope, and rise depicted in Figure 2.1) extends further than the 200-mile EEZ, a claim can be filed with the International Commission on the Outer Limits of the Continental Shelf. If the claim is upheld, that nation gains jurisdiction over seabed resources found on its continental shelf beyond 200 miles. The Truman Proclamation asserted similar authority but, because the U.S. has not formally acceded to UNCLOS, it cannot have such claims affirmed by the International Commission.

The High Seas, areas beyond national EEZs

This area, beyond the direct control of any nation, is where the traditional Freedom of the Seas is most applicable. The International Seabed

Authority, created by UNCLOS, oversees exploration, prospecting, and exploitation of marine minerals in the seabed and subsoil beneath the High Seas. A variety of other international agreements constrain certain behaviors in this area, such as whaling, the harvest of straddling or highly migratory stocks, and pollution of the high seas.

U.S. ocean agencies

The management of ocean space and resources developed along a different path than the management of public space on land. As will be discussed below, the federal land agencies were created to oversee designated *areas* within the public lands (e.g., forests, parks, wildlife refuges). In contrast, most federal ocean agencies are responsible for regulating particular *activities* throughout the EEZ and sometimes beyond.[6]

In 1969, the Commission on Marine Sciences, Engineering and Resources (generally referred to as the Stratton Commission after its chairman) examined the U.S. framework for ocean management, and found "little coordination of the many Federal, State, and local agencies with partial responsibilities" for coastal and ocean management, concluding that the nation "need[s] to establish the institutional framework and the scientific and technological foundation for assuring that [it] has access to those resources of the sea which it needs when it needs them" (CMSER 1969). In the three years following release of the Stratton Commission report, NOAA was created through executive action, and the Coastal Zone Management Act, National Marine Sanctuaries Act, and Marine Mammal Protection Act were all passed.

Thirty-five years later, USCOP (2004a) identified fifteen cabinet-level departments or independent agencies that included units with ocean responsibilities (see Figure 2.2). Many were established early in the nation's life to promote maritime safety and security (e.g., the Navy, Coast Guard, and Customs Service); some evolved from early bureaus and boards commissioned to explore, chart, and document ocean features and resources (e.g., NOAA); while a few were created in connection with broader legislative goals that include ocean elements (e.g., the Environmental Protection Agency).

The main regulatory functions in the EEZ, and the U.S. laws establishing them, include the following (note that these regulatory missions are also affected by dozens of international maritime treaties):

- fishery management through the MSFCMA;
- protections for marine mammals and endangered species through the Marine Mammal Protection Act and the ESA;
- control of pollution through the Clean Water Act, Clean Air Act, Ocean Dumping Act, Oil Pollution Act, Clean Vessel Act, Nonindigenous

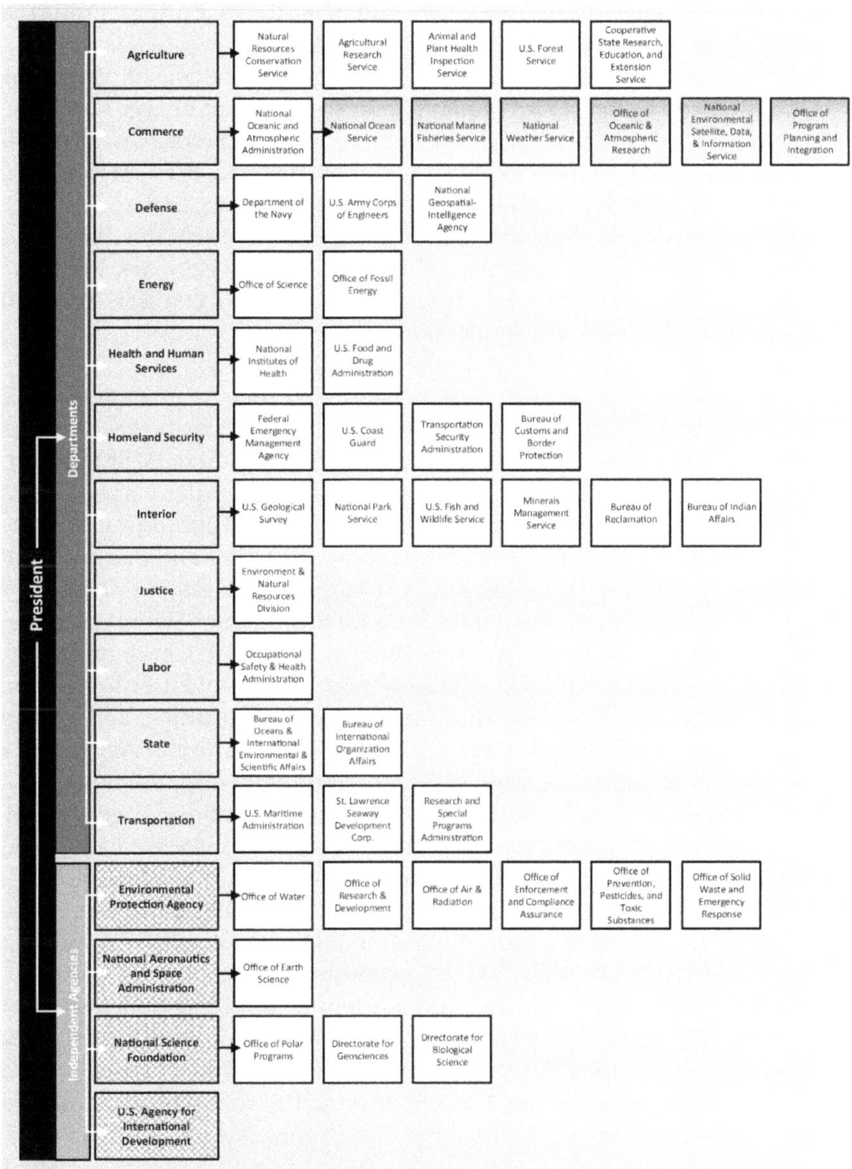

Figure 2.2 U.S. agencies with ocean and coastal responsibilities

Note: In 2011, the Minerals Management Service in the Department of the Interior was re-organized as the Bureau of Ocean Energy Management and the Bureau of Safety and Environmental Enforcement.

Source: USCOP 2004a.

Aquatic Nuisance Prevention Act, and the Act to Prevent Pollution from Ships;

- regulation of offshore mineral and energy production through the OCSLA, Deep Seabed Hard Mineral Resources Act, and Energy Policy Act;
- protection of cultural and unique ecosystem resources through the Abandoned Shipwreck Act, National Historic Preservation Act, National Marine Sanctuaries Act, and Antiquities Act; and
- safe and secure marine operations primarily through the Ports and Waterways Safety Act, Commercial Fishing Vessel Safety Act, Maritime Transportation Security Act, International Safe Container Act, and Hazardous Materials Transportation Act.

The federal agency most widely associated with ocean management is NOAA, created by Executive Order in 1970 pursuant to recommendations from the presidentially appointed Stratton Commission (CMSER 1969). Although the Commission had envisioned an independent agency that would incorporate virtually all non-military ocean and atmospheric functions, the Nixon Administration chose to create a smaller and less powerful organization within the Department of Commerce, with a focus on applied science. The new NOAA incorporated the Environmental Science Services Administration (primarily the Weather Bureau, Coast and Geodetic Survey, and a number of research labs), the Bureau of Commercial Fisheries, the Marine Sport Fishery Program, the National Sea Grant office, and several other data collection and research offices. Today it is organized into six line offices serving administrative, research, and regulatory functions.

As a result of this profusion of laws and treaties and the geographically overlapping jurisdictions of dozens of agencies, there have been repeated calls for better coordination of federal ocean management (e.g., NRC 1992; Pew Oceans Commission 2003; USCOP 2004a; Crowder et al. 2006). In 1997, Congress created the National Oceanographic Partnership Program (NOPP) (10USC§7901) to promote interagency cooperation, expand partnerships with industry and academia, and fund policy-relevant research. NOPP was to be overseen by the first cabinet-level, interagency ocean group, the National Ocean Research Leadership Council. Seven years later, in response to the USCOP report, President Bush convened essentially the same list of members as the Committee on Ocean Policy, preserving their high-level coordination function and broadening their scope to include resource management as well as research, but giving them no concrete mandate for action (IOPTF 2009, p. 6). Most recently, in 2010, President Obama established a very similar 26-member cabinet-level NOC "to ensure a comprehensive and collaborative framework for the stewardship of the ocean, our coasts, and the Great Lakes that facilitates cohesive actions across the Federal Government." The Council is tasked with nine "national priority objectives," the most concrete of which is "to implement comprehensive, integrated, ecosystem based coastal and marine spatial planning and management in the United States" (Executive Order #13547, July 19, 2010).

With this broad-brush sketch of the EEZ and its management in mind, we turn to the origins and current status of a different kind of federally controlled space: the public lands.

The U.S. public lands

Origins of the public lands

Since its formation, the U.S. government has at various times laid claim to and then given away huge tracts of land.[7] At its peak, in the 19th century, the federal government controlled 80 percent of the nation's area. That proportion gradually declined, leveling off at around 30 percent by 1970. Tables 2.2 and 2.3 portray this history of land acquisition—through appropriation, wars, treaties, donations from states, and purchases—and so-called land "disposal"—through homesteading allotments, donations to states, grants to private railroads and other interests, outright sales, and restitution to Native American tribes. These different phases illustrate evolving values and attitudes about the role of government and the best use of land.

Through the end of the 19th century, the U.S. government's primary goal was to encourage settlement of the West by European immigrants and their descendants, often involving the violent displacement of well-established Native American and Mexican inhabitants. One U.S. Senator in the 1840s boasted:

> We have gone on ... multiplying and advancing towards the Pacific, till the Aborigines of the country had disappeared before us ... Was not the hand of destiny seen in that? He who did not see it must be an infidel ... Where shall we find room for all our people, unless we have Oregon?
>
> (Quoted in Bryner 1998)

St. Martin (2009) notes that "the Jeffersonian project of gridding and enumerating the Western territories of the United States ... not only opened the frontier to settlement and capitalist expansion but simultaneously erased ... the community inhabitation and commons economies of Native Americans."

Expansionist ambitions fueled a drive to make federal land available to homesteaders and expanding railroad companies, who generally chose the most fertile, mineral-rich, low-lying, or accessible areas. By the end of this period of land transfer, the areas remaining under federal ownership tended to be dryer plains, desert zones, and steep, densely forested regions.

Table 2.2 Major acquisitions of the public domain, 1781–1867

	Land (acres)	*Water (acres)*	*Total (acres)*	*% of total U.S. land*[1]	*Cost*
State Cessions (1781–1802)	233,415,680	3,409,920	236,825,600	10.40	$6,200,000
Louisiana Purchase (1803)	523,446,400	6,465,280	529,911,680	23.30	$23,213,568
Red River Basin (1782–1817)	29,066,880	535,040	29,601,920	1.30	0
Cession from Spain (1819)	43,342,720	2,801,920	46,144,640	2.00	$6,674,057
Oregon Compromise (1846)	180,644,480	2,741,760	183,386,240	8.10	0
Mexican Cession (1848)	334,479,360	4,201,600	338,680,960	14.90	$16,295,149
Purchase from Texas (1850)	78,842,880	83,840	78,926,720	3.50	$15,496,448
Gadsden Purchase (1853)	18,961,920	26,880	18,988,800	0.80	$10,000,000
Alaska Purchase (1867)	365,333,120	12,909,440	378,242,560	16.70	$7,200,000
Total Public Domain in 1867	1,807,533,440	33,175,680	1,840,709,120	81.00	$85,079,222

[1]Total U.S. land area in 1867 taken as 2,271,343,360 acres.

Source: U.S. Department of the Interior, Office of the Secretary, Areas of Acquisition to the Territory of the United States, Washington, D.C., 1992.

In the late 19th century, the federal government shifted course again and began to "reserve" certain areas of publicly owned land (i.e., remove them from the pool available for grants or sales) that were deemed to have national importance. This practice began with establishment in 1872 of the first National Park, Yellowstone, and was followed by the creation of additional parks and Forest Reserves (later called the National Forests) between 1891 and 1910. By 1934, virtually all "disposal" of public lands had come to an end.

Under current law, public lands can be sold or exchanged only through an Act of Congress or administratively under very limited conditions. For the Forest Service, any sale must "achieve a desired national forest land ownership pattern that supports forest land and resource

Table 2.3 Disposition of the public domain, 1781–2010

Type	*Acres*
Granted or sold to homesteaders	287,500,000
Granted to States for:	
Support of common schools	77,630,000
Reclamation of swampland	64,920,000
Construction of railroads	37,130,000
Support of miscellaneous institutions	21,700,000
Purposes not classified elsewhere	117,600,000
Canals and rivers	6,100,000
Construction of wagon roads	3,400,000
Total Granted to Continental States	328,480,000
Granted to State of Alaska and ANCSA:	
State Conveyances	98,966,613
Native Conveyances	43,230,247
Total Granted to State of Alaska	142,196,860
Granted to railroad corporations	94,400,000
Granted to veterans as military bounties	61,000,000
Confirmed as private land claims	34,000,000
Sold under timber and stone law	13,900,000
Granted or sold under timber culture law	10,900,000
Sold under desert land law	10,700,000
Disposition by methods not classified elsewhere	303,500,000
Total Miscellaneous Dispositions	528,400,000
Grand total	1,286,576,860

Source: Public Land Statistics 2010. BLM, U.S. Dept. of the Interior.

goals and objectives, addresses fragmentation, reduces future management costs, and responds to urban and community needs" (USFS 2004). For the Bureau of Land Management (BLM), sales are only allowed to "serve important public objectives ... which cannot be achieved prudently or feasibly on land other than public land and which outweigh other public objectives and values, including ... recreation and scenic values" (FLPMA 1976).

Currently, the federal government controls approximately 653 million acres of land, about 40 percent of it in the Rocky Mountain region, 39 percent in Alaska, 14 percent in the Pacific region, 1.5 percent in the Appalachian region, and the remaining 5 percent scattered around the country.

U.S. public land management agencies

The oversight of this fluctuating inventory of government-owned land has also evolved over time, shifting from a focus on providing land to private parties to a vision of federal lands as a public trust to be managed for a mix of use and conservation that benefits all citizens. Beginning in 1812, all federal public lands were administered by the General Land Office (GLO), located first in the Treasury Department and moved to the Department of the Interior when the latter was created in 1849. The GLO's function was to keep track of the federal land registry and see that parcels were sold or given away as quickly as possible so they could be put to "productive" private use. Each subsequent land management agency was formed by reassigning GLO lands for some specified purpose.

As mentioned above, the first such reallocation came with the creation of Yellowstone National Park out of GLO lands in Wyoming in 1872. The park was to be controlled directly by the Secretary of the Interior as a "pleasuring ground for the benefit and enjoyment of the people." By 1916, forty more national parks had been carved out of GLO lands, leading Congress to create a new division within Interior, the National Park Service, whose mission was

> to conserve the scenery and the natural and historic objects and the wild life therein and to provide for the enjoyment of the same in such manner and by such means as will leave them unimpaired for the enjoyment of future generations.
>
> (National Park Service Organic Act 1916)

Since then, hundreds of additional sites occupying a total of 88 million acres have come under National Park Service management, including not only Parks, but National Monuments, Historical Sites, Battlefields, Seashores, Lakeshores, and Recreation Areas, all intended to advance a mission of conservation and sustainable recreation (www.nps.gov).

The second new purpose for GLO lands was declared in 1891 through presidential establishment of forest reserves. Codified in an 1897 Organic Act (16 U.S.C. Sec. 473), the forest reserves, initially under GLO management, were intended to "improve or protect the forests, ... secure favorable conditions of water flow, and furnish a continuous supply of timber for the use and necessities of the citizens of the United States." President Roosevelt's election in 1901 resulted in an acceleration of forest reserve designations and a push to have them taken out from under GLO oversight, culminating in the 1905 congressional creation of the Forest Service within the U.S. Department of Agriculture (USDA) and the transfer of all forest reserves (thereafter to be called National Forests) to this new agency. As early as 1908, 165 million acres of federal land in the West had been designated by President Roosevelt as National Forests—about 85 percent of their eventual total area. At that time, almost all forested lands in the Eastern states were in private hands and many had already been heavily harvested (Figure 2.3). To halt this trend and add an Eastern presence to the national forest system, two additional pieces of legislation (the Weeks Act in 1911 and the Clarke-McNary Act in 1924) authorized the Forest Service to purchase private lands that could be restored as viable forests, adding another 20 million acres of National Forest lands. Today, the Forest Service manages 175 National Forests and Grasslands, totaling 193 million acres (www.fs.fed.us).

Birds and game animals became the next target for protection through land set-asides. By the late 19th century, an expanding market for feathers in the fashion industry (primarily for use in ladies' hats) resulted in

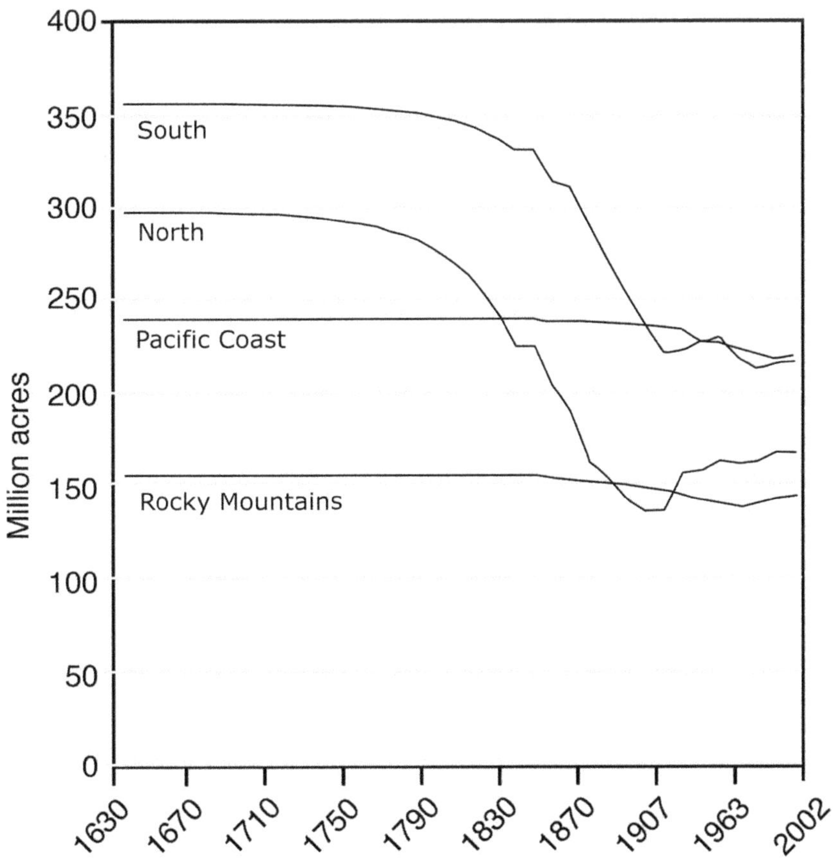

Figure 2.3 Change in forested area by region, 1630–2002

Source: Author's work based on Forest Service inventory figures.

intense harvests of herons, egrets, spoonbills and pelicans, particularly in the warm, swampy areas of Florida. Responding to aggressive lobbying by the American Ornithologists' Union, and in keeping with his lifelong interest in outdoor sports and wildlife, Teddy Roosevelt designated the federally owned, GLO-managed Pelican Island in Florida as the first federal bird reservation in 1903. The Division (later Bureau) of Biological Survey in the USDA was assigned the job of surveying resident bird populations and managing the new sanctuary. Roosevelt went on to add fifty-five other federal bird and game reservations to the Biological Survey's portfolio during his term. Throughout the next few decades, federal public lands continued to be set aside (through both Executive and Legislative action) to protect a variety of waterfowl, migratory birds, and larger game species. Finally, in 1940, Congress rechristened all these reservations as National Wildlife Refuges, and assigned their management to the newly created Fish and Wildlife Service (FWS) in the Department of the Interior. There are currently 556 units in the National Wildlife Refuge System, totaling 96 million acres (www.fws.gov).

The last pillar of today's federal public land management structure came about in response to widespread degradation of the remaining GLO lands, primarily due to water shortages and overgrazing. Over several decades, concerned legislators introduced bills to tighten regulations for grazing private cattle on public lands while leaders of the Forest Service (notably Gifford Pinchot, the first Chief Forester) lobbied to have GLO grazing lands transferred outright to their portfolio at the USDA. Successive Secretaries of the Interior who were protective of their turf, and ranchers who were comfortable with the lack of active management by the GLO, strongly resisted such efforts. In May 1934, a massive dust storm, set off by a combination of prolonged drought and poor land management, carried away some 350 million tons of soil from the northern Great Plains, casting a pall over cities along the Eastern seaboard. One month later, the Taylor Grazing Act was passed. The Act called for portions of the pasture on federal lands to be allocated to certain ranchers for grazing, with fees to be paid for this privilege. A new Division of Grazing (later the Grazing Service) was created within Interior to carry out these new management duties. The Grazing Service had relatively little clout; even minor proposed increases in grazing fees were successfully opposed by influential livestock owners who suggested that all remaining federal range lands should be turned over to private owners. Finally, in 1946, the lands administered by the Grazing Service plus all remaining GLO lands were consolidated under the new BLM, effectively ending the era of disposal of federal lands.

As a result of the shifting national goals embodied in the sequence of events outlined above, what we think of today as the federal public lands (Table 2.4) are overseen primarily by the National Park Service, the Forest Service, the FWS, and the BLM—agencies originating respectively from

Table 2.4 Public land agency holdings

	Jurisdictions in 1980	
Agency	*Acres (millions)*	*% of public lands*
BLM	254.9	40.1
Forest Service	189.0	29.7
FWS	82.9	13.0
National Park Service	68.5	10.8
Departments of the Navy, Air Force, and Army (except Corps of Engineers)	22.1	3.5
Corps of Engineers	8.2	1.3
Water and Power Resources Service (formerly Bureau of Reclamation)	6.6	1.0
Department of Energy	1.6	0.2
Remaining agencies, departments, and bureaus	2.6	0.4
TOTAL	636.4	100.0%

Source: Public Land Statistics 2010. BLM, U.S. Dept. of the Interior.

concerns about outdoor recreation and preservation; forestry and watershed protection; birding, fishing, and hunting; and cattle grazing. Despite these varied founding motivations and primary purposes, all the federal land management agencies are governed by multiple-use mandates that require them to balance many different constituencies and public desires. This tension is central to the comparison between federal lands and the EEZ.

Based on my examination of the histories, purposes, management approaches, and ecosystem characteristics of the four major types of public land, National Forests provide the most useful analogies to ocean space and are used as the basis for my comparisons between land and ocean governance. Many other authors have pointed to the National Forests as particularly interesting among the categories of public lands. Coggins (1981) provides a detailed comparison of the Forest Service and the BLM, finding that the former has more productive, healthier lands under its control, more diverse resources and resource users, has been allowed greater leeway in management experiments, including conservation, and has overall done a better job executing its mission. Another article states that "Although all the federal lands are a part of this story, we will primarily focus on the Forest Service and the national forests because that is where the major debates occurred that have profoundly influenced public land policy," particularly with reference to ecosystem management

(Caldwell et al. 1994). Although these authors do not make the link to ocean governance, their explorations of Forest Service challenges highlight issues strikingly familiar to ocean policy experts.

Comparing the U.S. EEZ and National Forests: a first sketch

This section presents eight elements that exhibit intriguing similarities between National Forest and ocean settings. As an expert who spent decades studying ocean policy, these are the elements that jumped out at me as being remarkably familiar as I began to learn about forest history. The discussion below serves as an introduction to these themes, and is thus more descriptive than analytic; later versions of the land–ocean comparison, to be developed in Chapters 3 and 7, will offer greater detail and build on common theoretical frameworks for public policy.

Multiple-use mandates

Both National Forests and the EEZ allow for many overlapping uses, including:

- living resource extraction (primarily timber and forage on land and fish in the sea);
- recreation (both motorized and lower impact);
- provision of water (with attention to quality, quantity, and location);
- energy production (oil, gas, and renewable);
- minerals mining (both high-value ores and various types of aggregates);
- transportation corridors (for commercial and recreational purposes);
- wildlife observing and harvest by recreational users; and
- preservation of relatively pristine natural areas for research, ecosystem services, and aesthetic or moral reasons.

Significantly, neither space has been assigned a clearly dominant use by Congress unlike, for example, the National Parks. Although there are processes in place to designate wilderness areas in forests and marine protected areas in the EEZ, they occupy a small fraction of the total space and rarely exclude all other activities. For the most part, managers are expected to accommodate a mix of potentially competing users.

Stressed but intact and diverse ecosystems

National Forests and oceans both include diverse, complex ecosystems (more so than, for example, BLM lands), with huge variability depending on latitude, altitude (or depth), nutrients, and water characteristics (availability on land, chemical composition and temperature in the sea). Both areas have experienced historic over-extraction of living resources and related habitat degradation (decades earlier in forests because of their greater accessibility to people), and agency managers have reacted by instituting a variety of more or less successful measures to slow or reverse the declines.

Conflicting stakeholders

Although public lands and ocean waters are to be managed for the benefit of all citizens, the values and interests among different industries, socioeconomic segments, and geographic constituencies often conflict, leading to thorny challenges for managers. In both settings, tensions arise between long-standing traditional users, generally loggers in the forests and fishers in the sea, and growing demands from newer users, such as renewable energy advocates. Communities that live near, or work in, forests and ocean waters often have strong, multi-generational ties to those areas but relatively little power, while national associations, representing commercial and environmental interests, press their agendas with the help of greater access and resources.

Transition from laissez-faire to more structured governance

As outlined earlier in this chapter, both National Forests and the EEZ experienced transitions over the 20th century from conditions of open access, with little centralized control, to heavily regulated spaces with complex combinations of property rights.

Public-trust responsibilities

Areas controlled by the federal government are intended, in a general sense, to be managed for the benefit of the nation's citizens. However, both public land and ocean scholars have long argued about how specific, binding, and actionable that obligation should be, and whether or not a strict "public trust doctrine" applies in these areas (e.g., Wilkinson 1980; Turnipseed et al. 2010).

Overlapping laws and authorities

Although public land agencies have been given designated areas to manage (e.g., National Parks, National Forests, etc.) while ocean agencies typically manage specific activities or functions within the EEZ (e.g., fisheries, shipping, safety), neither approach results in clear, undivided authority. In both arenas, conflicts arise among federal, state, tribal, and local authorities, administrative units responsible for different areas or uses, and elected bodies with different constituencies and values.

Limited data and understanding

Both land and ocean managers must make most of their decisions in the face of incomplete data and uncertain understanding. The uncertainties encompass everything from ecosystem functioning to social and cultural values and economic consequences. Because of the large, often inhospitable areas involved, additional data collection is quite expensive, particularly so in the ocean as one moves further from shore.

Human connection

Humans feel strong emotional connections to both forests and ocean spaces, as is evident from the proliferation of membership organizations advocating for the protection of both areas, ranging from small, local clubs to multi-million-dollar international organizations. Some observers (e.g., Barr and Lindholm 2000; Shackeroff et al. 2009) have suggested that human understanding, familiarity, and emotional connection with forests is greater than with the ocean, while others argue for a special bond between humans and the ocean (Wallace 2014). Because humans live on land but cannot survive for long in ocean waters, it seems plausible that a larger number of people over a longer time have been in closer contact with landscapes than with seascapes. But this has not prevented the ocean from playing a central role in the human story for millennia. Fish and seafood formed an important part of the early diet in coastal areas, the ocean has played a central role in literature, from Homer's *Odyssey* to Melville's *Moby Dick*, and ocean creatures are depicted in prehistoric art. The fact that fifteen of the world's twenty largest cities are along the coast (American Shore and Beach Association 2010) also attests to the fundamental role the ocean plays in human economic and social life.

Summary

This chapter presented the broad contours of two types of federally controlled space, the EEZ and the public lands, providing brief histories of each and summarizing their respective regulatory structures. Although the histories, physical characteristics, and biology of land and ocean ecosystems clearly differ in many ways, a number of intriguing similarities emerge, sufficient to justify further scrutiny and a more systematic analysis. Among the many types of public lands, the National Forests appear to be most comparable to the EEZ, for ecologic, social, and governance reasons. The next chapter presents a more structured approach for comparing these two locales, building on well-developed theories of policy analysis.

Notes

1 Figures compiled in 2001 by the Natural Resources Council of Maine based on data from the National Park Service Land Resources Division; U.S. BLM; Public Land Statistics; U.S. Forest Service Lands and Realty Management; U.S. FWS Division of Realty; Department of Defense Almanac; and U.S. Army Corps of Engineers Water Resources Projects. Accessed July 31, 2014 at www.nrcm.org/documents/publiclandownership.pdf.

2 There is some inconsistency in the literature about the use of the term "public lands." Some scholars (e.g., Coggins 1981; Wilkinson 1980) use it only in reference to areas managed by the BLM. Others, including most recent authors (e.g., McKinney and Harmon 2004), refer to all government-owned areas as public lands. I follow the latter usage.

3 This section summarizes detailed accounts of the evolution of ocean law as presented in Wenk 1972; Juda 1996; Steinberg 1999; Orbach 2003; and USCOP 2004b.

4 The term "Freedom of the Seas" derives from Hugo Grotius' 1608 treatise, *Mare Liberum*, but the underlying principles had been debated by scholars and philosophers for decades, if not centuries, before (Juda 1996).

5 Note that the U.S. and many other nations had already asserted control over fisheries and subsea resources out to 200 miles.

6 There are some specially designated areas in ocean waters. The Department of the Interior manages ninety-nine Marine Wildlife Refuges and ten National Seashores and NOAA manages thirteen National Marine Sanctuaries. Four recently established Marine National Monuments in the Pacific Ocean are jointly managed by Interior and NOAA. These areas occupy a small part of the total ocean space under U.S. jurisdiction and enjoy varying degrees of protection.

7 The history presented in this section has been synthesized from a variety of sources, including: U.S. Public Land Law Review Commission (USPLLRC) 1970; Culhane 1981; Nelson 1995; Nie 2008; BLM 2010; and Nickerson et al. 2011.

3

IS THE EXCLUSIVE ECONOMIC ZONE LIKE PUBLIC LANDS?

In Chapter 1, I suggested that ocean policy, and particularly the increasingly popular concept of marine spatial planning, may share important features with policies implemented over the last 100 years to manage publicly owned lands. An initial overview of ocean and public lands management history, as presented in Chapter 2, appears to support that claim, particularly with regard to human uses, economic and governance characteristics, and stakeholder composition. The two areas have experienced a number of similar policy changes over time, although these parallels have not been widely explored or exploited by managers. In this chapter, U.S. National Forests and the EEZ are compared in a more structured, systematic way than was done in Chapter 2—or than has been attempted by previous authors.

Anticipating that some of my less academically oriented readers may become impatient with the theoretical focus of this chapter, it is worth remembering why theory matters—even to the most practical among us. I have found it useful to consider an analogy to progress in the natural sciences, particularly the biological sciences. The invention and widespread adoption of the Linnaean system of species classification allowed the study of biology to progress beyond previous idiosyncratic, descriptive activities by creating a shared framework. This progress rocketed even further ahead after the discovery of DNA led to the routine application of genetic analyses that could describe and link disparate species in structured, replicable ways. In similar fashion, the study of natural resource institutions and governance is placed on firmer, less descriptive, ground by anchoring it to carefully developed theoretical frameworks that identify the most critical variables in policy development. As Schlager (2007) explains: "[Theoretical] frameworks bound inquiry and direct the attention of the analyst to critical features of the social and physical landscape."

This chapter reviews several widely adopted policy analysis frameworks, each of which is built around particular elements, or building blocks, that are deemed essential to understanding all policy situations. If the elements considered most important by the field of policy analysis prove similar in the forest and ocean settings, there is stronger reason to believe that the relatively long history of management successes (and failures) on land may be relevant to, and help inform, the still developing ocean management setting (de Jong et al. 2002).

Previous land–ocean comparisons

A small number of scholars have previously attempted to compare terrestrial and marine settings for the purpose of informing policy, although none of these efforts has been grounded in theory. One stream of comparative research accompanied the push to create marine reserves for ecosystem protection. It compares *ecological* processes on land and in the sea (e.g., Steele 1985; Carr et al. 2003; Kearney et al. 2012) to ascertain whether the design principles developed for establishing terrestrial parks would be helpful in the ocean. These papers identify significant biophysical differences in ecosystem connectivity, reproductive strategies, and physical habitat and, based on those differences, conclude that "land is fundamentally different to [*sic*] water" (Kearney et al. 2012) for the purpose of reserve design. However, these scientists do not examine any of the social, institutional, or governance considerations that would be likely to influence reserve approval, siting, or implementation. Barr and Lindholm (2000), who are also interested in fully protected marine reserves as a means to conserve ocean ecosystems, do look to National Parks and the Wilderness Preservation System on land as templates. They suggest that the legal tools available for conservation on land should be extended into ocean territory but, again, do not examine the underlying social and institutional factors that would facilitate or impede that option.

A second line of analysis corresponds with the surge of interest in marine spatial planning (MSP) over the last decade, as discussed in Chapter 1. These studies compare MSP to traditional municipal land-use planning, in part as a rhetorical device intended to ease concerns about MSP by placing it in a more familiar context (e.g., Tyldesley and Hunt 2003; Gopnik 2008). This tactic was particularly effective in Europe where land-use planning is well established and generally accepted as a desirable role for government (Tyldesley and Hunt 2003), but backfired in the U.S. context for political and cultural reasons. Land-use planning, and its implementation via zoning overlays, remains highly contentious in the U.S., where conservative commentators see it as unjustified government interference in the rights of property owners (see, e.g., Martin 1993). By adopting the European analogy between MSP and land-use planning, MSP proponents in the U.S. may have contributed to fierce opposition from property-rights advocates and conservative politicians (see, e.g., House Resources Committee 2011).

Whatever its rhetorical value, from an analytical perspective the analogy between MSP and land-use planning has serious weaknesses. Tyldesley and Hunt present a rather long list of differences, including issues of property rights, human population density, extent of ecosystem disruption (noting that most cities and towns have virtually obliterated the pre-existing ecosystem), presence of major infrastructure, and more. At their core, the differences revolve around the fact that a central function of land-use planning is to manage and harmonize uses of privately owned land in a crowded, human-occupied setting—not a central issue for ocean planners.

Acknowledging these fundamental differences, Kidd and Ellis (2012) use a different approach for extracting lessons for MSP from land-use planning in the United Kingdom, which they refer to as terrestrial spatial planning, or TSP. MSP proponents, they assert, have so far uncritically embraced TSP's "rationalist paradigm" of planning as "a positive, visionary, and reformist activity." However, to the extent that MSP wraps itself in this mantle of technocratic planning for the common good, it must also be open to the critiques of that model, subjecting itself to "the full rigor of ethical, methodological, and epistemological challenge" that has been levied against terrestrial planning. Kidd and Ellis review decades of accumulated theoretical and practical literature on TSP, describing how the notion of a value-free planning process has been widely challenged. In the eyes of critics, planning is "inherently political in character" and must be approached with flexibility and open-mindedness, draw on a broad range of expertise, and be sensitive to power imbalances among stakeholders. This thoughtful perspective and the profound questions it raises about the planning enterprise in general, and MSP in particular, are revisited in Chapter 7. However, for the purposes of this chapter, Kidd and Ellis's land–ocean comparison does not offer a structured, replicable template for systematically contrasting institutions and policies on land and in the ocean.

A third category of papers pinpoints public lands as the policy landscape most analogous to the ocean, similar to the premise advanced in this book. Gale and Miller (1985) relate the management of National Forests under the National Forest Management Act (NFMA) to fisheries management under the MSFCMA, drawing some interesting comparisons. However, their analysis fails to recognize the fundamental distinctions between managing a multiple-use *space* (National Forests) and a specific *resource* (marine fish) and makes no reference to the broader policy literature. Rather, as long-time scholars of forests and fisheries respectively, they admit that their discussion is based simply on "the ways in which we have observed these resource management systems to behave." One of the main conclusions they draw from their observations is that forest management is more "standardized, impersonal, and technical," while fisheries management is "less successful in separating subjective … from objective arguments"—claims that are not necessarily supported by other scholars, as will be discussed in Chapter 4.

Others have approached the comparison of public lands and ocean management from a legal perspective. A 2007 law review article by Salcido explores interactions between state and federal authorities on public lands and in the ocean. Based on a detailed exposition of the governing laws in both areas and a critical review of dozens of related court opinions, Salcido concluded that improved cooperation between state and federal authorities was key to achieving better results on land (based on both process-oriented and substantive measures) and that similar cooperation could benefit coastal and ocean management. In another law journal, Duff (2004) reviews the statutes that govern offshore fishing, oil extraction, and wind energy and concludes that this existing single-sector legal framework will be inadequate to deal with growing demands on ocean space and resources. In the final section, he states that "[the] models that ought to be considered in assessing ocean space/resource management issues are those models that have been employed to manage other public areas and resources," and suggests that government "may be able to emulate some of our public land successes while avoiding certain of our public land debacles" by mimicking the principles of public land law. The current study attempts in part to answer Duff's call.

Finally, Shackeroff et al. (2009) take a different approach, presenting an evocative portrayal of "oceans as peopled seascapes," stressing the importance of fully including humans in any exploration of ocean ecosystems. The authors discuss the strong sense of place experienced by coastal communities and advise decision-makers to "situate, or contextualize, marine management strategies socially, historically, and geographically." Although the essay does not set out explicitly to compare ocean and land, its conclusion proposes that "human–environment relationships in terrestrial environments" may be relevant to understanding the ocean, despite three distinguishing features:

1 more limited ecological data in the ocean (they do not call attention to even more severe limitations in social and economic data);
2 discrepancies in ecological and evolutionary processes, stemming from the open, three-dimensional nature of the ocean; and
3 "fundamental differences" in the way land-dwelling, air-breathing humans interact with the land and the sea.

Unfortunately, the authors do not explain why these three differences are deemed to be the most significant ones or explore further how they might be expected to affect policy development and implementation.

Most of the analyses described above, at some point in their text, provide a short list of selected social or ecological variables and explain how each one is manifested on land and in the ocean. These comparisons are thought-provoking and reveal certain telling overlaps, but the methods behind them are essentially ad-hoc, drawing on the particular experience, expertise, and viewpoints of their creators within the purview of their primary academic disciplines. In fact, they exhibit some of the common pitfalls of casual policy analysis identified by Imperial and Yandle (2005) and Sabatier (2007b), such as hidden assumptions, perceptual biases, and lack of analytic rigor.

To supplement these authors' efforts, and position the land–ocean comparison on more solid theoretical ground, this study looks to established findings in the field of policy analysis for guidance.

Theories of governance and public policy

Building blocks

The process of designing, advocating, implementing, and refining public policy is complex, involving interactions among many actors, with different needs, viewpoints, and authorities, at different scales, over extended time periods. When public policy also involves the use and protection of natural resources, these difficulties are exacerbated by the complexity of ecosystem behavior and our limited understanding of it.

Many scholars have attempted to discern and explain patterns in the initiation and evolution of public policy. Typically they construct a "framework" that identifies the variables and processes expected to be important. Frequently, they also propose a "theory" of how the framework elements are likely to interact to produce different outcomes. Before exploring these policy frameworks and theories, it is useful to set the stage by defining some common terms, as summarized in Box 3.1.

Box 3.1 The language of policy analysis

Just as a practicing brain surgeon is unlikely to use or understand the terminology of an academic neuroscientist, most policymakers and managers are unfamiliar with the vocabulary employed by policy scholars. Even within the academic community, some terms are not used consistently across investigators. Since a number of potentially unfamiliar or confusing terms will be used in this chapter, brief definitions are provided below.

Frameworks and Theories: *Frameworks* are used to organize inquiry by identifying and categorizing the factors (or elements, or variables) and processes deemed most relevant to understanding some phenomenon. *Theories* propose causal relationships among the elements in a framework, generating explanations and predictions about likely processes and outcomes. Theories are often based on particular assumptions about human behavior and the nature of policy change.

Note that the basic elements specified in a framework can be compatible with many different theories.

Rational Self-maximization and Bounded Rationality: Traditional economics assumes that individuals choose a course of action after rationally weighing all available choices and selecting the option that yields the greatest net personal benefit, i.e., it views people as *rational self-maximizers.* These assumptions have had to be modified by findings in behavioral psychology showing that real human decision-making is constrained by partial information, limited cognitive abilities, learned shortcuts, and tightly held biases, and that altruism can play a significant role in behavior, i.e., that our rationality is *bounded* by capacity, culture, and context.

Institution: The term institution is widely used in the policy literature, although it has not always been defined consistently. Hodgson (2006) takes 25 pages to answer the titular question "What Are Institutions?," concluding that "institutions are systems of established and embedded social rules that structure social interactions." McGinnis (2011) states that "institutions are human-constructed constraints or opportunities within which individual choices take place and which shape the consequences of their choices." In the policy analysis context, an *institution* (i.e., a set of rules) is distinct from an *organization* (a defined group of individuals with some common purpose), although the two are often treated as synonyms in popular usage (see, e.g., Merriam-Webster 2014).

Rules, Norms, and Strategies: As explained above, institutions are characterized by the set of rules they encompass. However, it is useful to break the broad concept of "rules" into more specific categories. Ostrom (2005) presents a detailed institutional grammar that distinguishes between rules, norms, and strategies. *Rules* determine: (a) who, (b) is required, permitted, or prohibited, (c) to do what, (d) under what conditions, and (e) what the consequences of rule-breaking will be. A rule is not always derived through a legislative or other formal process, creating a further distinction between actual rules-in-use (*de facto* rules) that apply in a given situation and rules-in-form (*de jure* rules) that are formally declared or written down but may or may not be commonly understood, followed, or enforced. *Norms* are cultural prescriptions that exist as part of the moral code in a community, sometimes called ethical codes or social obligations. Like rules, norms guide the choices and actions of individuals but, unlike rules, do not have an explicit enforcement mechanism beyond social pressure. Similar in effect, but less formal than rules or norms, *strategies* are habitual plans of action that guide what a participant does under certain conditions.

Governance: *Governance* is the process used for creating rules, norms, and strategies. Governance can be *self-organized* (community members actively participate in designing and modifying the rules that govern them), *monocentric* (the ability to make and change rules is vested in a single authority), or *polycentric* (overlapping or nested authorities interact to create rules).

Goods and Services: *Goods* are tangible things needed or desired by individuals or organizations, from iron ore for steel production to food and clean water. *Services* are actions that fulfill someone's needs, from car repair to climate regulation. Note that goods and services can be supplied by humans or through the functioning of ecological processes.

Sources: These definitions are drawn from Ostrom 2005; Hodgson 2006; Schlager 2007; McGinnis 2011; and Emerson et al. 2012.

Any discussion of institutions and policy change must be concerned with the nature of the *goods and services* being created, distributed, and exchanged. These can range from childcare in a metropolitan region (Bushouse 2011) to fish in a remote coastal setting (Basurto and Coleman 2010). Fortunately, there has been significant work dedicated to understanding and classifying such goods and services (e.g., Schlager and Ostrom 1992; Hanna et al. 1996). First, scholars identify two important characteristics of any resource. *Subtractability* is the extent to which one person's use of a resource diminishes its availability to another person. For example, fish stocks are highly subtractable (if I catch and eat a certain fish, you will not) while clean air is not (my intake of breath does not detract from yours except in extreme circumstances). *Excludability*, on the other hand, describes the ease of preventing access to a resource. A car is highly excludable (assuming a lock and key are available) while a wilderness hiking trail is not (barring hundreds of miles of fencing).

The four possible combinations of these two attributes create four types of goods and services, as shown in Table 3.1. However, these categories merely describe the nature of the goods or services themselves. They say nothing about the *property rights* assigned to a resource (i.e., who can use, manage, and sell it) or about the *management system* imposed in any particular institutional setting, such as a free market or communal system. For example, although federally owned spaces encompass primarily public goods and common-pool resources, the existence of leases, concessions, quotas, and similar management tools creates many private concerns and property claims. These important distinctions have often been overlooked, to the detriment of sound policy (McCay 1996; Imperial and Yandle 2005).

Table 3.1 Categories of goods and services

	Low subtractability	*High subtractability*
Low excludability	Public goods (e.g., clean air, hiking trails)	Common-pool resources (e.g., marine fish, grazing lands)
High excludability	Toll (or club) goods (e.g., cable television)	Private goods (e.g., a car)

Source: Adapted from Ostrom et al. 1994.

Another concept worth introducing in connection with resource management is the *public trust*. In the financial context, a trustee is required to "protect, conserve, and safeguard the assets of the trust for the benefit of all the [beneficiaries] ... [and] must take such action with respect to the trust property as will be most conducive to its welfare." Furthermore, the trustee is liable for any losses resulting from a failure to exercise care, prudence, and diligence or for misappropriation or waste of trust property (Applegate 1977, citing 90 CJS trusts §270). This definition of a trustee's duties and responsibilities accords with common usage of the term (see, e.g., Black and Garner 2009; Merriam-Webster 2014).

In the context of natural resources management, however, the public trust doctrine (PTD) descends from a long line of Roman and English common law that obliges "sovereigns" to hold certain lands and waters in trust for their citizenry. In the United States today, the PTD protects the public's rights to fishing, navigation, and commerce "on and over the beds of navigable waterways and submerged lands under tidal waters," which are governed by state law (Turnipseed et al. 2010). Many states have gone further by enshrining the PTD in their constitutions. For example, Article I, Section 27 of the Pennsylvania constitution states, "Public natural resources are the common property of all the people, including generations yet to come. As trustees of these resources, the [government] shall conserve and maintain them for the benefit of all the people."

Many legal scholars have explored the extension of the PTD to federal public lands (e.g., Sax 1970; Applegate 1977; Wilkinson 1980) and more recently to the federal EEZ (e.g., Babcock 2009; Turnipseed et al. 2010; Sun 2011). In both settings, the general conclusion has been that: (1) U.S. courts have not established the PTD in common law; (2) Congress has not enacted a statutory PTD; and (3) the U.S. constitution does not impose public trust duties on the federal government.[1] Nevertheless, many courts, including the Supreme Court, have used trust-like language in their opinions regarding resource management. As far back as 1911, the U.S. Supreme Court stated that "the public lands are held in trust for all the people of the United States" (220 U.S.C. 523, 1911). Wilkinson's (1980) review of cases since that time concludes that this kind of recurring use of trust language by courts "indicates an awareness that the special values of the federal lands ... have been gradually but indelibly imprinted on our national consciousness." Similarly, many environmental statutes appear to create trust-like duties for agencies. The Superfund Act of 1980 refers to the President as the "trustee ... [of] natural resources over which the United States has sovereign rights or natural resources within the territory or the [EEZ] of the United States." The National Environmental Policy Act also instructs the federal government to "fulfill the responsibilities of each generation as trustee of the environment for succeeding generations" (Turnipseed et al. 2010). In the context of public lands specifically, Wilkinson (1980) asserts that "modern statutes set a tone, a context, a milieu. When read together, they require a trustee's care." The Ocean Commission's report refers repeatedly to the federal government's "public trust" responsibilities toward ocean resources (e.g., USCOP 2004a, pp. 61, 76, 274, 333, 334). It has been suggested that the critical difference between such broad references to trust-like duties and a true PTD is enforceability (Turnipseed et al. 2010).

With the above definitions in mind, the following sub-sections summarize two of the most well-developed and widely accepted policy frameworks—Institutional Analysis and Design and the Advocacy Coalition Framework—followed by a discussion of amendments and critiques that have been suggested to improve those frameworks. A clear understanding of the structure and reasoning behind these approaches to policy analysis will provide a firmer basis for comparing public land and ocean management.

The Institutional Analysis and Design framework

One widely adopted rubric for policy analysis is the Institutional Analysis and Design (IAD) framework. Developed based on contributions from many scholars over several decades, the current conception of the IAD framework is laid out most thoroughly by Elinor Ostrom, who was awarded the 2009 Nobel Prize in Economics for this work. The intent behind her effort was to identify the basic building blocks of all policy situations, from U.S. government-run urban poverty programs to community-based forest management and small-scale fisheries. In Ostrom's words, "my deep conviction [is] that underlying the immense variety of surface differences, all repetitive situations faced by human beings are composed of nested layers composed of the same set of elements" (Ostrom 2005).

The IAD framework is based on the idea that all policy situations result from the cumulative actions of individuals who are boundedly rational (see Box 3.1), in pursuit of multiple goals for themselves and others, sensitive to context, fallible, and capable of learning over time. These individuals, sometimes gathered into small groups or organizations, operate as participants within what are called "action situations." Each action situation exists within the context of a number of exogenous variables and produces a set of outcomes (see Figure 3.1). This process is then repeated over time and at different scales.

The framework identifies three important contextual elements, or "exogenous variables" (on the left in Figure 3.1). First, the *biophysical setting*, which can be characterized by the type and nature of goods and resources present, including their extent, availability, mobility, subtractability, excludability, and other limiting features. Second, *community attributes* which include such elements as cultural history, shared knowledge, trust and reciprocity, language, values, diversity, size, inequalities, etc. Similar contextual factors are included in virtually all approaches to policy analysis. One distinctive contribution of the IAD framework is its careful elucidation of a third exogenous variable with huge ramifications on outcomes: the *rules* that guide participants' actions (see explanation in Box 3.1). Although participants in a given situation may not even be conscious of the potentially complex web of directives under which they operate, identification of such rules is crucial to understanding what outcomes are likely to occur and why.

Evaluation (the top right of Figure 3.1) is another important element of this framework, in keeping with the assumption that humans learn from experiences over time. Participants, as well as external observers, can use various evaluative criteria to analyze both the interactions that take place, i.e., the *process* used to reach outcomes, and the outcomes themselves. One approach to evaluating the relative performance of different institutional arrangements is to assess the transaction costs incurred, such

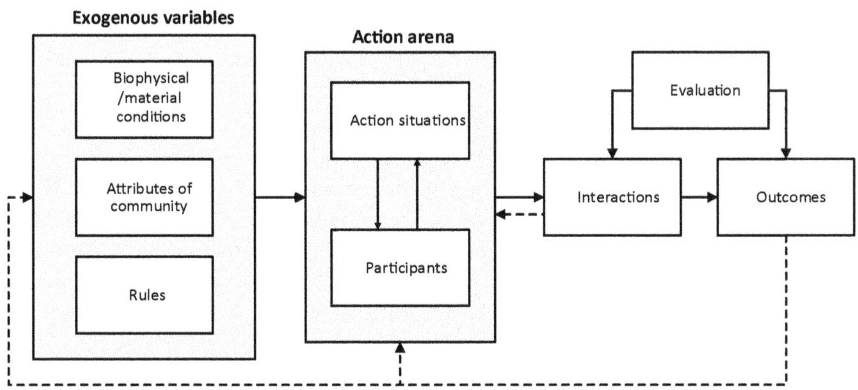

Figure 3.1 Components of the Institutional Analysis and Design framework

Source: Ostrom 2005.

as information costs, coordination costs, and strategic costs, assuming that participants will try to minimize such outlays. Outcomes can also be assessed by examining such features as efficiency, equity, accountability, adaptability, legitimacy, or sustainability (e.g., Ostrom et al. 1994; Imperial 1999; Imperial and Yandle 2005; Ostrom 2005). Whether evaluation is formal or informal, documented or unconscious, it provides essential feedback, allowing participants to learn and adapt their choices and actions over time. As explained by Ostrom (2005), "accrued learning and knowledge have led those with good information about participants, strategies, ecological conditions, and changes in technology and economic relationships over time to craft sustainable institutions."

The Advocacy Coalition Framework

Another widely adopted policy analysis tool is the Advocacy Coalition Framework (ACF), first proposed by Sabatier in 1986 and applied, tested, and modified by many others over the subsequent twenty-five years (Sabatier and Jenkins-Smith 1999; Leach and Sabatier 2005; Weible 2007). One thorough exposition of the ACF (Sabatier and Weible 2007[2]) incorporates several modifications made in response to critiques and suggestions from other scholars (e.g., Kingdon 1995; Schlager 1995; Weible 2007). Figure 3.2 illustrates the main elements and pathways in the current ACF.

As might be expected of two tools designed for the same general purpose, the IAD framework and ACF share similar concerns—such as why certain policies come into use and how they change—and include a number of related elements, such as features of the external context, the individuals and organizations involved in or affected by the policy in question, and the strategies and rules that produce particular outcomes. However, there are also important differences between the assumptions and foci of the two frameworks.

The ACF's basic unit of analysis, analogous to the IAD's action situation, is the *policy subsystem* (on the right in Figure 3.2), which is bounded by the geographic and substantive scope appropriate to the question being investigated, from global economic policy to the actions of a neighborhood association. Each policy subsystem is shaped by the biophysical, social, and governance systems within which it is located (the two boxes in the upper left of Figure 3.2), similar to the IAD framework's exogenous variables. Although policy subsystems can exist at many different scales, they are defined by the existence of an enduring community composed of some combination of government officials (legislative, executive, or judicial), interest groups, NGOs, media, and researchers, all possessing goals or expertise in a particular policy area.

Individuals are again assumed to be boundedly rational, with cognitive constraints as explained above. However, drawing on findings from

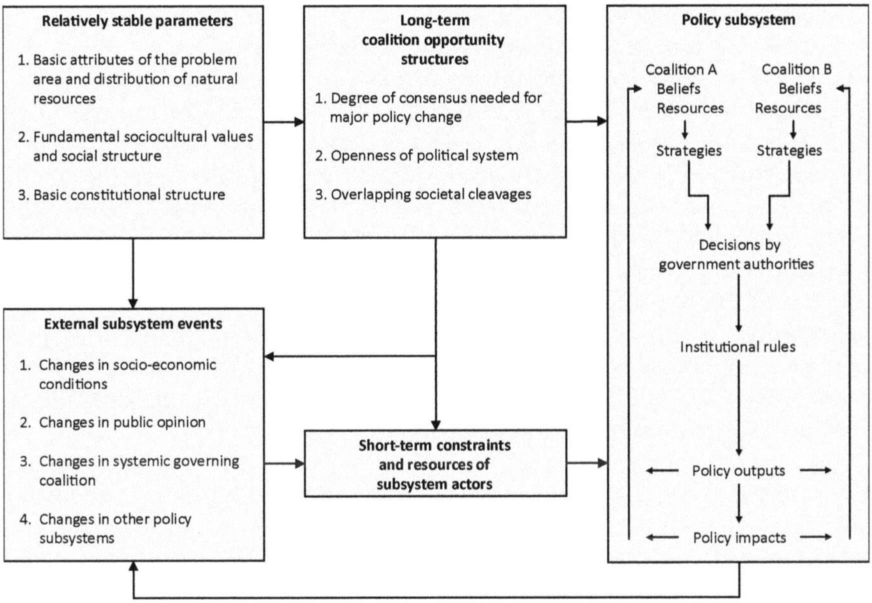

Figure 3.2 Components of the Advocacy Coalition Framework

Source: Sabatier and Weible 2005.

the fields of social psychology and behavioral economics (e.g., Quattrone and Tversky 1988; Munro and Ditto 1997), the ACF considers individuals' internal *belief systems* to be an essential explanatory feature for policy development.[3] Personal beliefs are known to filter available information, exaggerating the influence and bad motives of opponents and magnifying an individual's perceived losses relative to gains. In fact, when beliefs are sufficiently strong, research suggests they can outweigh more tangible material self-interest (Weible 2007).

The ACF posits three levels of belief: *deep core beliefs*, a participant's fundamental enduring values; *policy core beliefs*, normative views about policy options that will be slow to change; and *secondary beliefs* that are empirically based and amenable to change in light of new information. These ideas about human belief systems undergird the central element of the ACF, the *advocacy coalition*. Advocacy coalitions are composed of those members of a policy subsystem who develop trust as a result of overlapping core beliefs and are thus willing to invest in coordination to achieve shared policy goals—a particular form of collective action. Examples might include wilderness advocates, loggers, commercial fishermen, marine protected area proponents or opponents, small business owners, etc. The degree of investment and coordination in the coalition will be proportional to the extent of overlap in core beliefs.

For a coalition to be successful, it requires (1) adequate resources, (2) access to suitable venues of influence and decision-making, and (3) a setting that makes change possible. The first element, *coalition resources*, may take many forms, including political access, public support, data and information (such as scientific studies, polls, or legal analyses), members, leadership, and, of course, money, which can often be traded for the other resources. Strong leaders, also referred to as "public entrepreneurs" (McGinnis 2011), can be particularly important in crafting new policy paradigms and solutions, attracting other resources, and recognizing when the moment is ripe for change. With resources in hand, coalitions must seek out *venues* where they might have influence, such as electoral politics, referenda, legislative hearings and bills, grassroots organizing, media outlets, administrative appeals, or judicial proceedings.

As a result of ongoing resource imbalances and differential access to key venues, policy subsystems may become dominated by one advocacy coalition. However, given sufficient resources, appropriate venues, the right context, and time, it is possible to achieve *minor policy change*, i.e., changes to a specific policy within a larger policy subsystem. To achieve *major policy change* that fundamentally alters the policy subsystem, more profound shifts are needed. In its original formulation, the ACF saw *external shocks*, i.e., major socio-economic changes, shifts in public opinion, a turnover in the governing coalition, or impacts from other policy subsystems (the lower left-hand box in Figure 3.2), as the only avenues for major change. Because the ACF assumed that core beliefs were fairly intransigent, external shocks were considered necessary to shift power toward a minority coalition.

Since that time, critiques of the ACF and additional research have led ACF practitioners to add two more pathways for major change (not shown in Figure 3.2). The first is via *internal shocks*, landmark events that reveal a fundamental failure of the policy subsystem—for example, the 2009 oil spill in the Gulf of Mexico that exposed serious flaws in the offshore drilling regulatory system. Such shocks can alter core beliefs even within the dominant coalition and may increase the resources—particularly public opinion and new information—available to the minority coalition.

The second newly recognized pathway to major change is through *negotiated agreement* accompanied by long-term *policy-oriented learning*. ACF scholars have drawn on two decades of practical and theoretical progress in the field of Alternate Dispute Resolution (ADR) (e.g., Susskind et al. 1999; O'Leary and Bingham 2003) to help develop this component of the framework. Both the ACF and the ADR proponents consider coalitions of individuals with similar beliefs and a distrust of outsiders to be central elements of the policy system, and both believe that policy change will be difficult unless such tightly held beliefs can be modified. But ADR research has found that negotiated agreements *can* be reached even between opposing coalitions, particularly when a "hurting stalemate" develops whereby no one is happy with the status quo but no coalition has the ability to force change on its own. Additional findings from the field of ADR, many developed in overcoming disputes related to National Forest management, are discussed below.

Other policy elements of interest

Although the two policy analysis frameworks discussed above have been identified as the most well developed and widely adopted (Schlager 2007), other scholars have suggested additions, modifications, and alternative formulations to better account for elements they consider under-represented or ignored by the main frameworks. Because some of these perspectives are highly relevant to the public land and ocean settings, three additional streams of policy analysis are discussed below: local public economy (LPE) studies, social construction theory, and collaborative governance.

Employing many of the same elements found in the IAD framework, the study of LPEs focuses on situations characterized by overlapping, multi-jurisdictional, polycentric governance arrangements (Oakerson and Parks 2011). Originally developed to understand metropolitan areas where a complex web of governmental agencies and private and nonprofit organizations provide a mix of goods and services to residents, Oakerson and Parks propose that some LPE research findings may also be applicable to policy analyses of large ecosystems, including their human components, which often exhibit similar institutional complexities. They suggest that "LPE analysis is a logical extension of IAD's micro-level work to a meso-level populated by multi-organizational, nested structures of governance." Three concepts are highlighted as particularly important in the extension of LPE ideas to natural resource governance contexts.

First, a distinction is drawn between the *provision* and *production* of goods and services. In other words, one entity may be responsible for ensuring that a service is available while another actually renders the service. For example, municipal trash collection may be organized by either individual building managers, neighborhood associations, or city governments (provision) while the trash is picked up by either public employees, monopolistic service companies, or multiple private contractors (production). Similarly, the Forest Service (or Regional Fishery Council) typically determines the locations and volumes of timber sales (or fishing), while logging companies and mills (or fishermen and fishhouses) harvest and process the wood (or seafood).

Second, LPE scholars have looked closely at the phenomenon of political and functional *fragmentation* within communities, a characteristic of most ocean management, which has been criticized as disjointed and including too many competing authorities (e.g., USCOP 2004a; Crowder et al. 2006). However, LPE research refutes the blanket vilification of fragmented governance, finding that it can instead exist as a well-adapted, geographically and functionally differentiated, polycentric structure where "multiple independent actors interact to produce an outcome that is commonly valued" (Oakerson and Parks 2011). For such a system to function well, however, the different centers of authority must recognize their mutual interdependence, and some higher, constitutional-level mechanism must exist to modify the structure of authorities if needed.

From this follows the third LPE concept highlighted by Oakerson and Parks: the role of *citizen voice* in shaping the provision and production of services. The strength of citizen voice depends on local governance institutions (i.e., the rules that guide local decision-making, equivalent to the IAD framework's collective choice level) and how they can be amended (the rules for changing local rules, or the IAD constitutional level). Polycentric governance systems are generally thought to provide more "civic space" for non-governmental actors to participate in governance. As will be seen in later chapters, citizen voice has played a major role in National Forest management. These three concepts (provision vs. production, fragmentation vs. polycentricity, and citizen voice) are likely to be useful in understanding the management of large eco-regions on land and in the ocean that also provide environmental goods and services through multi-jurisdictional arrangements.

Another category of amendments to the dominant policy frameworks comes out of social constructivist perspectives. As explained by Clement (2010), a major limitation to the application of the IAD framework is its "inadequate consideration of the role of power" in crafting institutions. Who holds power, how is that power exercised, and what historical context created the current distribution of power? Different experiences of power will alter—if not determine—participants' perceptions of their options. Steins and Edwards (1999) agree, suggesting that outcomes from action situations will depend critically on "how actors 'socially construct' their everyday reality"—in other words, how they understand their social, political, and physical circumstances. This situation is certainly evident in the ocean setting, with its conflicts between individual users and multinational companies, local and global environmental agendas, commercial and recreational fishermen, and others.

Clement (2010) suggests that policy analysts look more closely at the nature of community *discourse* as an indicator of prevalent social constructions and their role in constraining policy alternatives. Ingram et al. (2007) go further to propose an alternative policy framework that focuses foremost on how social constructions and political power influence, and are reinforced by, policy decisions. Schlager (2007) argues that this Social Construction *Framework* actually belongs within the category of *theory* (see definitions in Box 3.1) since it attempts to explain *why* policies evolve as they do, rather than simply identifying underlying building blocks. But if the variables of "discourse" or "participant power" are not specified by the analytic framework, their influence is likely to be overlooked. The concepts of power, social construction, and policy discourse have been extensively explored within the fields of sociology and political ecology. However, for the purposes of this study I will follow Clement's relatively simple "fix" by thinking of these as additional types of external variables, i.e., new boxes on the left-hand sides of Figures 3.1 and 3.2. Although an argument could be made that these variables are implicitly included under the broad heading of "Attributes of Community," social constructivist scholars make a good case that their frequent neglect by mainstream policy scholars dictates that they be explicitly called out.

The theories and practice of Alternate Dispute Resolution (ADR) and its sister discipline Environmental Conflict Resolution (ECR) (Wondolleck and Yaffee 2000; Daniels and Walker 2001; O'Leary and Bingham 2003; Marshall 2005) have served as another source of policy framework modifications. The section explaining the ACF above described how ADR findings led to an additional proposed pathway for policy change: negotiated agreement. ADR and ECR researchers have identified several conditions that appear to make negotiated agreement possible even among staunch opponents, such as the existence of a "hurting stalemate," visionary leadership, incentives for participation, uncertainty about future conditions, and perceived interdependence of the parties. There are also certain process elements generally associated with successful collaborative outcomes, including trust building, transparency, and development of shared understanding (Bryson et al. 2006; Ansell and Gash 2008). These findings offer new elements to be considered when analyzing coalition behavior and policy change under the ACF.

Another group of ADR/ECR researchers has specifically adapted the IAD framework to study collaborative governance, or multi-party, multi-level collaboration (Emerson et al. 2012). Similar to what is seen in LPEs, collaborative governance occurs when people become engaged across agencies, levels of government, and public and private spheres in order to attain shared outcomes—a situation frequently found in public lands and ocean settings. The IAD modifications suggested by Emerson et al. are shown in Figure 3.3. The system context (outermost box, corresponding to the exogenous variables in Figure 3.1) creates initial *drivers* for collaboration (left-most arrow), while characteristics of the policy actors—engagement, capacity for action, and shared motivation—can either propel or deter collaborative actions and outcomes. The "Collaboration Dynamics" box in Figure 3.3 can be thought of as an additional element or step between "Exogenous Variables" and the "Action Arena" in Figure 3.1. The new framework elements are derived from ADR/ECR theory and research and are supported by the results of a meta-analysis of 137 case studies of successful and unsuccessful collaborative processes (Ansell and Gash 2008).[4]

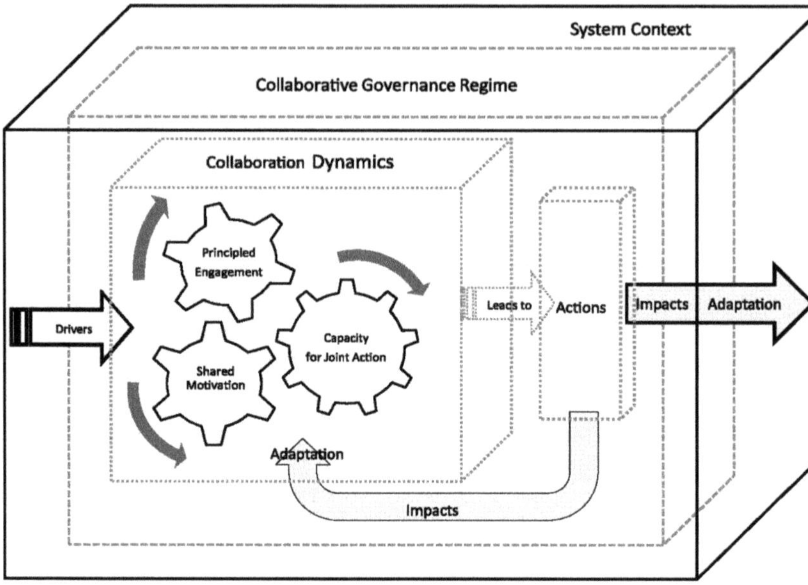

Figure 3.3 The Integrative Framework for Collaborative Governance

Source: Emerson et al. 2012.

Comparing the U.S. EEZ and National Forests: a systematic approach

At the end of Chapter 2, public lands and the EEZ were compared in broad, descriptive terms, revealing sufficient similarities to merit further exploration. This section returns to that comparison using a more systematic approach, underpinned by the major theoretical frameworks and their variations described above. In Table 3.2, three central components of policy analysis (and sub-elements within them) are evaluated in both public lands and ocean settings. Similarities continue to be evident, although the comparison remains incomplete and will be re-visited in Chapter 7, building on the more thorough investigation of National Forest management developed in Chapters 4–6.

Defining the scope of inquiry

The first step in any policy analysis is to determine the scope of the system to be studied. Up until now, the two systems of interest in this comparative study have been described as "U.S. National Forests" and the "U.S. EEZ," but those terms are too general for this phase of the inquiry. After all, the U.S. EEZ comprises over 4 million square miles of the ocean, with portions extending from

Table 3.2 Policy framework elements on land and in the ocean (Differences are highlighted in bold italics. This comparison is developed further in Table 7.1.)

Framework element	*Public land*	*Ocean*
Scope	A U.S. National Forest, plus closely linked human communities and ecosystem components	An ecosystem-based region of the EEZ (3–200 nm from shore), plus closely linked human communities and ecosystem components
Ecological setting	Widely varied ecosystems generally include harvestable trees, related mid-story and ground cover species, and diverse animal assemblages, often including one or more threatened or endangered species	Species assemblages extremely variable depending on location, depth, latitude, chemistry, etc. ***Typically higher mobility and connectivity than on land.*** Fewer marine endangered species
	Migratory species, waterways, and airborne features extend ecosystem beyond forest boundaries	Migratory species, ocean currents, and airborne features extend ecosystem beyond defined boundaries
	Some vertical variation, from subsurface resources, through a multi-layered ecosystem, and including airborne species and atmospheric phenomena	***Extreme vertical variation from the seafloor, through several ocean ecosystem zones, and into the atmosphere***
	"Natural" ecosystem subject to major shifts due to fire, flooding, geologic events, and disease	"Natural" ecosystem subject to major shifts due to storms, geologic events, and disease
	Ecological status ranges from highly impacted to near pristine. Main threats are from overharvesting, habitat modification, invasive species, disease, fire, and climate change	Ecological status ranges from impacted to near pristine. Main threats are from overharvesting, habitat modification, invasive species, and climate change
	Monitoring and mapping are extensive and ecological understanding has improved greatly over time	***Monitoring is patchy at best***, with greatest focus on marine mammals and commercially desirable fish species; ***mapping is limited*** to coastal areas. Ecological understanding is limited, but growing

Continued

Table 3.2 Policy framework elements on land and in the ocean, *continued*

Framework element	*Public land*	*Ocean*
Goods and services	Goods: Timber, forage, other natural products, wildlife for recreational hunting, fossil fuels, hard rock minerals. Most goods provided by federal agencies but produced by private parties	Goods: Fish and seafood, other natural products, recreational fishing, fossil fuels, minerals and aggregates. Most goods provided by federal agencies but produced by private parties
	Services: Non-extractive recreation, water and climate services, renewable energy, transportation (resource-related and thruways), wilderness and existence value. Combination of natural and human-created services	Services: Non-extractive recreation, water and climate services, renewable energy, transportation, wilderness and existence value. Combination of natural and human-created services
	Access to resources is dependent on road construction	***Access to resources is highly challenging, but not tied to linear, manmade transportation routes***
Social setting	Humans can live within and immediately at forest boundaries	***Humans live at some distance from EEZ and access ocean space only temporarily for work or recreation***
	Long history of human habitation and use throughout the area	Long history of human uses in coastal zone, extending further offshore in recent decades
	Historically small, resource-dependent communities have undergone population growth and diversification over time	Ocean-dependent coastal populations increasingly displaced by residential and tourism-related communities
	Variable and complex discourses concerning forest resources and related communities; conflicting conceptions of problems and solutions (discussed further in Chs. 4–6)	Variable and complex discourses concerning ocean resources and related communities; conflicting conceptions of problems and solutions
	Longstanding interest in forest policy among the general public and distant communities	***Relatively recent interest in ocean policy among the general public and distant communities***

Framework element	*Public land*	*Ocean*
Social setting (*continued*)	Incentives for collaboration present due to interdependence of authorities, motivated leaders, scientific and policy uncertainties, plus "hurting stalemates" in many locations	***Infrequency of direct conflicts and agency independence provide little incentive for collaboration***
	Uneven access to information and expertise and varied sources of knowledge among participants	Uneven access to information and expertise and varied sources of knowledge among participants
Governance setting	Forest Service has primary authority, but other state and federal agencies have jurisdiction over specific activities, issues, or regulatory requirements. Nested and polycentric governance	Sector-specific authorities dispersed among many parallel federal agencies. ***Complex rights and international authorities from 12–200 nm.*** New NOC may promote greater coordination
	Dozens of independent and overlapping laws in operation	Dozens of independent and overlapping laws and conventions in operation
	Trust-like duties but no formal PTD	Trust-like duties but no formal PTD
	Explicit multiple-use mandate in law	***No legal mandate to accommodate multiple uses***
	Privately owned lands often interspersed with federal lands	***No private ownership within the EEZ***
	Primary venues for influence include the media, courts, elections and lobbying, administrative proceedings, and occasional collaborative settings	Primary venues for influence include the media, courts, elections and lobbying, administrative proceedings
	Management includes technocratic, market-based, and participatory approaches	Management primarily technocratic and regulatory, with limited market-based approaches. Some authority devolved to Regional Fishery Councils
	Major emphasis on area-wide, multiple-use planning	***No area-wide planning in EEZ; 2010 Executive Order calls for multiple-use spatial planning***
	Enforcement difficult	Enforcement very difficult

Continued

Table 3.2 Policy framework elements on land and in the ocean, *continued*

Framework element	*Public land*	*Ocean*
Participants	Local, state, and national legislators	State and national legislators; ***selected international bodies***
	State and federal courts	State and federal courts; ***international adjudication***
	Agency staff	Agency staff
	Local and national media	Local and national media
	Scientists	Scientists
	Longtime and recent residents, frequently of different socio-economic status	Longtime and recent coastal residents, frequently of different socio-economic status
	Forestry workers (resident and migratory); recreation-related workers; energy/mineral industry owners and workers	Fishermen (nearby and distant); charter boat owners; other recreation-related workers; shipping industry owners and workers; energy/mineral industry owners and workers; “new” users (e.g., aquaculture, wind energy)
	Environmental NGOs	Environmental NGOs
	Collaborative dynamics historically poor; growing collaborative leadership from agencies and communities, with an emphasis on trust-building, shared discovery, joint deliberation, and multi-agency decision-making	***Collaborative dynamics generally poor.*** Some fishery councils, coastal communities, and regions have demonstrated elements of engagement and shared motivation.

Framework element	*Public land*	*Ocean*
Coalitions	Parties interested in: • commercial timber • recreational fishing and hunting • fossil fuel extraction • conservation/sustainable use • wilderness preservation • market mechanisms and states-rights • local and state economic development • traditional native claims • national security/military priorities • ***fire management/suppression***	Parties interested in: • commercial fishing • recreational fishing • fossil fuel extraction • conservation/sustainable use • no-take marine reserves • small government/"freedom of the seas" (anti-regulation) • coastal economic development • traditional native claims • national security/military priorities • ***coastal protection from storms, erosion***

Source: Author's work.

Guam in the Western Pacific to Puerto Rico in the Caribbean and from the Arctic Ocean down to American Samoa. Likewise, the 155 National Forests cannot usefully be treated as a unified whole.

In the ACF, a policy subsystem is "characterized by both a functional/substantive dimension and a territorial one" (Sabatier and Weible 2007). Mature policy subsystems include "a set of participants … who share an expertise in a policy domain and who have sought to influence public policy in that domain for an extended period" and "the agencies, interest groups, and research institutions that have had sub-units specializing in that topic for an extended period." In the IAD framework, an action arena refers to "the social space where individuals interact, exchange goods and services, solve problems, dominate one another, or fight (among the many things that individuals do in action arenas)" (Ostrom 2007). Although these explanations of the scope of policy analysis focus on slightly different features, they are complementary. In the remainder of this study, two systems will be considered and compared:

1 a representative U.S. National Forest, including the natural and manmade resources located within it, plus the people who depend on, interact with, manage, and study it, as well as external but closely linked ecosystem components (such as contiguous state or private forests, waterways, and wildlife habitats that span the forest boundary); and
2 a three-dimensional, ecosystem-scale portion of the U.S. EEZ, including the natural and manmade resources located within it, plus the people who depend on, interact with, manage, and study it, as well as nearby or linked ecosystem components that affect it (such as watersheds, coastal waters, migratory species, and large-scale currents).

There is inevitably some arbitrariness in the delineation of any study area. Many scientists and policymakers have struggled to define an appropriate scale for ocean policy analysis and implementation. USCOP (2004a) and others (e.g., Hennessey and Juda 2001) have recommended using large marine ecosystems (LMEs)[5] as the unit of study, although they emphasize that some problems may need to be addressed at larger or smaller scales. Others (e.g., Cicin-Sain et al. 1998) have cautioned that ocean areas should not be considered separately from the watersheds that feed them. However, the scale of LMEs, a concept originated and advanced by ecologists, is not nearly as useful for exploring governance issues. As explained by Hennessey and Juda (2001), "the divergence between 'ecologically defined space' and 'politically defined space' gives rise to a host of management problems …" On the other hand, the inclusion of coastal watersheds in an analysis of the EEZ introduces many additional agencies and communities that, while consequential, may not be intimately involved in the EEZ-focused action arena.

Whatever boundaries are selected, policy analysts need to remain conscious of related processes operating at larger and smaller scales. As will become evident in later chapters, the actual dimensions of the two policy arenas defined here can range from hundreds to hundreds-of-thousands of square miles and their boundaries are highly porous. Global climate patterns and distant political events affect forests in important ways, just as watershed features and international law influence the U.S. EEZ. Such factors will be considered implicitly and explicitly as part of the broader setting for each action arena.

Contextual settings

Every policy analyst recognizes that the setting in which the policy action takes place, the *system context* or set of *exogenous variables,* is extremely important and includes physical (including geological and chemical) conditions, ecological factors, a variety of manmade and natural goods and services, and complex political, economic, and cultural dynamics. Again drawing on the frameworks discussed above, some of the most important context variables to be considered are listed here. Note that because broad community attributes are inextricably linked to the characteristics of the individual and group actors within the policy system, there are overlapping elements between this section and the next.

Ecological setting

- Main species, habitats, processes.
- Ecological status, from pristine to degraded.
- History of depletion and restoration.
- Availability of data and level of understanding.
- Ease of monitoring.

Goods and services

- Available goods and their characteristics (common pool, public, private, toll).
- Nature of property rights (including public trust duties).
- Available services and their means of provision and production.

Social setting

- Cultural history.
- Community diversity, nature of inequalities, presence of hierarchy.
- Socio-economic status, employment opportunities.

- Levels of trust, conflict, connectedness.
- Nature of discourse/social constructions concerning community members, resources, problems, and solutions.
- External interest in the policy subsystem and connections with other policy subsystems.
- Presence of collaborative drivers.

Governance setting

- Authorities (parallel, sequential, nested, fragmented, polycentric).
- Types of rules-in-use, formal and informal.
- Monitoring and enforcement provisions.
- Venues for influence, decision-making, and conflict resolution.
- Access for citizen voice.
- Accessibility of information.
- Decision-making levels.
- Prior governance successes or failures.
- Significance of public trust duties.
- Institutional support for collaboration.

Table 3.2 provides a first look at how the elements identified above might be characterized in forest and ocean arenas. As later chapters delve more deeply into U.S. forest and ocean features, additional details will emerge, leading to an updated table in Chapter 7.

Participants and their interactions

At the heart of any action situation (a.k.a. policy subsystem, LPE, or collaborative governance regime) are *participants*: the actors whose decisions and interactions lead to certain outcomes. Each participant occupies one or more *positions*, each of which grants certain kinds of authority, offers different choices for action, and imbues its holder with certain cultural attributes. Some important and frequently occurring positions include elected official, agency professional, journalist, scientist, judge, resource user, interest group leader, citizen, indigenous group member, and policy entrepreneur. Other potentially significant characteristics of participants include their access to information, relative power or vulnerability, and contributions to (or victimization by) community narratives or discourse. Participants are likely to have very different ideas about the costs and benefits, real or perceived, that accrue to them under different outcomes.

Although participants are often conceptualized as individuals, they can also be formal or informal organizations, including the dominant and minority advocacy coalitions proposed by the ACF. Enduring ACF-style coalitions are linked by a shared set of beliefs and access to resources, although temporary coalitions can be formed based on mutually desired outcomes, even if they are motivated by very different beliefs.

When some form of multi-party, multi-agency, or multi-level collaboration is desired or necessary—the norm in the complex settings being explored here—the participants' collaborative dynamics (the "gears in the machine" in Figure 3.3) become important. According to Emerson et al. (2012), certain conditions have been found to accelerate the collaborative process. *Principled engagement* is propelled by (1) shared discovery of interests, concerns, and information; (2) agreement on objectives and expectations; (3) joint deliberation, relying on reasoned communication and "the exercise of meaningful voice" by all parties; and (4) group determinations about process and substance. The next dynamic, *shared motivation* (sometimes referred to as social capital), is boosted by (1) building trust; (2) generating understanding and respect for differences; (3) establishing the legitimacy of the process, through transparency and demonstrations of credibility; and (4) fostering group commitment to an ongoing process over time. Finally, the participants' *capacity for joint action* is increased when there are (1) institutional arrangements to manage repeated interactions over time; (2) leadership that supports collaboration; (3) a knowledge base that is jointly derived and accepted; and (4) resources such as funding, time, technical support, expertise, and power that are distributed among participants to ease transaction costs. A broad-brush description of participants, coalitions, and collaborative drivers in the National Forest and ocean settings is provided in Table 3.2.

Variation over time

One critical feature of the policy elements and interactions discussed above is their variation over time. Some are thought to change very slowly as a result of changes in the surrounding political and social climate (e.g., the ACF category of deep core beliefs), some can change due to deliberate collective action by participants (e.g., the rules-in-use within the IAD framework), while other features may adjust rapidly and continuously (e.g., coalition resources). Considering how and why important policy elements, interactions, and outcomes change over time is central to policy analysis.

In addition to the models of change embedded in the frameworks discussed above, other scholars have advanced important ideas about policy change. One commonly discussed issue is the concept of "path dependence," a term coined by David (1985). Its subsequent development and use is well described and analyzed in Pierson (2000). In its simplest form, path dependence merely reminds us that "history matters": previous choices and events affect those that come later. A more significant form of path dependence occurs when yesterday's choices result in structures or institutions that are both difficult to change and that limit current choices in ways that are inefficient or undesirable (Liebowitz and Margolis 1995). The most frequently cited example is the persistence of the QWERTY keyboard layout. Originally designed deliberately to slow typing on mechanical machines with moving parts, its familiarity makes it the continued choice, even though modern computers could easily accommodate more efficient layouts that could speed typing. Although the concept of path dependency was originally developed to explain such market inefficiencies, it has also been employed by historians and political scientists to understand persistent social patterns (e.g., Page 2006; Torfing 2009).

One perspective on policy change over time led to the Multiple Streams Framework, developed by Kingdon (1984), applied and extended by others (e.g., Zahariadis and Allen 1995), and summarized in Sabatier (2007a). In brief, proponents of the Multiple Streams Framework posit that significant policy change occurs when three events coincide (the "merging streams"): (1) a particular problem, through new data or framing, becomes salient; (2) a feasible solution is available; and (3) policymakers are paying attention. This presumably infrequent occurrence is thought to create a "window of opportunity" that can then be exploited by savvy "policy entrepreneurs" with an interest in addressing that problem. Although the Multiple Streams Framework appears to explain certain policy patterns, at least ex post facto, many critics (see Sabatier 2007b; Schlager 2007) consider it incomplete as an explanation for policy development.

Another effort to analyze how policy changes over time, first proposed by Baumgartner and Jones (1993) and updated and summarized by True et al. (2007), relies on the application of punctuated equilibrium theory to public policy. Observations of U.S. policy, particularly the budgeting process, led these researchers to conclude that policy change is generally slow and incremental but is punctuated with brief periods of major change precipitated by the actions of a few influential individuals backed by group mobilization. The effect is not unlike the course of erosion, which generally proceeds steadily and gradually due to the effects of wind or water, and then advances in sudden leaps as a result of storms and floods. As will be discussed in Chapter 8, there is some evidence that the adoption of marine spatial planning as a policy option exhibited similar features (Merrie and Olsson 2014).

Although I do not apply the specific theories of change over time discussed above to my analysis of forest and ocean policies, the factors identified as potentially important—such as major shifts in elected, appointed, or populist leaders (e.g., during the New Deal), the evolution of popular culture (e.g., the growth of the progressive movement), and significant bio-physical events (e.g., the 1930s Dust Bowl)—are noted and related to both immediate and later policy developments. Figure 3.4 compares the timelines of major policy events in the U.S. ocean and forest settings, illustrating both the lag in active ocean management and the different time periods in which these events took place.

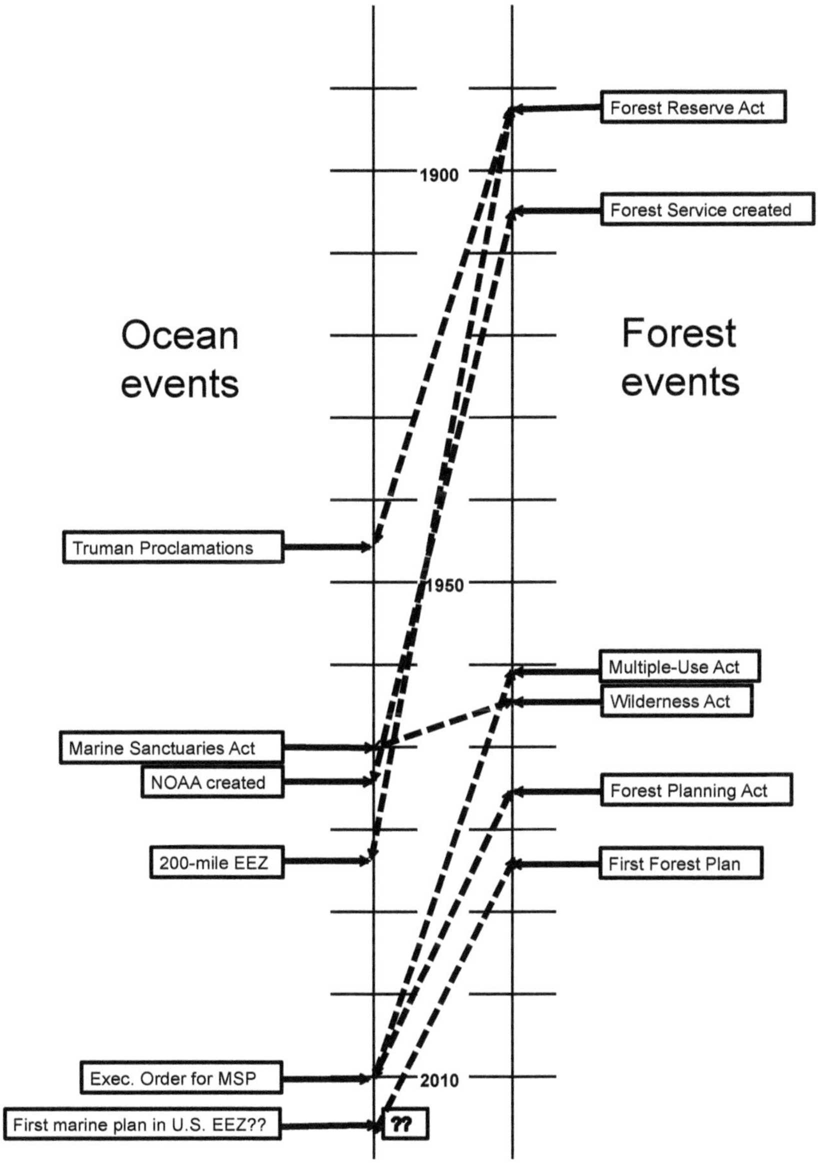

Figure 3.4 Comparison of ocean and forest timelines

Source: Compiled by author.

Summary

In this chapter, I reviewed several well-developed frameworks for policy analysis in order to devise a less descriptive, more theoretically grounded approach for comparing the governance of public lands and the EEZ. Using this approach, I conducted a preliminary analysis of the ecological, social, and governance settings, goods and services provided, and participants and coalitions engaged in each location, concluding that the similarities are significant. The next step, which I pursue in Chapters 4–6, is to delve more deeply into the history of the U.S. National Forest system, exploring developments over the last 100–150 years, examining how they influenced social and ecological outcomes, and identifying any lessons that might be applied in the less well-developed ocean context.

Notes

1 Sun (2011) suggests that public trust rights reside in the catch-all Ninth Amendment to the U.S. Constitution: "The enumeration of certain rights shall not be construed to deny or disparage others retained by the people," although others have not embraced that expansive view.
2 Appendix 7.2 in Sabatier and Weible (2007) provides an extensive list of ACF-based studies.
3 The IAD framework does not attempt to assess participants' internal beliefs. However, the identification of shared social norms that influence behavior, one subset of the institutional rules, may play a similar role in the analysis.
4 The theory behind, and additional elements of, the Collaborative Governance Framework are explained in detail in Emerson et al. (2012), with a particularly helpful table showing the underlying logic model on page 7.
5 According to Sherman and Alexander (1986) LMEs are "regions of ocean space encompassing coastal areas from river basins and estuaries on out to the seaward boundary of continental shelves and the seaward boundary of coastal current systems. They are relatively large regions on the order of 200,000 km^2 or larger, characterized by distinct bathymetry, hydrography, productivity, and trophically dependent populations."

4

THE STORY OF THE U.S. NATIONAL FOREST SYSTEM

Previous chapters showed that the U.S. EEZ and National Forests exhibit many similarities in their underlying, policy-relevant features. In this chapter, I look in greater depth at the history of the National Forests to ponder what occurred and why, and to uncover positive and negative developments that might be translatable to the ocean context. Ocean policy experts—and all those familiar with the ocean management context—should read this chapter carefully. Although the details may be new, as they were for me, there are many eye-opening parallels and startlingly familiar scenarios that emerge.

The National Forests and their administrative home in the U.S. Forest Service were built up over many decades and are now enshrined in a number of laws and firmly lodged within the federal bureaucracy. But what *are* National Forests? How and why did they come about? What value (and values) do they embody? How have they been used and managed and what challenges has that posed for government agencies and the public? Like most organizations, the story of the Forest Service has been told by many different people over time, with different memories and perspectives, relying on different records. This chapter presents a condensed account of some of the major themes and events in Forest Service history, each one presented in roughly chronological order.

Hundreds of scholars have spent distinguished careers studying and theorizing about National Forest management; their analyses and writings are heavily referenced below. My purpose is not to reinvent that body of work but rather, through the eyes of a marine policy specialist, to see what themes emerge that might be relevant to the management of another valuable public space: the ocean.

The shift from "disposal" to "reservation" of public lands

Chapter 2 described the late 19th-century shift from an era of rapid *disposal* of U.S. government-controlled lands, through grants and sales to other entities, to an era of *reservation* of those lands, i.e., maintaining them under federal ownership for specified national purposes.[1] That shift established what we now think of as the public lands and created a role for the federal government in managing land for the benefit of the nation as a whole, rather than transferring land to private owners. The concept of government-run forests, in particular, was enshrined in the 1891 Forest Reserve Act and further clarified in an 1897 Organic Act (see timeline in Table 4.1), stating that Forest Reserve managers were to "regulate occupancy and use and preserve the forests thereon from destruction." In 1905, the Division of Forestry, previously in the Department of the Interior, was renamed the Forest Service and moved to the USDA where other "crops" were managed.

Table 4.1 Timeline of major laws and regulations affecting National Forests

Date	*Event*
1891	Forest Reserve Act declares that certain forested GLO lands can no longer be sold or given away
1897	Organic Act clarifies that the Forest Reserves are intended to protect forests, supply timber, and maintain watershed functions
1905	Forest Service created and moved to the USDA
1911	Weeks Act authorizes Forest Service purchases of degraded Eastern forest lands
1916	Wildlife Refuges created on Forest Service lands
1922	General Exchange Act allows National Forest managers to exchange lands with other landowners to consolidate holdings
1924	Clarke-McNary Act encourages and facilitates purchases of additional Eastern forest lands
1960	Multiple-Use Sustained Yield Act (MUSY) tells Forest Service to manage for timber, water supply, wildlife, grazing, and recreation; authority over mining and oil and gas remains in the Dept. of the Interior
1964	Wilderness Act creates 9 million acres of fully protected Forest Service lands and sets a process for further designations
1966	Freedom of Information Act (FOIA) allows greater public access to agency records
1969	NEPA requires environmental impact analyses for federal actions
1969	ESA grants heightened protection for listed species
1970	Binding regulatory provisions added to the 1963 Clean Air Act require additional impact analyses
1972	Federal Advisory Committee Act (FACA) regulates external advisory bodies
1972	Clean Water Act
1974	Forest and Rangelands Renewable Resources Planning Act (RPA) calls for periodic resource assessments on federal lands
1976	NFMA instructs Forest Service to create a plan for every forest that achieves balanced, multiple use (as called for in the MUSY Act), with revisions every 15 years
1982	NFMA planning regulations issued. These regulations have governed forest plans for 30 years as all subsequent proposed revisions were challenged and withdrawn or rejected by courts
2012	Revised NFMA planning rule issued and immediately challenged in court

Source: Compiled by author.

This transition took place against the backdrop of several competing philosophical, economic, and administrative perspectives. Late 19th-century politics in the U.S. were dominated by a small number of wealthy capitalists promoting an aggressive free-market approach toward natural resources, supported by a utilitarian philosophy that sought to maximize economic gains (Culhane 1981). By the end of that century, the widespread and visible degradation of forests, rangelands, farmland, and wildlife—not to mention the economic and political stranglehold of the few over the many—created strong public support for a new president, Theodore Roosevelt, and a new approach referred to as *progressive conservationism* (Pinchot 1947).

The conservationists (with President Roosevelt and his friend Gifford Pinchot in the lead) believed that some portion of the land and resources should be kept under government ownership, to be managed in the interests of the public. Furthermore, they thought this could be admirably accomplished by professional staff within government agencies, relying on rational, scientific techniques. Based on this philosophical orientation, and his training under French and Prussian foresters, Pinchot proposed that National Forests could be efficiently managed as well-run "tree farms" that would produce large yields indefinitely (Kennedy et al. 1998).

Around the same time, a competing perspective, *preservationism*, was being advanced by well-known thinkers and writers who viewed undisturbed nature as valuable in its own right, rather than as a source of goods for people (Meyer 1997). They sought to preserve areas that they saw (incorrectly) as untouched by civilization, believing that "in God's wildness lies the hope of the world—the great fresh, unblighted, unredeemed wilderness" (quote from John Muir's 1890 *Alaskan Journal*, see Muir 1979).[2]

These three competing goals—free enterprise, progressive conservation, and preservation—continued to jostle for dominance in American attitudes toward natural resources over the next 100 years and to this day (Culhane 1981; Bryner 1998).

Trees as a crop

The early days of the Forest Service, with Pinchot as Chief Forester, epitomized the ascendance of progressive conservation. In an era when notions of efficiency, professionalism, and science were greatly valued, Pinchot made it his priority to advance the field of professional silviculture in America. He helped create (and fund) the Yale School of Forestry and founded the Society of American Foresters. He believed that the forests should be overseen by government, but harvested by private interests according to specific guidelines in exchange for fees. In this, he was opposed by both the timber companies, who resented perceived government interference in their business (Balogh 2002), and by preservationists like John Muir, who were opposed to the commodification of nature. Muir (1917) referred to the forests as "lordly monarchs proclaiming the gospel of beauty like apostles."

Through the 1930s, timber harvest levels on federal lands were relatively low (Figure 4.1) and the role of the Forest Service was considered largely custodial. One of its main tasks was to control wildfires, which burned from 20–50 million acres annually in 1930 (see Figure 4.2). These fires often originated on private lands, but the damage to public forests led the Forest Service to devote significant resources to their prevention, detection, and rapid suppression. In his 1933 book, Marshall depicted forest rangers as larger than life, heroic figures and exhorted the U.S. government to initiate a major program of purchasing private forest lands and converting them all to the "excellent" stewardship of the Forest Service. The purchase of private forest lands in Eastern states was initiated in 1911 under the Weeks Act and accelerated in 1924 with passage of the Clarke-McNary Act.

Through the early 20th century, owners of private forestlands had been rapidly cutting their trees to satisfy national needs for timber. Beginning around the time of World War II, and accelerating through the 1950s and 1960s as post-war housing construction boomed, the timber industry increasingly looked to National Forests as an additional source of wood products. The Forest Service obliged by steadily increasing the allowable cut (see Figure 4.1). Their incomplete ecological understanding, faith in technocratic management, and persistent view of trees as agricultural crops to be actively managed combined to convince Forest Service staff that these harvest levels could be sustained, and even increased, if they were accompanied by systematic replanting. By clearcutting entire stands, and replanting them with denser monocultures, foresters believed they were executing efficient, science-based, modern management. As late as 1947, Pinchot continued to proclaim that "forestry is tree farming" (Pinchot 1947). This perspective was reinforced by pressure from industry groups and a strong message from Congress, through hearings and appropriations, that a critical Forest Service job was to help boost local and national economies through timber sales.

In some ways, the 1950s may have been a high point for the Forest Service image, internally and externally. A 1952 article in *Newsweek* magazine stated that "in 47 years, the foresters have been untouched by scandal," and a book written in the late 1950s (Kaufman 1960) concluded that the Forest Service could be considered a model of "an efficient and effective government agency." But by the 1960s, the consequences of the escalating harvest were beginning to be felt. Twice as much timber was cut between 1950 and 1966 as during the previous forty-five years of Forest Service existence. Meanwhile, the mood of the country was beginning to shift and the forces of opposition were getting organized.

In 1969, a Forest Service study of Douglas fir in the Pacific Northwest concluded that existing harvest levels could not be sustained (USFS 1969).

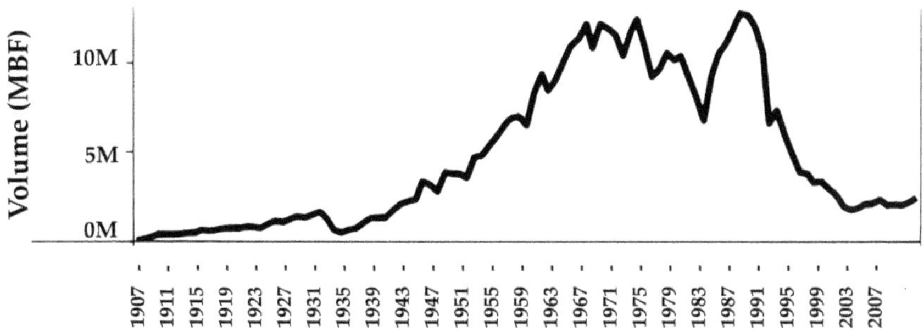

Figure 4.1 Timber harvest on National Forests, 1905–2011

Source: Author's work based on Forest Service harvest data.

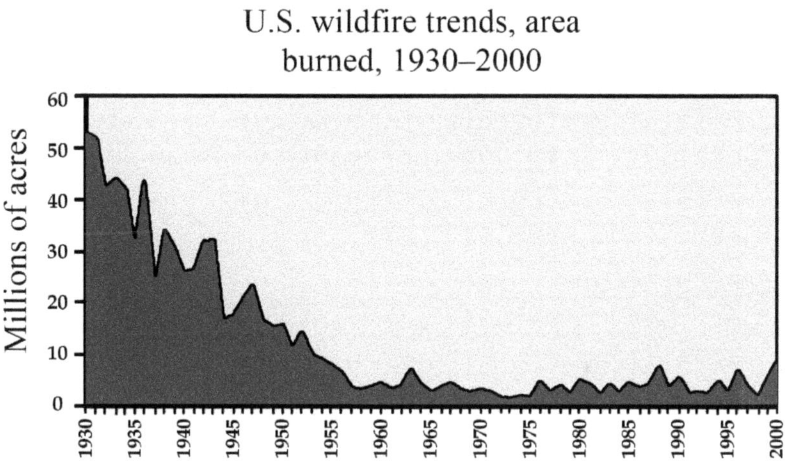

Figure 4.2 Area burned by wildfire, 1930–2000

Source: U.S. Wildfire Statistics 2001, USDA, Forest Service.

Nevertheless, rather than *decreasing* allowable timber sales, Congress instructed the Forest Service to intensify its active forest management efforts with the hope of increasing future yields—in other words, the Service was to continue high levels of cutting, dense re-planting, and heavy use of herbicides and pesticides (Fedkiw 1999). The timber harvest on National Forests rose by another 92 percent from 1952 through 1986, before plummeting by 84 percent through 2001 as the debates and conflicts described in the sections below developed (Smith et al. 2004).

Currently, about one-third of the United States' land area, 755 million acres, is forested. Of that, 56 percent is privately owned and the rest is controlled by federal, state, county, or municipal agencies. The Forest Service manages 193 million acres (60 percent of the public forest lands and 8.5 percent of the total U.S. land area), divided into 155 National Forests and 20 national grasslands, located in 44 states (Figure 4.3), which range in size from the diminutive Calaveras Big Tree National Forest in California at only 379 acres, to the massive Tongass National Forest in Alaska at 17 million acres. The great majority of National Forests are located in the Western states. Despite this large forest area under federal ownership, privately owned forests currently provide 92 percent of the nation's timber harvest, with National Forests contributing only 2 percent (Smith et al. 2004).

Navigating a multiple-use mandate

In addition to the original purposes of timber harvesting and waterway maintenance, other uses of Forest Service lands emerged and grew over time. From the first establishment of Forest Reserves, homesteaders and settlers were permitted to extract timber, stone, fodder, and wildlife from the National Forests for domestic use, free of charge. In 1905, when

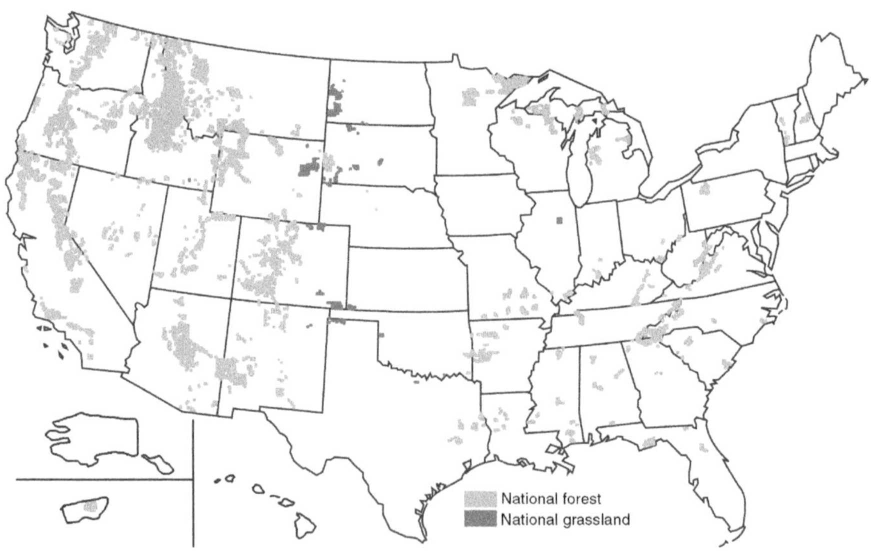

Figure 4.3 Distribution of National Forests

Source: www.fs.fed.us/maps.

the Forest Reserves were transferred to the Department of Agriculture, livestock grazing was stipulated as an additional acceptable use. A law in 1915 specifically authorized the construction of summer homes and related recreation on National Forests. Then, in 1916, wildlife refuges were established on Forest Service lands, and fishing and hunting were recognized as allowable uses. Thus, by 1916 the Forest Service was already responsible for managing "the five Ws" (Hall 1963): wood, water, wildlife, range, and recreation.

As early as 1907, Pinchot had recognized that National Forest uses might "sometimes conflict a little" but had to "fit with one another so that the machine would run smoothly as a whole" (as quoted in Fedkiw 1999). As the Forest Service grew, institutionalized its operating procedures, and developed an organizational culture, it sought ways to fulfill its sometimes contradictory responsibilities by attempting to "balance" all the allowed uses. The term "multiple use" is found in Forest Service speeches and documents starting in around 1933 and was increasingly incorporated into Forest Service practice and guidance from that time forward (see Table 4.2; Fedkiw 1999).

In 1936, an article was written for the farming community to explain the value of intercropping, exemplified by the ancient Native American practice of mingled cultivation of the beans and corn used in succotash; as an analogy, the author asserted that "the best illustration of this is the National Forests." This resonated with Forest Service thinking at the time, and the article was widely praised and circulated among Forest Service staff (as recounted in Behan 1967). The idea that multiple uses could not only co-exist but actually enhance each other came to be accepted as the justification for multiple-use management. By 1963, the Forest Service Manual continued to maintain that "compromise and limitations are acceptable because of the greater total benefit," an unverified assumption that Behan referred to as the "Succotash Syndrome."

For the next several decades, uses continued to increase and forest managers took a proactive role in facilitating and encouraging them. Intensive, technocratically driven forest harvesting practices were described in the previous section. A similar philosophy governed efforts to build up herds of desirable, big game animals for hunters, such as deliberate predator control and selective forest thinning, and to ensure adequate fish stocks for anglers by stocking rivers with native and non-native species. To compete with the popular and expanding National Park system, recreation was enthusiastically promoted in the forests, including construction of facilities to support camping, automobile touring, hiking, river rafting, and skiing.[3]

Table 4.2 Evolution of multiple-use management and planning in National Forests

Date	*Event*
1897	Organic Act for Forest Reserves clarifies that they are intended to protect the forests, supply timber, and maintain watershed functions
1905	Transfer Act creates the Forest Service and moves it to the USDA; grazing is specified as an allowable use in a letter from the Secretary of Agriculture
1915	Term Lease Law allows summer homes on forests; beginning of recreational uses
1916	Wildlife Refuges created on Forest Service lands; five major Forest Service goals—wood, water, wildlife, range, and recreation—now enshrined in law
1934	Montana's Regional Forester writes an article explaining that Forest Service practice is to manage multiple uses in one place, as a farmer would
1958	Forest Service manual adds a new section on multiple-use management
1960	MUSY Act confirms previous practice, instructing Forest Service to manage for wood, watershed, wildlife, range, and recreation, but does not give them authority over mining or oil and gas. Bill does not mention wilderness as a use
1974	RPA requires National Forest assessments for each region
1976	NFMA expands on RPA. Instructs Forest Service to create a plan for each forest that achieves balanced, multiple use for the five MUSY goals, plus wilderness. Calls for plans to be revised no later than every 15 years
1979	First NFMA regulations issued
1982	Revised NFMA regulations issued. These rules still govern forest plans because all subsequent versions were withdrawn, revised, and/or blocked in court
1983	First forest plans completed
1990	Forest Service releases the "Critique of Land Management Planning" (USFS 1990)
1995	Last forest plan completed; early plans being revised
1999	USDA Committee of Scientists releases report on Forest Service planning, "Sustaining the People's Lands"(Johnson et al. 1999)
2012	Revised NFMA planning rule issued after extensive public consultation but immediately challenged in court

Source: Compiled by author.

Post-war affluence and mobility sent Americans flocking to the public lands. Annual visits to National Forests went from 5 million in 1920, to 18 million in 1946, and 93 million in 1960 (MacCleery 1992). Even adjusting for population growth, this means that in the year 1920 there was an average of one forest visit per twenty-one U.S. residents, while forty years later that annual rate had increased tenfold, to one forest visit for every two residents. Of course, forest visits are not distributed evenly over the population, but the growing highway system, cheap gas, and subsidized facilities did make National Parks and Forests affordable vacation spots for an expanding middle class.

In 1960, the Forest Service's original 1897 Organic Act was finally updated to formalize the full range of uses allowed in National Forests and describe how they should be managed. The MUSY Act reaffirmed that the National Forests exist "for outdoor recreation, range, timber, watershed, and wildlife and fish purposes" and enshrined the Forest Service's authority to "administer the renewable surface resources of the National Forests for multiple use and sustained yield of the several products and services obtained therefrom."

In fact, many additional uses were accepted, and continue to occur, on Forest Service land. From the start, the 1897 Organic Act for the Forest Reserves allowed prospecting and mining to continue in the forests under the very permissive General Mining Law of 1872, administered by the Department of the Interior and in effect to this day (Fedkiw 1999). Although this use doesn't occupy large areas of the forest, it can be very damaging locally. One Forest Service scholar referred to the anomaly of leaving mining out of the broader multiple-use structure as "a bad idea that has been amazingly persistent" (Davis 2001). In addition, rights of way for pipelines, power lines, public roads, and hydropower installations—mostly managed by other agencies—are allowed in National Forests under "general occupancy and use" regulations that were not overridden by the 1960 MUSY Act. Finally, the extensive network of logging roads constructed to ease access to and removal of timber, although not treated as a separate "use," created serious problems for other users, hindered conservation, and became a major source of contention.

The Forest Service had lobbied in favor of MUSY and considered its passage a significant accomplishment since it essentially codified what they had been doing for the past four decades. Significantly, Congress did not establish any priorities among the allowed uses in case of conflict, nor did it specify how the Forest Service was intended to make such choices.

As defined in MUSY, "multiple use" means:

> The management of all the various renewable surface resources of the National Forests so that they are utilized in the combination that will best meet the needs of the American people; making the most judicious use of the land for some or all of these resources or related services over areas large enough to provide sufficient latitude for periodic adjustments in use to conform to changing needs and conditions; that some land will be used for less than all of the resources; and harmonious and coordinated management of the various resources, each with the other, without impairment of the productivity of the land, with consideration being given to the relative values of the various resources, and not necessarily the combination of uses that will give the greatest dollar return or the greatest unit output.

Its companion term, "sustained-yield," was defined as "the achievement and maintenance in perpetuity of a high-level annual or periodic output of the various renewable resources of the National Forests without impairment of the productivity of the land." A careful reading of these definitions makes it clear that MUSY creates a very difficult balancing act for the agency, requiring a high level of agency judgment and discretion. In effect, the Forest Service's job had become to define "the needs of the American people" and "the most judicious use of the land" (Reich 1962; Behan 1967).

The gradual adoption, and eventual codification, of multiple use as the guiding principle for management of the National Forests represents a victory for the progressive conservationists' conviction that science-based, apolitical, federal agencies would be in the best position to make decisions that achieve "the greatest good for the greatest number of people over the long run." It was also a victory for agency leaders who wished to preserve administrative flexibility and control over "their" lands (Hall 1963). MUSY still governs Forest Service lands, although the relative mix of uses occurring there, and the interpretation of "balance," have drastically changed in many forests.

Making room for wilderness

As discussed previously, the expansion of timber harvesting and other National Forest uses was continually challenged by advocates of the preservationist perspective, rooted in the writings of philosophers and writers such as Ralph Waldo Emerson, Henry David Thoreau, John Muir, Bob Marshall, and Aldo Leopold, who saw wilderness as a place of spiritual sustenance and "the essential fabric of a distinctive American culture" (Scott 2001).[4] Although the concept of "untrammeled wilderness" is a human invention—virtually all of the U.S. land area has been inhabited or in some way used by human communities for hundreds or thousands of years—the desire to identify and set aside "unspoiled" areas has endured and expanded over the last century.

One response to this yearning to preserve natural landscapes was the creation of the National Park System, starting in the late 1800s and expanding through the 1930s. Although largely protected from extractive uses, the parks were intended to promote recreation. The Park Service encouraged and accommodated visitors by building roads, lodges, campsites, and trails, all of which necessarily impinged on natural areas. As a result, advocates for preservation looked to the Forest Service to set aside some of its lands as true wilderness areas, asserting that this could be considered a legitimate "highest use" under multiple-use principles. In 1924, the Gila Wilderness Area in New Mexico became the first so-designated, created at the urging of Aldo Leopold who served as a Forest Service ranger there.

Additional National Forest wilderness designations moved forward in 1929, when Regulation L-20 established a formal process for the Forest

Service Chief to designate "primitive areas" within National Forests that would "maintain primitive conditions of transportation, subsistence, habitation, and environment *to the fullest degree compatible with their highest public use* with a view to conserving the values of such areas for ... public education and recreation" (emphasis added; Wilkinson and Anderson 1987). Seventy-five such areas totaling 14.2 million acres were designated over the following ten years. However, as the regulation made clear, these primitive areas were still considered available for other uses. Debates took place within the wilderness community in the 1930s about which approach was preferable: primitive areas designated by the Forest Service, which offered greater wilderness protection for the moment, but no long-term security, or National Parks, which would be more permanent because of congressional designation, but open to a wide range of recreational users (Scott 2001; Harvey 2005).

In the late 1930s, two new National Parks (Olympic and Kings Canyon) were carved out of Forest Service lands. Perhaps in reaction, the head of the Forest Service Recreation and Lands division, Bob Marshall, another wealthy, influential wilderness advocate and founder of the Wilderness Society, pushed hard for more stringent protection of selected areas within the forests. The so-called U-regulations, issued in 1939 (36 CFR Sec. 251.20, 1939), stated that new "wilderness areas"—as opposed to the "primitive areas" formerly created by Regulation L-20—would exclude all new roads, motorized transportation, commercial timber harvest, and any special uses such as resorts and related public facilities. Such areas would be selected by the Secretary of Agriculture (rather than the Forest Service Chief) and all existing "primitive areas" would be evaluated for possible re-classification as wilderness.

Despite this growing administrative designation of wilderness areas, the drive for permanent preservation of "natural" spaces remained strong. In 1945, the Wilderness Society (endowed through a substantial bequest from Marshall's estate) hired a new director, Howard Zahniser, to draft and build grass-roots support for federal wilderness legislation, working with other like-minded groups. A January 1956 Sierra Club Bulletin proclaimed that "[wilderness areas] are great reservoirs of the serene order of nature, where things work the way they ought to" (quoted in Scott 2001). The first attempt to pass a Wilderness Bill in Congress was met with strong opposition from commercial timber interests, the leadership of the National Park Service and Forest Service, many members of relevant House Committees, and the Eisenhower Administration. Although MUSY had specified that "the establishment and maintenance of areas of wilderness" was allowed within National Forests—and by 1963, 14.5 million acres of either "Primitive" or "Wilderness" areas had been carved out under the L- and U-regulations—a permanent, statutory approach remained the preservationists' goal. After several more attempts, fierce media campaigns, setbacks, and compromises, President Johnson signed the Wilderness Act into law in 1964, shortly after taking office.

The Act defines wilderness as "an area of undeveloped Federal land retaining its primeval character and influence without permanent improvements or human habitation and which generally appears to have been affected primarily by the forces of nature, with the imprint of man's work substantially unnoticeable" and, more poetically, "an area where the earth and its community of life are untrammeled by man." Areas designated as wilderness were exempt from the multiple-use paradigm, governed instead by the preservationist belief in the inherent value of nature with no human presence. (At that time, arguments for wilderness did not include the value of ecosystem services and system resilience to *humans*, as they would later on.)

The new Act immediately brought 9.1 million acres of administratively designated Forest Service wilderness areas into the new National Wilderness Preservation System, despite the fact that some of those areas were far from "primeval," and set up a ten-year process for all the federal public land agencies (including the Forest Service, BLM, FWS, and National Park Service) to review areas under their jurisdiction and make recommendations for further wilderness. The Forest Service's resulting Roadless Area Review and Evaluation (RARE) and its successor, RARE-II, examined 62 million acres of forest land, recommending 15 million of them as additional wilderness.

Early drafts of the Wilderness Bill had proposed that agency recommendations be automatically adopted, unless vetoed by Congress. However, in an ironic twist of history, opponents of the Act who wanted to make it difficult to add new wilderness areas insisted on a provision specifying that only Congress could make such designations (Scott 2001). Although considered a bitter pill to swallow by preservationists at the time, this feature of the Act later proved a blessing: wilderness advocates found it easier to exert political pressure on Congress than to alter the deeply ingrained multiple-use mindset and slow pace of the agencies. What's more, Congress was able to interpret its own definition of wilderness much more loosely than the courts may have permitted the agencies to do (Kelson 1998). In subsequent years, Congress included many areas in the system that fell far short of the statutory definition of wilderness. In lobbying for designation of one such area in California, proponents admitted that this was "the logical means of precluding timber-harvest activities in the watershed" (MacCleery 2001). Such stretching of the law was particularly common in Eastern forests, most of which had been acquired by the government after they had already been heavily harvested.

The Wilderness Act was one of the first pieces of environmental legislation to include extensive public participation requirements. As a result, the process of agency wilderness review, which took place from 1964 to 1974, an already tumultuous time at the height of the pro-environment, anti-war activist movements, was closely scrutinized and became highly politicized. In 1968, "hundreds of grass roots citizen leaders ... travelled to Washington ... to lobby their congressional delegations and to testify for their own wilderness proposals" (Scott 2001).

After passage of NEPA in 1969, environmental groups maintained, and the courts agreed, that an environmental impact statement (EIS) would henceforth be required for any activity proposed to take place in part of a National Forest subject to the roadless area review process, whether that area had yet been formally designated as wilderness or not. Recognizing the enormous delays such assessments would create, the timber industry and other forest users instead agreed to support dozens of state-specific wilderness designation bills. Although these bills included even more wilderness area than recommended under the RARE-II process, they simultaneously exempted any remaining roadless areas in those states from NEPA's EIS requirements.

Between 1978 and 1998, twenty-four wilderness designation bills were passed by Congress, including the Alaska National Interest Lands Conservation Act which added over 56 million acres to the Wilderness System, by far the single largest addition.[5] In some instances, legislators created whole new categories of protected public lands (such as National Preserves, Conservation Areas, Scenic Areas, and others) when they wished to remove areas from multiple use but could not plausibly assert that they satisfied the statutory definition of wilderness (Kelson 1998).

As of 2012, 30 percent of the National Forests are maintained as Roadless Areas and another 19 percent (37 million acres) are part of the National Wilderness Preservation System. Another 73 million acres of wilderness are located on lands under the BLM, FWS, and National Park Service management.[6] Of the entire land area of the United States, about 5 percent is now protected as wilderness, much of it in Alaska.

The role of forest planning

Although the first formal regulations requiring a plan for every National Forest were not issued until 1979 (see Table 4.2), the notion of nationwide and unit-specific planning had been around for some time before then. The Forest Service had a long history of conducting resource assessments and drafting work plans with varying levels of detail (Coggins and Evans 1981), but it was the MUSY Act of 1960 that "created the impetus for multiple-use planning" (MacCleery 2008).

To fulfill MUSY requirements—and to address a series of court losses related to MUSY implementation—the Forest Service developed an agency-wide planning process in the 1960s and early 1970s whereby broad multiple-use objectives were established by the Chief in D.C., further elaborated in Regional guides, used by Forest Supervisors and their staff in preparing forest plans, and implemented by requiring projects and actions at the district level to be "consistent" with those plans. A case study from that time (Martin 1969) concluded that "through the preparation of plans … multiple use can become a decisional rule for the future."

In fact, despite improved coordination among some uses, MUSY did not lead to a consistent, integrated, nationwide planning system, nor did it constrain Forest Service discretion at the project level in a way that could shift the balance of uses away from its historic emphasis on timber harvesting. For example, in 1970 the Bolle Committee, an independent panel named after its chair, the Dean of the School of Forestry at the University of Montana, evaluated the status of the Bitterroot National Forest and concluded that "multiple-use management, in fact, does not exist as the governing principle on the Bitterroot […] Consideration of recreation, watershed, wildlife, and grazing appear as afterthoughts" (Bolle et al. 1970).

In an attempt to give non-timber uses more even-handed consideration, Congress passed the 1974 RPA, which required the Forest Service to periodically assess the long-term supply and demand for all renewable resources and to plan accordingly, but this bill too failed to significantly change Forest Service practice. Two years later, under growing pressure from environmental advocates and a game-changing Court Order that declared all clearcutting to be inconsistent with the 1897 Organic Act, Congress passed NFMA. As evidence of the sense of urgency behind this bill, it was introduced, debated, and passed within just three months. Upon its passage, Senator Hubert Humphrey declared that:

> The days have ended when the forest may be viewed only as trees and trees viewed only as timber. The soil and water, the grasses and the shrubs, the fish and the wildlife, and the beauty that is the forest must become integral parts of resource managers' thinking and actions.
> (1976 Congressional record, cited in Wilkinson 1997)

NFMA provided extensive guidelines for long-term management of National Forests, requiring planning to be conducted by interdisciplinary teams, including an "integrated plan for each National Forest," and calling for increased participation by the public and the external science community (Applegate 1977; Fedkiw 1999). Moreover, NFMA specified for the first time that, once a forest plan is in place, subsequent management actions must be consistent with its elements. Although NFMA's supporters hoped that the process would "help to resolve the differences between environmentalists and timber, mining and livestock-grazing communities" (MacCleery 2001), and others thought planning could insulate forest managers from criticism by "reducing political pressures … and providing a consistent rationale for on-the-ground decisions" (Coggins and Evans 1981), subsequent events dashed such optimism.

NFMA set out extremely detailed elements to be included in forest plans, deemed at the time to be "some of the most specific forest management requirements ever enacted into law" (Applegate 1977). For the Forest Service to issue suitable implementing regulations, they would have to include guidelines concerning precisely how, when, and where to cut timber, how to achieve diverse plant and animal communities, and how to include the public. The first set of regulations, issued in 1979 and revised in 1982, has governed forest planning ever since, during which time all subsequent proposed updates have been withdrawn, revised, and/or blocked in court. On March 23, 2012, the Forest Service at last issued a revised planning rule, finalized after more than two years of public consultation and comment. The rule was immediately criticized by environmental groups and, shortly after, challenged in court by a coalition of industry groups.[7]

Integrated multiple-use planning did not turn out to be the panacea for which some had hoped. It became increasingly clear that there were no "optimal solutions," just different ways of balancing competing interests (Yaffee and Wondolleck 2003). An in-depth review of the first decade of planning recognized both its promise—"planning is the gateway to meeting both the spirit and intent of the many laws governing natural resources"—and its limitations—"some of the problems we want planning to solve are intractable" (USFS 1990). That same review defined the essential elements of planning as: determining resource capabilities, identifying current and future demands, finding the best match between capabilities and demands, and educating everyone involved. It then concluded that people inside and outside the Forest Service had unreasonable expectations about how easily those tasks could be achieved.

The impact of planning on conditions in the forests has also been uneven. In some forests, plans were written, implemented on the ground, and revised with relatively little conflict (see the Eastern Forest case study in Chapter 6). In others, lawsuits under the NEPA, ESA, Clean Air Act, FACA, or Clean Water Act dominated the debate, overwhelming any focus on the forest plan. And in the Pacific Northwest, site of the infamous "owls vs. jobs" debacle, planning was taken to a whole new level, including active involvement by the President of the United States, as described in the first case study in Chapter 5.

One interesting side effect of NFMA and later environmental laws was a significant change in the Forest Service workforce. Although foresters still formed the largest group of employees, many other specialists—in fields such as wildlife biology, landscape design, ecology, hydrology, soil science, environmental economics, planning, sociology, and archaeology—were brought in to help prepare EISs and forest plans (Farnham and Mohai 1995). By the late 1980s, foresters comprised only 50 percent of the professional staff (Sabatier et al. 1995). As the new staff became absorbed into the agency culture and began to move into management positions, pressure from within helped nudge the Forest Service toward a more holistic, multi-faceted view of its mission (Thomas and Mohai 1995). By 1993, a wildlife biologist, Jack Ward Thomas, became the first non-forester appointed as Chief of the Forest Service.

In 1998, in the midst of the Forest Service's ongoing failure to craft updated NFMA rules that could withstand public and judicial scrutiny, a committee of scientists was appointed by the Secretary of Agriculture to fundamentally rethink the Forest Service's approach to planning (Committee of Scientists 1999). Its central recommendations were to shift Forest Service *goals* from commodity outputs to broader ecological sustainability, and its *approach* from primarily internal, technically driven decision-making to an open, collaborative planning process. These two themes are discussed in the following sections.

New forestry, new perspectives

Starting in the 1960s, accelerating by the time of the first Earth Day on April 22, 1970, and continuing through the rest of that decade, scientists and environmental advocates began exploring new paradigms for natural resource management. This new movement combined elements of progressive conservation (e.g., belief in science-based management) and preservation (e.g., desire for undisturbed wilderness) with new scientific findings about ecosystem complexity and a growing mistrust of traditional, agency procedures (Keiter 1994). As early as 1970, Caldwell noted that "the natural processes of physical and biological systems ... do not necessarily accommodate themselves to the artificial boundaries and restrictions that law and political economy impose upon them." That same year, Forest Service Chief Edward Cliff opined that "an ecosystem approach to multiple-use management, [to] our National Forests, and [to our] rangelands can contribute to a better living for present and future generations" (as quoted in Fedkiw 1999). But adoption of EBM as a guiding principle by Forest Service leaders would not come for another twenty years.

In the meantime, there were many practical reasons to conclude that existing approaches to management were making it difficult to achieve desired results. One recurring debate involved impacts on designated wilderness areas from outside their boundaries. How could the "primeval character" of these lands be maintained if roads and clearcuts were allowed immediately adjacent to them? Efforts to create "buffer zones" around wilderness areas were resisted by the Forest Service, asserting the primacy of the multiple-use approach on all Forest Service land unless otherwise instructed by Congress. This was affirmed in Congress's 1980 Colorado Wilderness Act which declared that "the fact that non-wilderness activities or uses can be seen or heard from within the wilderness shall not, of itself, preclude such activities or uses up to the boundary of the wilderness area." Similar language was included in twenty-one state wilderness acts (Kelson 1998). In other words, only Congress could draw the limits of wilderness on the map, and there they would remain. Even more complicated legal and political issues surrounded debates about how to manage water and the complicated system of water rights in, near, or with impacts on wilderness areas.

The traditional Forest Service approach to fire management also appeared to be breaking down. As a result of decades of deliberate and highly successful fire suppression (see Figure 4.2), by 1960 the number of wildfires and the total area burned had dramatically decreased. However, the resulting buildup of flammable materials, with dry wood on the ground, standing dead wood, thick undergrowth, and densely planted replacement stands, made forests highly susceptible to large-scale fires as well as insect and disease outbreaks. By the 1980s, many areas that had once experienced frequent, slow-burning fires were now witnessing uncharacteristically intense, wide-ranging, and destructive wildfires (Figure 4.4). The expansion of residential development in previously rural areas near forests exacerbated the resulting costs in human lives and property damage. Counter to all their training, rangers were forced to wonder whether some fires should be allowed to burn.

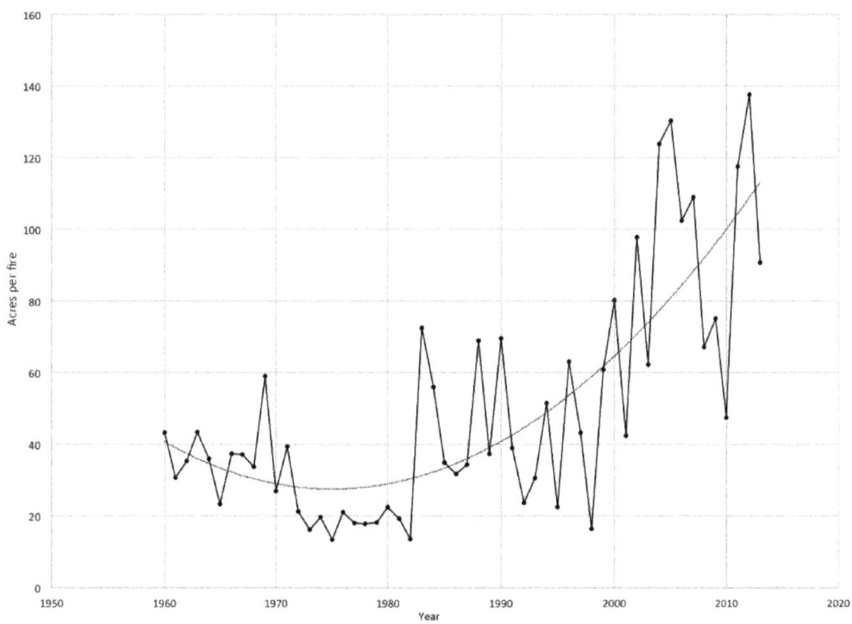

Figure 4.4 Trend in average acres burned per wildfire (1960–2013)

Source: Western Institute for Study of the Environment, based on data from the National Interagency Fire Center.

The ESA, which regulates activities that might harm threatened or endangered species, provided perhaps the clearest example of the limitations of business-as-usual management. By making species protection trump virtually all management goals except national security, the ESA forced federal agencies, particularly the Forest Service, to change their ways. The Act explicitly linked species conservation to preservation of suitable habitat, and scientists were realizing that isolated parks and wilderness areas would not be adequate to prevent further losses (Keiter 1994).

By the mid-1980s, the northern spotted owl had become the symbol for species that need large areas of old-growth forest for their survival. In 1991, a federal judge issued an injunction against all timber harvest on forests within the range of the northern spotted owl (i.e., western Washington and Oregon and northern California). He found that the Forest Service had not complied with provisions in NFMA that required agency plans to provide for maintenance of "viable populations of existing native and desired non-native vertebrate species." Around the same time, several blue-ribbon scientific committees issued reports projecting how much federal land would need to be preserved, and what level of timber harvest could be allowed, to maintain viable spotted owl populations (Thomas et al. 1990, 1993; FEMAT 1993). These panels invalidated the longstanding assumption that high production forestry and species protection were compatible (MacCleery 2001). As a result of these scientific and legal developments, a new tri-state, multi-agency, regional approach to management was enshrined in the Northwest Forest Plan, resulting in drastic declines in timber sales (additional details and discussion of the Northwest Forest Plan are provided as part of the case studies in Chapter 5).

The public upheavals described above were accompanied by similar turmoil within the Forest Service staff. In 1989, fourteen forest supervisors from Montana and northern Idaho sent a letter to Forest Service Chief Dale Robertson complaining that continued high harvest levels were opposed by many stakeholders and were placing other resources at risk. Jeff DeBonis, a timber sale planner, sent a similar letter to Chief Robertson and launched the Association of Forest Service Employees for Environmental Ethics (AFSEEE, later shortened to FSEEE), a forum for dissenting employees. A Forest Service biologist, Jerry Franklin, began to sketch out and promote a "New Forestry" that would incorporate emerging findings in ecosystem science while maintaining timber production (Kohm and Franklin 1997). For example, he suggested that foresters could maintain more diverse habitats by leaving some downed logs, standing dead trees, and clumps of live trees within harvested areas—a major departure from standard practice. More generally, New Forestry would require managers to look at forests as complex, adaptive ecosystems, not tree farms (Gillis 1990). Predictably, criticisms were lobbed at this new idea from all directions: the Wilderness Society rejected it as a weaker alternative than straight-out preservation, and the Forest Resource Alliance, an industry trade group, thought it would only be acceptable if previously fully protected lands were also opened up for partial harvest to make up for the lower yields.

Building on New Forestry ideas, Chief Robertson launched the "New Perspectives" initiative in 1992 to put ecosystem concepts into practice Service-wide, including a commitment to end clearcutting as a standard practice on all National Forests (MacCleery 2001). The following year, President Clinton appointed a new Chief, Jack Ward Thomas, a biologist who had become famous for his work on spotted owls, and Thomas adopted the term "ecosystem management" as an overarching goal. In 1994, the Forest Service issued a National Framework that defined ecosystem management as an approach that "blends the needs of people and environmental values in such a way that National Forests and grasslands represent diverse, healthy, productive, and sustainable ecosystems" (USFS 1994). The accompanying action plan operationalized ecosystem management by "allowing multiple-use benefits to be realized within the capabilities of ecosystems" (Fedkiw 1999).

As the New Forestry, New Perspectives, and ecosystem management initiatives unfolded, prospects for their successful nationwide implementation appeared decidedly mixed. One optimistic observer (Keiter 1994) believed that these new approaches could force managers to break down "the man-nature or utilitarian-preservation dichotomy that has characterized natural resources policy for so long." He went on to identify five core principles for success: cooperative interagency processes; reliance on cutting-edge research; a focus on biological diversity; broad public participation ("with national interests prevailing over local interests in the case of irreconcilable conflict"); and sustainable resource use to maintain local economies. But others noted significant technical, legal, and organizational obstacles, including confusion about what ecosystem management was ("a dung pile is as much an ecosystem as a watershed" [Haeuber 1996]), concern about how it might affect existing statutory mandates, and lack of Forest Service staff training, expertise, and, in some cases, willingness (Davis 2001). Keiter and others (e.g., Haeuber 1996) noted that ecosystem management had no explicit statutory support and thus remained vulnerable to the shifting winds of agency leadership and public attention. In fact, the midterm elections of 1994, which gave Republicans control of the U.S. House and Senate for the first time in forty years, resulted in a whole new set of committee chairs who made it clear that ecosystem management was not on their agenda (Davis 2001).

But there was no possibility of retreat from ecosystem science and management principles once they had been introduced. Internal and external attitudes toward resource management agencies and their professional personnel had changed for good (Kennedy et al. 1998). Changes were also evident on the ground. Natural wildfires were now allowed to burn unless population centers were at immediate risk. Controlled burns were deliberately introduced to mimic natural processes and clear out accumulated fuels. Restoration forestry (in other words, using selective timber removal to contribute to the rebuilding of degraded ecosystems) had become popular as a way to marry conservation with economic production. Based on a large-scale study of the Forest Service, Butler and Koontz (2005) found that the agency had "incorporated numerous ecosystem management components into its objectives." The greatest success was achieved in integrating new biological findings and deploying collaborative techniques, but the agency continued to struggle to incorporate social science findings and implement adaptive management.

In twenty years, resource management had forever changed from a focus on harvesting resource units on designated parcels of land, using technical and engineering solutions to maximize production, to "an ecosystem-scale perspective where [managers] collaborate with a range of groups to manage for a broad set of values" (Yaffee and Wondolleck 2003).

Evolving approaches to public participation

An insider's game

A 1905 letter to Chief Forester Pinchot from his new boss, the Secretary of Agriculture, informed him that, in the National Forests, "local questions will be decided upon local grounds. Industry will be considered first, but with as little restriction to [other] industries as may be possible" (Wilkinson and Anderson 1987). In this context "industry" referred to the timber industry, whose well-being was the raison d'être for the Forest Service. In keeping with the dominant progressive conservation philosophy of the time, the expectation was that specially trained foresters would use their expertise to efficiently and scientifically make timber available to private logging companies into the indefinite future. Because the purpose of public lands was to facilitate resource use, early laws also assumed that extractive users would have a strong voice in setting the rules.

This approach prevailed through the first half of the 20th century. One observer concluded that early public land laws created "a number of private privileges, which morphed into expectations, and became a sense of entitlement among commodity users" (Nie 2008). Jurisdictions surrounding the forests were also accommodated with extra opportunities for review of proposed activities and, perhaps more important, a share of the revenue raised from timber sales. Broad participation by the general public in Forest Service decisions was neither sought out nor expected.

By the 1960s, environmental groups advocated increasingly loudly for more public involvement in the fate of public lands whose management was deemed "too important to leave to professionals" (Hall 1963). New substantive laws concerning forest management (e.g., MUSY, the Wilderness Act, RPA, NFMA, and others) and broader environmental protections (e.g., under the Clean Air Act, Clean Water Act, ESA, etc.) changed both the goals and procedures for land management, including greater attention to ecological impacts and explicit requirements for citizen participation. At the same time, new process-oriented laws (the Administrative Procedures Act, FOIA, and NEPA) were intended to facilitate public scrutiny of government. One forester, unhappy with these changes, exhorted his colleagues to "retrieve the prerogatives that rightfully belong to us ... and return decision making in forestry matters to professionally trained men from [those] who have usurped these prerogatives" (Hunt 1966).

Increased citizen participation has been justified on a variety of philosophical and practical grounds, including such notions as natural rights, direct democracy, government accountability, procedural justice, consciousness-raising, and legal necessity (Germain et al. 2001; McKinney and Harmon 2004). Unfortunately, increased public participation in Forest Service efforts did not always achieve the *substantive* changes that some assumed would ensue. For example, a careful study of 227 public meetings held in conjunction with the 1977 Roadless Area Review found no evidence that public comments had an effect on the final Forest Service decision (Mohai 1987). Applegate (1977) complained that the Forest Service thinks "EIS comments, occasional public meetings, and infrequent advisory councils satisfy the need for citizen involvement."

Many of the new environmental laws also authorized individuals and NGOs to bring lawsuits against federal agency actions,[8] creating a visible and controversial role for them as enforcers of environmental law and involving the U.S. courts to a much larger extent than previously in reviewing Forest Service decisions (Burns 2001). Of course businesses and workers, whose profits and jobs were threatened, also turned to the courts for redress against unfavorable Forest Service decisions. One study found that, over the time period examined, "every major Forest Service decision was appealed by environmental and/or timber harvesting groups" (Sabatier et al. 1995). Whether this development is seen as a positive expression of citizen empowerment or a questionable instance of courts "setting environmental policy through judicial interpretation" (MacCleery 2001) is, of course, a matter of perspective.

It is impossible to review the history of stakeholder input to the Forest Service without mentioning the so-called "capture–conformity debate." Early in Forest Service history, advocates for progressive conservation created the Forest Reserves to keep wealthy industrialists and property owners of the time from wiping out forest resources. They believed that Forest Service employees should "conform" their decisions to the latest technical and scientific standards so as not to be "captured" by external influences. In keeping with this philosophy, Forest Service employees were transferred frequently, both to enlarge their knowledge and experience and to maintain their primary loyalty to the agency, not the community. Promotions were (and still are) almost always associated with a move to another forest or region.

But the goal of impartial objectivity proved impossible, since management within a multiple-use context demands that choices be made which transcend the purview of science. There is convincing evidence that varying degrees of agency capture by industrial interests did take place at least through the 1950s (Feller 1995). Building on the ACF and punctuated equilibrium theory discussed in Chapter 3, Davis (2001) explains events from that time as being controlled by a "policy subsystem" wherein a small cadre of Congressional committee members, agency staff, industry representatives, and academics with industry funding supported and reinforced each other's views, distributing a public resource to a small number of beneficiaries with little outside interference.

In subsequent decades, increasing competition for forest access by recreational users, and the rise of the environmental movement with its legal challenges, grassroots advocacy techniques, and media exposure of public land issues, created a strong counterbalance to industry pressure. A detailed study by Culhane (1981), drawing on hundreds of surveys and dozens of interviews administered to Forest Service and BLM personnel and a wide range of other stakeholders in three regions around the country, found that individuals associated with the timber and grazing industries were convinced that environmental groups had undue influence over the agencies while environmentalists believed the reverse. Agency staff saw themselves as trying to balance the two viewpoints—and even play them off against each other—to achieve their statutory mandates. Culhane's analysis of respondents' attitudes is presented in Figure 4.5, providing some support for the agency viewpoint.

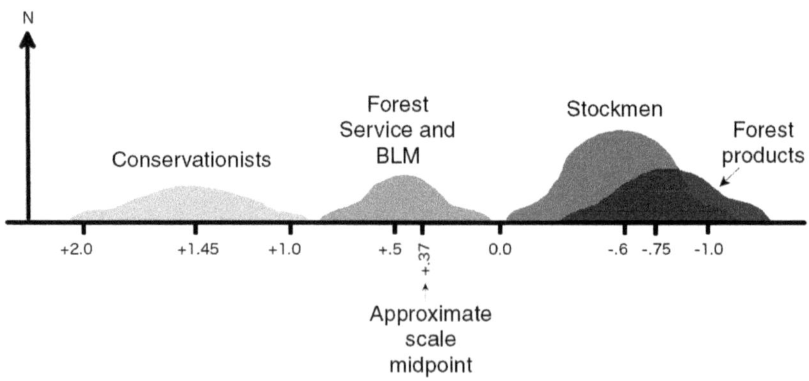

Figure 4.5 Forest participant scores on "environmental–utilitarian" attitude scale

Source: Adapted from Culhane 1981.

By the early 1990s, another large-scale study conducted in forty-four National Forests (Sabatier et al. 1995) found that the best predictors of timber harvest targets were (1) previous years' output levels—in other words, the status quo—and (2) influence from environmental groups or agencies, but found little correlation with factors including the personal attitudes of forest staff, budget considerations, or the views of industry, Congress, or Forest Service leadership.

The rise of partnerships and collaboration

As we have seen, the 1980s and 1990s were tumultuous years for the Forest Service. Criticism was coming from Congress, the courts, the scientific community, the public, and even from within its own ranks. Protests to protect old-growth timber and adopt an ecosystem perspective grew in intensity, while Congress resisted any reductions in timber sales. Meanwhile, rural communities whose economies were tightly linked to harvests from National Forests suffered real economic hardship. Towns that had been encouraged by the Forest Service to locate and expand near National Forests in the late 1950s and early 1960s based on promises of reliable supplies of timber, felt betrayed and helpless when harvest levels dropped precipitously (Dietrich 1992). The changing landscape, both physical and political, engaged politicians and Congressional committees that previously had played no role in public lands management. The national media sent gripping images of ugly clearcuts and shouting protesters directly into most American homes. For better and for worse, management decisions were increasingly fought out in very public and often acrimonious ways. Mandated public participation, interpreted by the Forest Service in narrow, legalistic terms, merely contributed further to "a loss of public trust and ... crisis of conflict" (Germain et al. 2001).

This confluence of events led a few frustrated forest stakeholders to explore new ways to build trust, discover common goals, and potentially resolve seemingly intractable conflicts. The Forest Service also realized it must do a better job of engaging a broad range of stakeholders upfront—and then responding to what they heard—in order to reach more appropriate and durable decisions (Fedkiw 1999). Burns (2001) found that "an absence of well-grounded consensual problem solving [was] harming the social and economic fabric of communities and regions." He went on to explain that the very nature of forests as public spaces "generates a set of conflicting values and intentions" that can damage communities *and* forests if left unresolved.

Early efforts at collaboration, such as the much-dissected Applegate Partnership in Oregon (e.g., KenCairn 1995) and Quincy Library Group in California (e.g., Braxton 1995; Blumberg and Knuffke 1998), plus many less well-known examples, often got their start when a few individuals on opposite sides of a forest issue decided to cross the barricades and talk (Wondolleck and Yaffee 2000; Yaffee and Wondolleck 2003). Some bitterly divided communities slowly came together to explore common interests and shared goals of social, economic, and ecological sustainability. Other parties, from industry, environmental groups, the Forest Service, and eventually Congress and the White House, took notice, suspicious of the new collaborative's motives, wary of altering a system they knew how to navigate, and afraid of potentially losing the power and influence they already had.

Both participants and outside observers have struggled to determine when and why collaboration occurs and how to evaluate the sociological and environmental outcomes of collaborative efforts (e.g., O'Leary and Bingham 2003; Bryson et al. 2006; and many others). Today the Forest Service has embraced the notion of collaboration, including it as one of the agency's five "management principles" in its 2010 strategic plan. The role of collaboration in the management of public space appears prominently throughout the case studies presented in Chapters 5 and 6, and will be revisited in Chapter 7.

Summary

The 120-year history of National Forests summarized in this chapter reveals a record of ongoing struggles to define and realize "the public good." A trio of articles—"The Myth of the Omnipotent Forester" (Behan 1966), "Has the Myth of the Omnipotent Forester Become the Reality of the Impotent Forester?" (Luckert 2006), and "From Omnipotence to Omnipresence: The Evolution of the American Forester" (Argow 2009)—each one responding to the previous authors, succinctly encapsulates these changes in the role of the Forest Service over time. They document a progression from "omnipotence" to "impotence," to "omnipresence"—in other words, from sole decision-makers, to mistrusted and often overruled bureaucrats, to multi-disciplinary facilitators of a complex process to implement societal values and choices.

To shed further light on how the broad Forest Service themes described above played out in specific places, the next two chapters present the results of two regional case studies, covering three different National Forests: the Siuslaw and Willamette Forests in Oregon and the Croatan Forest in North Carolina.

Notes

1 The terms "disposal" (giving land to non-federal owners) and "reservation" (maintaining land under federal ownership) are terms-of-art in the public lands literature that are not widely used in day-to-day conversation. The latter term in particular should not be confused with the common usage of the term "reservation" to refer to land owned by Indian Nations.

2 The romantic notion of untouched wilderness ignored the fact that virtually all U.S. government lands had previously been occupied and used for centuries by Native Americans and, in some areas, by Spanish and Mexican descendants (Bryner 1998; Kosek 2006).

3 In 1987, 54 percent of downhill ski lift capacity in the U.S. was actually located on National Forest land, operated under special-use permits from the Forest Service (Wilkinson and Anderson 1987).

4 These thinkers were also wealthy, privileged, white men of European descent whose less well-known writings reveal disturbing currents of racism. Their love of "untrammeled" nature was linked to a notion of the white man's destiny in the New World and a willing blindness to the thousands of long-standing inhabitants who had been displaced or forcibly removed from much of that land (Bryner 1998; Kosek 2006).

5 A study of the particular circumstances surrounding Alaskan public land management and wilderness could fill several books—and does. Those issues are not explored in this study.

6 Data compiled from agency statistics: available at www.wilderness.net, and managed by the University of Montana and partner federal agencies. Accessed March 20, 2012.

7 For details, see www.biologicaldiversity.org/news/press_releases/2012/national-forests-03-23-2012.html and http://ens-newswire.com/2012/09/11/enviros-fight-industry-lawsuit-over-u-s-forest-planning-rule. Both accessed February 22, 2014.

8 This trend was accelerated by the 1980 Equal Access to Justice Act (5 U.S.C. § 504; 28 U.S.C. § 2412) which reimbursed "eligible individuals and small entities" for expenses associated with successful lawsuits against the federal government under certain conditions. Parties are considered to have prevailed if "they are successful on at least one significant issue that achieves at least some of the benefit the parties sought." Unlike many other countries, the converse is not true: U.S. citizens and NGOs are not required to cover the government's legal costs when their litigation is unsuccessful.

5

PACIFIC NORTHWEST FORESTS

Case Study #1

Study approach

The previous chapter sketched the broad contours of 120 years of U.S. forest management, synthesizing expert observations and analyses to uncover significant events and themes. To complement that broad-brush portrait, I conducted in-depth case studies of three National Forests to illustrate how the national themes played out in these unique social and ecological settings. Although the case studies corroborate the broader findings, they also draw attention to the variability that occurs among systems within the same country, ostensibly governed by the same laws, regulations, and management procedures.

To develop this more place-based perspective on National Forest management, I focused on two regions with very different biological, historical, and community settings: the Pacific Northwest, presented in this chapter, and the Mid-Atlantic Coast, portrayed in Chapter 6. In addition to examining important historical documents, I spent time in each region getting a feel for the landscape and listening to the people who live near, work in, and think about these forests, including Forest Service staff, community members, local issue advocates, and academics.

As in the previous chapter, I recommend that those interested primarily in *ocean* issues read these case studies carefully. Despite the differences in setting, many of the events, participants, management processes, and conflicts should strike a familiar chord. For example, as you read about changing attitudes toward timber harvesting, keep the fishing industry in mind. When you see how wilderness designations sparked conflict, think about debates over marine protected areas. And while you learn about the goals and subsequent implementation challenges of NFMA, think about the recent Executive Order calling for marine spatial planning in U.S. waters.

Background and general features

My first site visit focused on two forests in Western Oregon, the Willamette and Siuslaw National Forests (see Figure 5.1 and Table 5.1). For thousands of years this region had been inhabited and its resources used by Native American tribes. But by the 19th century, the Cascade Range in Oregon was becoming a gateway for pioneers rushing westward in search of land and riches, with the main Oregon Trail passing just south of Mount Hood. As happened elsewhere, the native peoples were forcibly displaced and the land was considered free for homesteading claims, living and non-living resource extraction, railroad construction, and, toward the end of that century, conversion to government ownership (Bryner 1998).

The lush forests that covered the Western Oregon mountains were among the first in the country to be set aside as national Forest Reserves. In 1893, the Cascade Range Forest Reserve was created along the length of Oregon's Cascade Mountains, followed in 1907 by the Umpqua and Tillamook Forest Reserves on the coast. In 1908, shortly after the establishment of the U.S. Forest Service within the USDA, the Cascade Reserve was divided into five National Forests, one of which later became the Willamette, while the Tillamook and part of the

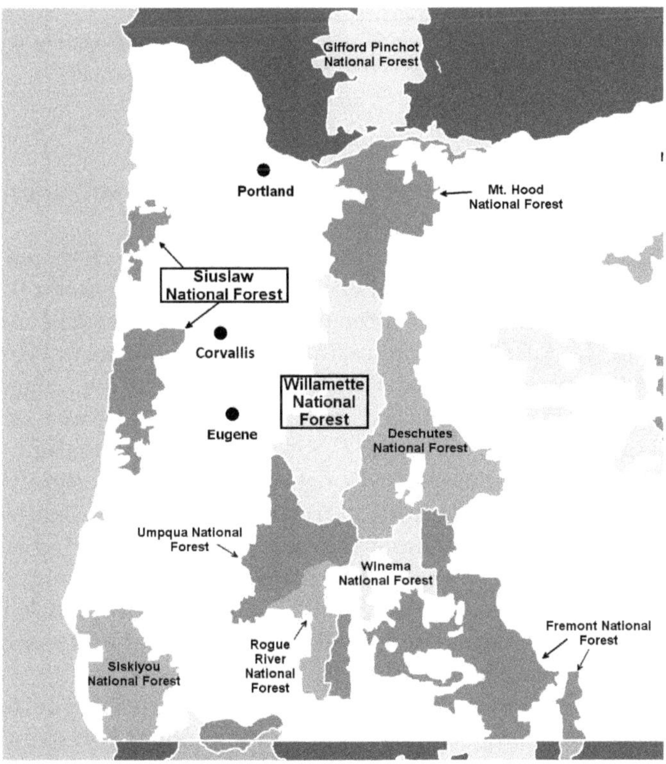

Figure 5.1 Map of National Forests in Western Oregon (this chapter focuses on the Willamette and Siuslaw Forests)

Source: Author's work.

Table 5.1 Basic facts about the Willamette and Siuslaw National Forests

	Siuslaw	*Willamette*
Year established*	1908	1933
Total area (acres)	630,000	1,675,000
Highest elevation (ft)	4,097	10,495
Wilderness area (acres) *(proportion of total area)*	16,000 *(3%)*	381,000 *(23%)*
1978 timber harvest (MMBF)	315	693
harvest intensity (BF per non-wilderness acre)	*513*	*536*
2008 timber harvest (MMBF)	28	31
harvest intensity (BF per non-wilderness acre)	*46*	*24*
Decrease in harvest, 1978–2008	91%	96%

* The dates shown indicate establishment under the current name; forests in the area were combined, re-divided, and renamed several times before then.

Source: Compiled by author from various sources.

Umpqua Reserves were linked to form the two non-contiguous pieces of the current Siuslaw National Forest.

The Willamette Forest is characterized by narrow, steep-walled river valleys and heavily timbered slopes. Large contrasts exist between the eastern and western slopes, with heavy precipitation in the West and much drier conditions in the East as Pacific weather systems move from West to East. Although the Siuslaw National Forest also includes steep rugged slopes in its interior, it is a more temperate coastal forest and one of only two National Forests in the continental U.S. that borders the ocean.[1]

Both forests are dominated by Douglas fir trees, with a significant presence of other conifers. Sitka spruce grows in the seaward, coastal areas of the Siuslaw, where milder temperatures, frequent rain, strong winds, and thick fog are prevalent. The forests provide habitat for a huge variety of freshwater and anadromous fish, resident and migratory birds including bald eagles and the endangered northern spotted owl and marbled murrelet, and larger animals including elk, bears, and deer.

Private lands immediately adjacent to the Western Oregon forests are not as densely populated as those near many National Forests in the East, but residents of the Greater Portland area (60 miles from Mt. Hood; pop. over 1 million), Eugene (in the Willamette valley; pop. 155,000), and

Corvallis (50 miles from the coast; pop. 51,000) rely on forest watersheds for water supplies and are heavy users of hiking trails, downhill ski resorts, and other recreational amenities in the National Forests. Smaller towns in and around the forests were traditionally tightly linked to the timber industry but have become increasingly dependent on tourism and retirees for economic sustenance.

Issues and challenges

Western Oregon forests went through most of the phases and experienced the many challenges described in Chapter 4. As shown in Table 5.2, they were:

- among the first areas set aside as Forest Reserves in the late 19th century;
- designated as National Forests in the early 20th century;
- focused on fire suppression as their central mission for decades;
- dominated by skyrocketing timber harvests, including massive clearcuts, from the 1950s to the 1980s;
- prime locations for non-timber uses, including wilderness set-asides, in the 1970s and 1980s;
- heavily affected by non-forest-specific laws, such as the ESA and NEPA;
- at ground zero of internal and external challenges to traditional forest planning and management through the 1980s and 1990s, including major interventions by the courts and elected officials;
- the birthplace of the New Forestry movement in the late 1980s and early 1990s; and,
- perhaps as a result of all the above, incubators for new approaches to collaboration and partnerships in the 1990s and into the 21st century.

Through the 1930s, harvest levels remained low in Oregon's National Forests, as elsewhere. Depression-era job programs such as the Civilian Conservation Corps and Works Progress Administration supplied workers to fight fires and build fire lookouts, ranger stations, and recreational facilities. (The Timberline Lodge, located at 6,000 ft. elevation on the southeast side of Mount Hood and still in active use, was built in 1936 and has been designated as a Historic Landmark.)

Intense harvests started in the 1940s, accelerated through the 1960s, and were maintained through the 1980s (Figure 5.2). At their peak, timber sales on the medium-sized Willamette exceeded those on any other National Forest in the country. Clearcutting followed by large-scale herbicide applications became standard practice, both to simplify the timber harvest and to facilitate dense replanting of more "desirable" species, typically Douglas fir.[2]

Table 5.2 Selected events in Western Oregon National Forest history

Date	*Event*
1893	Cascade Range Forest Reserve established
1907	Umpqua and Tillamook Forest Reserves established
1908	Cascade Range Reserve broken into five National Forests (including the precursor to the Willamette); Tillamook and part of Umpqua Reserves joined to create the Siuslaw National Forest; Congress allocates 25 percent of timber revenues from National Forests to local counties
1933	Willamette National Forest named
1964	First Wilderness Act passed
1970	NEPA passed; requires EISs for Forest Service actions
1976	NFMA passed requiring a detailed plan for each National Forest; Congress creates the Payment in Lieu of Taxes program to provide federal funding to counties to offset lost property taxes due to federal land holdings
1984	Oregon Wilderness Act creates 29 new wilderness areas
1990	Northern spotted owl listed as endangered
1990	Siuslaw and Willamette Forests issue their Land and Resource Management Plans
1992	Marbled murrelet listed as endangered
1993	Snowy plover listed as endangered
1993	Clinton hosts Environmental Summit, Portland
1993	Forest Ecosystem Management Assessment Team (FEMAT) report released
1994	Region-wide Northwest Forest Plan finalized with major reductions in harvest
1996	Previous forest plans (from 1990) amended to comply with Northwest Plan
1998	Congress passes Wyden Amendment authorizing stewardship contracting
2000	Secure Rural Schools and Community Self-Determination Act provides direct funding to affected counties to replace lost timber revenues

Source: Compiled by author from various sources.

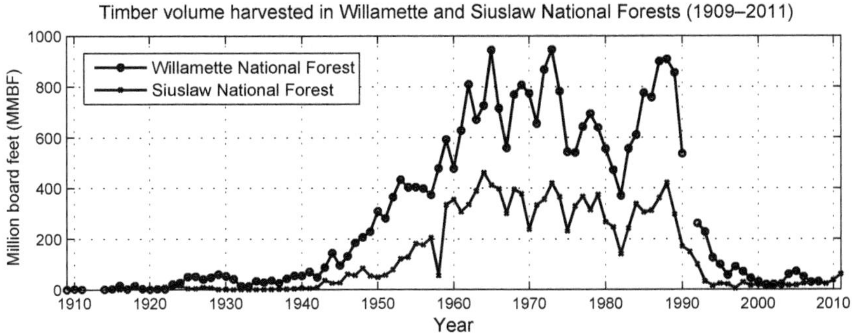

Figure 5.2 Historical trends in timber harvest on the Willamette and Siuslaw National Forests

Source: U.S. Forest Service.

Many reasons have been given for the Forest Service's promotion of harvest levels and methods that most observers now agree were unsustainable. Some of those explanations include:

- pressing demands for timber to supply the post-war, baby boom-driven housing industry;
- limited yields from already depleted Eastern Forests;
- exhaustion or development of many privately owned forest lands;
- tight links between Forest Service staff and private industry;
- unduly optimistic estimates of "sustainable yield," based on over-simplified assumptions and models; and
- political pressure to extract cash from the National Forests, both for federal coffers and for local communities that received up to 25 percent of harvest revenues.

In the late 1960s, mirroring national trends, citizens became increasingly vigilant about the fate of Oregon's National Forests. The burgeoning environmental movement, combined with new ecological research findings, led to protests and lawsuits about logging techniques and chemical applications. Researchers at the University of Oregon documented a diverse and growing recreational user community, which included everything from individual solitude seekers to well-organized hunters and motorists, finding that they were often in conflict with industrial users as well as with each other (Rakestraw 1991).

Debates about forest road-building—Where should they run? How wide and long? Paved or not?—became a flashpoint, as the presence of roads inevitably increased activity of all sorts in the forests and accelerated erosion. Road construction was also tightly linked to ongoing fights about wilderness designation. The Forest Service RARE and RARE II processes (discussed in Chapter 4) included many areas throughout the Northwest Oregon forests and generated strong public interest. The draft EIS associated with RARE II generated 59,000 comments from Oregon residents alone, out of 260,000 nationwide, and the final EIS was challenged and rejected in court. In one district of the Siuslaw forest, a 1984 lawsuit resulted in an injunction against any logging that would require new road construction. A news story from that time makes it clear that this result was not universally supported, ramping up the community discord that would grow even fiercer in subsequent years.

> *Associated Press,* July 21, 1985
> FLORENCE, Ore.—Signs at the city limits read "Florence, Ore., Closed—Blame National Wildlife Federation" as the town shut down for four hours to protest a halt in nearby logging ... "This talk of shutting down the timber industry is talk about the death of this city as we know it," said Wilbur Ternyik, mayor of the coastal town of about 4,000 residents. About 1,000 people gathered ... to castigate the National Wildlife Federation ... the major plaintiff in a lawsuit that led to an injunction prohibiting timber sales in the Mapleton Ranger District.

In 1984, after the RARE II process failed and things appeared to be at a standstill, Congress passed the Oregon Wilderness Act, hoping to satisfy both sides. The Act created significant new wilderness areas in all of the Northwest Oregon forests while keeping remaining areas open for other uses. Instead, neither faction felt their concerns had truly been heeded. A pro-harvest individual complained at the time that "ninety percent of the wilderness that exists in Oregon is not used by anybody" (quoted in Rakestraw 1991), echoing a widespread misunderstanding about the purpose of wilderness designation. On the other hand, conservation advocates, angry about continued logging in areas that had *not* been protected, began an era of tree sitting, harvest disruptions, and other acts of civil disobedience intended to halt all logging of old trees, particularly in the Willamette.

The forests in this area became testing grounds for new research into concepts such as ecosystem resilience, complexity, and biodiversity. The Andrews Experimental Forest, 16,000 acres carved out of the Willamette in 1948, was home to much of the research on the spotted owl, the functioning of old-growth forests, and other studies that provided the foundation for the "New Forestry," described by one of its founders as a way to "manage land to accommodate ecological values and allow for the extraction of commodities" (Franklin 1989). Western Oregon is also where Jeff DeBonis was working as a timber planner in 1991 when he created Forest Service Employees for Environmental Ethics (see Chapter 4) in reaction to the ecosystem damage he witnessed and the pressure he experienced to forge ahead with large timber sales. He was not alone. A large-scale survey of Forest Service employees conducted in 1993 found that only 29 percent of those who worked in Region 6 (Washington and Oregon) agreed with the statement "We can sustain our forests' current level of resource use for 100 years" (Boyle et al. 1994).

In 1990, the northern spotted owl was listed as an endangered species. Shortly afterward, Oregon forests issued their Land and Resource Management Plans, as required under NFMA following NEPA procedures. Acknowledging the ESA listing, the plans all included set-asides of old-growth habitat for owls. For example, the 1990 Siuslaw plan protected 31,000 acres of old-growth habitat (5 percent) while maintaining projected harvests of 332 million board feet (MMBF)/yr, and the Willamette plan protected 365,000 acres (22 percent) while setting harvest levels at 491 MMBF/yr. Although the set-asides were larger and the harvests smaller than in previous years, environmental scientists and advocates believed even these modifications would be insufficient to save the owl from extinction. The courts agreed, and all timber sales on old-growth forests in the region were halted pending completion of new forest plans and EISs. Addressing the tradeoffs between ecological and economic considerations, the court found that "the argument that the mightiest economy on earth cannot afford to preserve old-growth forests for a short time, while it reaches an overdue decision on how to manage them, is not convincing today [and] would be even less so a year or a century from now" (Seattle Audubon v. Evans, 771 F.Supp. 1081, W. Dist. Wash. 1991, p. 1096).

Communities in Washington, Oregon, and Northern California were near the breaking point when President Clinton convened a high-profile forest conference in Portland in April 1993, followed shortly after by release of the interagency Forest Ecosystem Management Assessment Team's report (FEMAT 1993). In 1994, the formal "Record of Decision for Amendments to Forest Service and Bureau of Land Management Planning Documents within the Range of the Northern Spotted Owl," commonly known as the Northwest Forest Plan, was issued. This new plan was a major departure from previous efforts due to its focus on biological, economic, and cultural sustainability—very different from the old commodity-oriented goal of "sustained yield" (Wilkinson 1997).

The Plan found that the northern spotted owl's range encompassed 24.5 million acres of federal lands in Oregon, Washington, and Northern California, including parts of nineteen National Forests, seven BLM districts, six National Parks, and smaller areas on Wildlife Refuges and military lands. To protect the owl, the Plan created seven types of land allocations within those areas. Four categories excluded all logging: Congressionally Reserved Lands (occupying 30 percent of the total area); Late Successional Reserves (30 percent); Riparian Reserves (11 percent); and Administrative Withdrawals (6 percent). The remaining 23 percent—Matrix Lands (16 percent), Adaptive Management Areas (6 percent), and Managed Late Successional Areas (1 percent)—could be logged subject to a variety of caveats and conditions.

Because much of the Forest Service's funding was linked to logging revenues, budgets and staffing levels in the affected forests were drastically reduced as a result; surrounding counties that had received a portion of the timber revenues were also seriously affected. From 1990 to 1994, dozens of lumber mills throughout the region closed, many of them family businesses that had been operating for half a century or more. The wood products industry increasingly looked to private and state lands for timber, state and local officials lobbied for subsidies from Congress to replace logging revenues, and many environmental groups remained opposed to *any* continued logging of older trees.[3] These tensions and contradictions remain evident to the people in the region with whom I spoke, with some hints at possible ways forward.

Voices from today's forests

In speaking with local forest stakeholders, including forest managers, industry representatives, environmental advocates, watershed council members, and other residents, everyone recognized that major changes had taken place in Pacific Northwest forests over the last twenty years, and most, but not all, were cautiously optimistic that these changes would turn out to be for the better. The following subsection explores respondents' general views on recent events and the current status of the forest. Subsequent subsections then explore three topics that elicited particularly lengthy and sometimes emotional answers: (1) the meaning of multiple-use planning in forest management; (2) the difficulties of coordination within and among responsible agencies; and (3) the role of the public in decision-making. The final section of this case study summarizes the future hopes and fears of Oregonians with whom I spoke. To maintain confidentiality, as promised, quotes throughout are identified by the general affiliation of the speaker: Forest Service staff (FS), state government (ST), environmental group staff (environmental non-governmental organization [ENGO]), community member (COMM), or industry representative (IND).

The lay of the land

As explained previously, the 1994 Northwest Forest Plan excluded 77 percent of federal lands within the range of the spotted owl from logging (Rapp

2008). However, the Plan has not played out quite as it was conceived. Crafted as a compromise between protecting sufficient habitat for owls while allowing continued commercial logging of large trees in some areas, ongoing lawsuits and ecological uncertainty have altered that balance.

The Plan envisioned that more than 900 MMBF of timber could continue to be sold each year from designated federal lands in the Plan area. However, much of that harvest was expected to come from forests more than 200 years old, an outcome that never materialized. As a result, 2003 timber sales for all forests in the Plan were less than half the original targets, and less than 25 percent of 1980s levels. In some places the reduction was even more extreme. For example, the 1996 Siuslaw Forest Plan, revised according to the mandate of the Northwest Forest Plan, excluded all but 1.5 percent of its area from timber harvest. Local people were acutely aware of these disparities, whether they applauded or condemned them.

> [Under the Plan] a million acres of old growth occurred in the "matrix" land allocation, and we did not want to see that cut. (ENGO)
>
> The active management side [of the Plan] was never implemented … [When] we try to start doing something to get that eight hundred million [allowed board feet of timber], they sue you every step! Because they don't want that to happen either … For 20 years I've been saying, "Let's protect old growth, but free up the rest of the land!" (IND)

The new balance of power (or stalemate, depending on your perspective) also created new opportunities. The Forest Service, particularly within the Siuslaw National Forest, but in other Oregon forests as well, redirected much of its effort toward "restoration forestry," i.e., taking the dense, uniform-age, single-species stands that were the legacy of clearcutting and agricultural-style planting and selectively thinning them in an attempt to restore complex, late successional forest habitats and natural streamflows. These restoration-oriented projects also supply a small but stable flow of small-diameter timber for commercial use, around 30–60 MMBF/year. Not surprisingly, this new direction is described in different terms by different participants:

> [We brought] a huge lawsuit which basically shut everything down in about 2000 … And at that point, [the Forest Service] realized that the best place to get volume in the short term … was thinning young stands. And they realized that there's a lot more of that opportunity than they even imagined, so old-growth logging really never got restarted in a big way after about 2000. (ENGO)

> "Restoration" is the 2000 buzzword. It was "New Forestry" before and it was something else before that ... To restore something, there has to be something broken or wrong ... They are going in there thinning out young stands because that is the least common denominator ... that these environmental groups will allow. (IND)

A side effect of the restoration approach was that it often fostered partnerships with local communities. Existing Watershed Councils got involved and new "Stewardship Groups" sprung up, typically unincorporated, flexible gatherings of community members with varied backgrounds but a shared interest in maintaining both economically viable communities and healthy ecosystems. These groups worked with forest managers to think about landscape-level goals and needs.

> The Siuslaw has a longer history of building trust with the communities and stakeholders ... because of its unique position under the Northwest Forest Plan. If you can't log old-growth trees anymore, you're going to start building common ground towards doing other things. (ENGO)

Based on these pilot projects, in 1999 Congress authorized a five-year "stewardship contracting" program (PL 109–54, Sec. 434), dubbed the Wyden Amendment after its main proponent, Oregon Congressman Ron Wyden. The program allowed rangers to design timber sales that would spur the regeneration of old-growth habitat and then use the resulting revenues to support projects on nearby lands that could provide "tangible benefits to federal land"—a major departure from previous practice. The restoration harvest proceeds are passed through a locally based, unaffiliated non-profit organization that then awards grants or contracts to carry out the agreed-upon non-federal projects. As a result, "a revolution blossomed on the ground. [Environmental groups] formerly opposed to logging on public land helped design timber sales instead of blocking them. Logging profits financed the restoration of salmon habitat. Environmentalists worked with timber giants like Georgia-Pacific instead of fighting them" (Payne 2007).

> Of all of the forests [under] the Northwest Forest Plan, the Siuslaw National Forest is the one that most consistently hits [its] harvest targets [and] it's all coming from thinning! The other side of that is that it's been probably a decade since this forest has had a harvest project appealed in court. (COMM)

Multiple benefits of forest restoration and stewardship projects are cited such as:

- re-establishment of forest and stream habitats for threatened, endangered, or iconic species;
- a focus on watershed and landscape scales, including a mix of private, federal, and state-owned lands;
- greater involvement of communities in decision-making; and
- access to a marketable product that can sustain timber-related jobs.

As might be expected, the new spirit of collaboration and common purpose did not prevail everywhere or among all participants. Although community residents and watershed council members touted the results of collaborative stewardship and restoration forestry, a more adversarial tone remained among some advocates on both sides.

> If you have a big old-growth tree that has a lot of clear and big dimension from it, you will be able to sell the product that comes out of the tree for a lot more money ... Being limited to cutting very few, small trees per acre means that you're selling things at minimum rate. (IND)
>
> The counties [are] so used to that traditional role of "rah, rah, logging" that they can't stop. [And the timber industry] says "we need to maintain our current infrastructure of mills, and if you don't let us log more, we're going to have to lay off more people, we'll have to close mills!" ... The counties need to [get] their paychecks from the treasury rather than from timber receipts. (ENGO)

Forest Service employees also remain acutely aware of the fact that the new paradigm is less than perfect and represents a tenuous truce.

> There are people who believe the environmental community's goal still is to go out and basically decommission all the [forest] roads, use thinning to pay for it, and then ... to never do anything again. (FS)

Although restoration forestry and stewardship projects also take place on the larger, less recreation-oriented Willamette Forest, traditional timber sales continue to be proposed on these "matrix" lands—and are often challenged. As a result, total harvests on the Willamette are roughly equal to those on the Siuslaw, despite its much greater size and fewer explicit restrictions under the Northwest Forest Plan (Table 5.1). One recently proposed timber sale in the Willamette, the so-called Goose Project, has been generating old-style conflict and media attention. The narrative being played out includes virtually all of the themes that have characterized decades of Pacific Northwest forest disputes.[4] By May 2012, a lawsuit was filed to halt the project citing concerns about potential impacts on wilderness areas, streams, and endangered species. The most recent Forest Service response concludes by saying, "In future projects, we are looking forward to incorporating public concerns upfront in our planning process through better initial outreach, field trips, community meetings, and personal contacts," demonstrating that old lessons must often be learned anew.

The role of multiple-use planning

As discussed in Chapter 4, National Forests are required by law to be managed in a way that provides for balanced multiple uses—the wood, water, wildlife, range, and recreation called for in the MUSY Act. To achieve this, NFMA instructs each forest to create a spatial plan (its Land and Resource Management Plan) describing where and how each use may be carried out. However, neither MUSY nor NFMA sets *priorities* among the uses, or specifies how an appropriate balance among uses is to be achieved.

> It isn't fashionable politically to talk about the Multiple-Use Sustained Yield Act with some of our constituents [but] Congress hasn't rescinded or repealed any of [it] … How do we produce the amenities (clean water, clean air, recreational opportunities for hunters, for fishermen, for snowboarders) and the commodities (which, depending on what part of the country you're in, could be oak veneer, could be saw timber to build houses, could be grass that feeds and grows cattle, let alone oil and gas leasing, mining molybdenum that's in steel, or rare metals that are in catalytic converters …) that Americans rely on? … Those are impactive activities and they always will be … What's an *acceptable* cost is where the discussion is. (FS)

> The Forest Service for far too long looked at multiple use as really just a bunch of extractive uses, with a few non-extractive uses glued on for decoration. Now it's a lot of non-extractive uses, with a few extractive uses that look funny. And still, they haven't figured out any great way to harmonize those. (ENGO)

Confronted by the challenges of pursuing a multiple-use mission while protecting endangered species associated with old-growth forests and navigating seemingly intractable conflicts among stakeholders, the Northwest Forest Plan departed from the forest-by-forest planning envisioned in NFMA to craft a solution that attempted to achieve overall regional balance, while allowing certain forests to focus almost exclusively on habitat restoration. There is no doubt that managers on this latter category of forests had an easier time meeting their goals.

> There comes a point in time where it's better off as, "If you're gonna make a change give us a full change, rather than a partial change that we cannot meet." ... We were kind of thankful ... that we did not have to continue to look for timber production [on the Siuslaw]. (FS)

But the businesses, individuals, and communities that had long relied on jobs and revenues associated with extractive activities on the National Forests suffered, and now argue vociferously that the balance has tipped too far toward conservation.

> It amazes me that we as a country feel so rich that we can throw away 750 million board feet a year off the Willamette National Forest alone. That we feel so rich that we don't need that natural resource. (IND)

Few would dispute that proactive planning can be beneficial for organizations and projects of all types, but it is an endeavor that draws on both art and science (Kidd and Ellis 2012). The people I spoke with expressed very mixed feelings about the appropriate timeframe for revising plans, the value of forest planning relative to its cost, the relationship of plans to actual projects on the ground, and the most suitable spatial scale for planning.

> No one envisioned, when the National Forest Management Act was passed in 1976, that decades would go by before revision of a forest plan would take place ... You take, what, 114 National Forests, and we all spend \$7–\$10 million on plan revisions—is that a reasonable investment for the taxpayer? (FS)
>
> I've seen a bunch of plans be adopted, but none of them ever implemented. (IND)
>
> Planning at primarily the forest level, you end up with sort of a Balkanization; you have a whole bunch of different rule sets. One of the beautiful things about the Northwest Forest Plan is that ... it's one set of rules, it's like an overarching scheme ... It limits the ability of local politics to drag the plans down. (ENGO)
>
> There's an image of, well, you do planning at all scales and it just cascades down. But do you do NEPA and all of the bureaucracy of planning at all scales? And the answer is: if you did you would never, ever, ever be done. (FS)

Coordinating multiple authorities

Another topic that has received considerable attention from policy analysts is how coordination does or does not occur within and between authorities (Bardach 1998; Thomas 2003), an issue of direct relevance to National Forest management. Because the boundaries of National Forests are primarily political creations, the ecosystems being managed typically extend beyond them and include lands controlled by other federal agencies, state and local authorities, Indian tribes, and private landowners.

> The area I work in is [mostly] Forest Service, but there's a moderate amount of BLM land, and a modest amount of state forest land, and just under 40 percent industrial timber companies, and the remainder is non-industrial private ownership—and the management [on each] is radically different. (COMM)
>
> From my personal experience, I don't think [the federal agencies] are very well coordinated ... We would talk with one resource area and we made the assumption that the information ... would be transmitted and transferred to the other resource areas on the same district, and it was not. (COMM)

Even within the boundaries of a particular forest, agencies other than the Forest Service control certain activities (such as mining, fossil fuel extraction, and hunting permits) or enforce particular laws (such as the ESA, Clean Air Act, Clean Water Act, etc.). In fact, even when a decision is solely under Forest Service jurisdiction, tensions arise between different specialist groups *within* the Service, such as planners, foresters, ecologists, archaeologists, and administrators, each of which has its own training, culture, and constituency. These struggles were evident to all those with an interest in Oregon's National Forests.

> The Forest Service does not have full authority, even over the resources of the National Forests ... For some of those laws, the agency with jurisdiction ... is a different agency of federal government. The Endangered Species Act is probably the leading case like that, but the U.S. Army Corps of Engineers has jurisdiction over floodplains and wetlands and that affects our management ... We do a lot of cooperative work with the BLM. (FS)
>
> The district rangers have lots and lots of independence to do their job as they see fit ... [There are staff] that feel that their job is to just provide ecological benefits and recreation opportunities and all that. Then there are others who think their job is to provide counties with money and provide jobs and stuff. Others are focused on land restoration because "we have a bunch of bugs and insects and stuff and my job is to restore the land." It varies by personality. (IND)

In the forests of the Pacific Northwest, endangered species in particular became the poster children for interagency conflict since the ESA requires the Forest Service to consult with, and listen to, other agencies in different Cabinet departments, including the National Marine Fisheries Service (NMFS) and the FWS.

> We have had a fair amount of tension, on the natural resource side, with [the] National Marine Fisheries [Service] … It has sometimes led to projects that have had huge community support, including environmental groups, including industry … getting gummed up in the consultation process for substantial amounts of time. (FS)
>
> Historically, the way it worked on public lands here is that the agency would put forward a project … and then they would consult with U.S. Fish and Wildlife or with NOAA Fisheries … after they designed the project. And NOAA Fisheries, or U.S. Fish and Wildlife, would then determine whether it was a take or not a take … Those agencies held the big stick; they could stop the project. (COMM)

One proposed solution to such Balkanization is to shift planning and decision-making to larger scales. For example, a professor at a prominent Oregon university believes it is necessary to "move toward landscape-level management that involves many districts, agencies, and private landowners." In contrast, others believe that decisions should remain at a *local* level, where participants have the most immediate understanding of, and attachment to, the landscape, and where constituents and agencies can be engaged in multi-party dialogue and other collaborative techniques.

> Instead of having NOAA Fisheries and U.S. Fish and Wildlife come in after the project's been designed, we've had [them] at the design table, helping guide the process rather than reacting to the process. And they've really appreciated being included up front … It's going to streamline what's being done. (COMM)
>
> U.S. Fish and Wildlife sits in on almost every one of our meetings … Their thoughts are being incorporated into the planning process up front … It was really driven by the communities of place coming to the table and saying, "How can we do this?" … It hadn't been in the institutional thinking. (COMM)

Engaging the public

As discussed in Chapter 4, the role of the public in Forest Service decision-making went from minor through the 1950s, to extensive, formal, and legalistic, starting in the 1970s. In some places and in connection with certain issues, public involvement has gone further over the past ten to twenty years, approaching something akin to a partnership between those who care about a particular forest. Western Oregon was in the forefront of this most recent phase, and the concepts of public engagement and collaboration were very much on the minds of people there.

Many community members were dissatisfied with the traditional, statutorily driven public participation process wherein the Forest Service proposes an action, presents its plan for public comment (typically through a Federal Register notice and advertisement in a "newspaper of record"), and then incorporates external input as they deem appropriate.

> I think there's a culture of, "We know exactly what's right for this piece of land, this is our plan, this is what it's going to end up being. Whatever the public has to say, we either already thought of it and dismissed it or we know better than them." So the outcome is exactly what they wanted, it's predetermined. (ENGO)
>
> I was on a federal advisory committee for the Forest Service some years ago ... The agencies would set the agenda, the agencies would set the place of the meeting, and the rest of us would show up ... We had issues we thought needed to be brought to the table that we couldn't get there. (COMM)

Of course, it can be hard to distinguish between being ignored and simply being unhappy that one's views were not adopted. Based on my dozens of hours of interviews in Western Oregon, there was a widespread feeling among community members, industry representatives, and Forest Service staff that this tendency is particularly common among environmental advocates. In fact, one ENGO representative essentially agreed.

> We didn't see eye-to-eye with the agency and they weren't willing to change ... If they go into it with a more "open arms" approach, then the outcome is something that the community will be more supportive of ... And by saying "the community," I mean us, the environmentalists. [*laughs*] I want them to listen to *us*. (ENGO)

Some of those who criticized the typical public participation process also admitted that it was at least familiar—a known quantity—for regular participants in Forest Service decisions. They expressed ambivalence about the fundamental fairness of such a system, but were reluctant to upset the status quo.

> If you understand the process, you can work the process. If you know how to get input in appropriate places ... then the process is open and accessible to the public ... But there are a lot of people around who have differences of opinion but don't know how to

> work within that structure, and if you asked *them* they'll tell you that [the Forest Service] never listens to anybody. (COMM)

The post Northwest Forest Plan shift toward restoration forestry and stewardship contracting, combined with a determination in some communities to overcome decades of conflict, helped launch a new movement. Although it goes by many names and the social science that underpins it is still developing, collaborative resource management has taken root in Western Oregon. This approach changes the timing of public participation from commenting on Forest Service proposals after they are formulated, to working together with the Forest Service and other stakeholders to craft a shared vision for the forest before any decisions have been made. Praise for the power of collaboration was a persistent theme among some community members, and its supporters were eloquent in their endorsements.

> In [one] National Forest ... they brought all the radicals from either side together and came up with a way to treat this district ... It took about five years to develop, because they really took it slow and got a lot of buy-in from a lot of different people ... It worked great ... Now there's a lot of trust built, a lot of relationships built, and that forest is moving forward. (ENGO)

> If you have all people at the table that think the same way, you're going to get only one answer. What's really important is that you need to get the broad range of diversity ... The folks at the environmental extreme have some good points that need to come to the table, and the folks at the industry extremes have some points that need to come to the table, and somewhere in the middle we can start to find solutions. They're not always going to be perfect solutions, but I think they're going to be better solutions than the win–lose scenario. (COMM)

> I think the wave of the future, especially as we live in constrained budget environments, is how and to what degree do our constituents themselves, who are very diverse, talk about the kinds of activities that we want to do ... We don't have the assets to play the technocratic role that [in the 1950s] typified the Forest Service ... We don't have all the answers nor the capabilities of gaining all the answers. (FS)

Not everyone was equally convinced of the value of collaboration. Within the highly charged context of old-growth forest management, with ongoing litigation and nationwide lobbying campaigns, some individuals expressed concerns about both the collaborative *process* and the impact it might have on management decisions. Four recurring themes ran through these critiques:

(1) Anxiety about the legal underpinnings of collaborative efforts
With the exception of the Wyden Amendment process, collaborative efforts currently have no statutory authority. Any decisions reached are binding only in so far as participants wish to maintain good relationships. The applicability of the Federal Advisory Committee Act, whose purpose is to prevent special interest influence over federal decisions, remains particularly unclear.

> The precondition for collaboration is usually to lay down your sword. We don't want to put down our sword 'cause without the threat of litigation we are powerless. (ENGO)
>
> We have been at the center of the storm around FACA. When we first started we had both the BLM and the Forest Service sit on our board. [But] … we actually had a representative from the Attorney General's office come here from Washington, D.C. to inform us and our agency partners that we were in violation of the Federal Advisory Committee Act. (COMM)

(2) Unease with a perceived focus on process rather than results
The vocabulary of collaboration, with its emphasis on trust building, active listening, and achieving consensus, can seem obfuscatory to some participants, particularly those from industry who are more bottom-line, action oriented.

> Management has been reduced to the least common denominator, meaning we can only do the thing that everyone agrees on, and since a bunch of people don't want you to do anything, that's where it's tended to … Say you're a farmer and you want water for 100 acres and someone says, "I'll give you water for one." Why would you block the one? … We do what we got to do. (IND)
>
> The old guard—"The purpose of this forest is to cut down trees, and it used to cut down trees, and now it doesn't so much anymore, and bring back the good old days"—is a voice that's still out there … Some of those people choose to participate in the local collaboratives … and some of them don't because they [say], "This is a bunch of namby-pamby hand-holding about restoration and I want to bring back the good old days." (FS)

(3) Conflicts between local and national agendas, values, and priorities
A widely circulated and much discussed 1999 article by Michael McCloskey, then Chairman of the national Sierra Club, attacked place-based collaborative efforts as undemocratic and susceptible to capture by local economic

interests. Others fought back, arguing that local communities were in the best position to understand and protect nearby resources (e.g., Kemmis and McKinney 2011). The latter view dominated among my primarily local respondents, although one Forest Service staff member acknowledged the opposing viewpoint.

> We found that [the ENGOs] loved us when they needed us [but] they were very fickle lovers. We're finding the same thing with the timber interests; they herald us as the next best thing since sliced bread until they see an opportunity to get a better deal [through Congress]. (COMM)
>
> A national red alert went out both from the Sierra Club and the Audubon Society for their membership to not participate with groups like [ours] … What it meant was that these organizations were going to have to … become involved at the community level, and they didn't want to. (COMM)

(4) Distrust among stakeholder groups and fears that some participants will not act in good faith

Effective collaboration depends fundamentally on trust (Daniels and Walker 2001). Where trust has not been built up, or is fractured by specific events, it will be extremely difficult to find common ground.

> [Collaboration] was tried on the Willamette … It failed miserably. Mostly because of the players who came to the table. There were some people who just did not want to see it work. (ENGO)
>
> There wasn't a rule that everything your group did had to be in alignment, but that you wouldn't *surprise* each other. But [one of the participants] sued and they forgot to tell the partners. I would say that was almost the end of the whole partnership. (FS)
>
> Place-based conservation assumes that everybody is going to come with a certain sense of integrity, is willing to discuss beyond position … and really commit to exploring genuine shared interest … They're experiencing some growing pains with an entity or two in the environmental community that's like … "We're gonna be incredibly strong positional advocates, and if our position can't be satisfied … we're not going to play." (FS)

The misgivings discussed above align with critiques leveled against collaborative governance within the academic literature. Nevertheless, supporters of collaboration felt that most of the concerns were either invalid, or could be overcome.[5] They believed that the key to long-term success—and their recommendation to others exploring collaborative decision-making—was to focus on patient, long-term relationship building and small but tangible successes.

> Management agencies respecting and learning from their constituents, their public, is an important factor—actually taking into account the legitimate views of all these stakeholders. It's important that they actually listen, that people feel valued and empowered in the process, that's definitely something I've learned here. (ENGO)
>
> One of the challenges with these groups, it takes a long time to build trust. Many of the people who are engaged are not getting paid to be there ... It takes finding areas of common interest, and being able to come together around them ... You've got to have the little successes and you've got to have them fast. (FS)
>
> The Siuslaw is cutting edge when it comes to stewardship and ... collaboration. Over time, it has gone from being ... something that they were new to, to becoming so ingrained that ... they don't even think about collaboration or about public input as being separate ... I take it for granted ... that we would be involved, and the public at large would be involved, and that there's that understanding. (COMM)

The future

Marcot and Thomas noted in a 1997 article that the Northwest Forest Plan lacks "goals for maintaining intergenerational equity" and wondered whether this would become "a point of contention in public forest management." Today, it's clear that people are still worried about what future generations will face.

> So often, our environmental decisions are based on short-term economic gains, rather than long-term economic *sustainability* that may require lower levels of economic gain [now]. A lot of the issues related to harvest today, we're having to make up for those short-term decisions of the past that maximized production and income for that generation. (FS)

With this in mind, all interviewees were asked how they imagined the future of Oregon's National Forests and surrounding communities. Did they believe the situation was getting better or worse, and why? What were the biggest opportunities and threats? And what would "success" look like from their perspective? In general, timber representatives want access to more and bigger trees, see themselves as having lost substantial control to the ENGOs, and hope to shift the balance of Forest Service priorities back toward their interests. Most environmental advocates hold on to a vision of fully protected National Forests with little if any continued logging. Members of community groups are typically open to both logging and conservation efforts, but want to maintain local flexibility to determine the appropriate balance. And Forest Service employees, frequent targets of criticism from all sides, look to capacity building, strong relationships, and an inclusive decision-making *process* as the keys to adapting to whatever changes might come.[6] Each constituency's interpretation of looming "threats" reflects these perspectives, with loggers fearing the end of "active" forest management, environmentalists worried that Northwestern forests could again be viewed in commercial terms, local communities anxious about external interference, and agency staff acutely aware that their priorities are forever subject to shifting political winds.

> [The biggest threat is] to stand back and not manage 24 million [acres], not manage our National Forests, and let nature burn where it's going to burn, and let the new trees come in … I don't believe that's why [National Forests] were created; I don't believe that's what we should do as man[kind] … We should take charge. If we want this forever and ever, let's get a plan and let's operate under that plan. (IND)
>
> As long as you can make money off logging the forests … they will never be permanently saved. Money is the root of all evil, greed runs the pressure to extract our natural resources over what is sustainable … If you're a little bit greedy, there'll always be that pressure to extract. (ENGO)
>
> I see threats from D.C. or the region[al office]—their interpretation of how things are done or are not allowed. When I talk to people who are in the environmental movement … they want to see *less* flexibility in how the Forest Service can work … Here, we're looking at [flexibility] as a *good* thing 'cause our forest works so well and we can do what we want. (COMM)
>
> If suddenly the direction from the administration was [that] we need to cut 400 million [board] feet again every year … that would affect our ability to maintain our collaboratives and relationships and would undermine what we've done here … Our hope is that whatever the future looks like that we can continue to be relevant in providing things that society values in both an ecosystem and in a human community way. (FS)

Finally, each respondent was asked to imagine what a successful future would look like on the National Forests they cared about. Their answers revealed a dichotomy between those who cared primarily about attaining certain desired *outcomes* and those who wanted to ensure that a workable *process* was in place that could allow decisions to be made while sustaining the social fabric of nearby communities. A sampling of a few of these replies provides a fitting wrap-up for this case study.

> If the science says that our ecosystems are restored, our streams are healthy, we've done what we can, our native wildlife is thriving, including salmon, we've reintroduced fire into fire-dependent ecosystems … that would be a great success. (ENGO)
>
> Let's make sure we are growing new trees today that are going to be there, and we are thinning the young trees so they can stay healthy so they can get [big]. (IND)
>
> In thirty years, success I really think is, "Have we held onto the ability to continue to collaborate with people and work together?" [If] we lose that, it doesn't matter what causes change. We [could] get a 9.0 earthquake … We could have the really large fire that occurs every 350–400 years. What will get people through is the ability to communicate and work together based on relationships … If we can keep up those communications, that's where we have to measure our successes and failures. Not in individual outputs. (FS)
>
> If things don't get worse and if we manage to all still get along somewhat and have this fairly positive collaboration … that's gonna be success … The only way that anything ever progressed was when people communicated … outside of their comfort zone. (COMM)

Notes

1 An area of coastal sand dunes was "mysteriously" (Tonsfeldt 2010) included in the original Umpqua Forest Reserve, although it met none of the relevant criteria. To this day, the Oregon Dunes Recreation Area remains a strange fit within the Siuslaw National Forest.

2 A special case of this agricultural approach to forest management took place in coastal areas of the Siuslaw. Foresters knew that some species of pine trees would thrive if the sand dunes could be stabilized and enriched. To achieve this, they implemented a phased approach, first planting European beach grass to hold the sand in place, then Scotch broom to fix nitrogen in the sandy medium, and finally Monterey pines since the native shore pine was not considered desirable as timber. All three of the planted species were non-native. In the end, much of the Monterey pine succumbed to disease and, to this day, the Forest Service continues to fight the invasive beach grass and Scotch broom (Tonsfeldt 2010).

3 There is significant scientific and political debate about what constitutes an "old-growth" forest. Should it be defined according to the age of the oldest

trees in the stand or its previous logging history, whether never cut, selectively cut, or clearcut and replanted? Alternatively, as some environmental advocates suggest, should old-growth forests simply be defined self-referentially as any habitat suitable for "old-growth dependent" species such as the spotted owl? (Dietrich 1992).

4 Different versions of the Goose Project dispute are presented by the Forest Service (www.fs.usda.gov/willamette); community opponents (www.savemckenziebridge.com); and the local newspaper (www.willamettelive.com/2012/news/community-outraged-by-surprise-logging-launch).

5 On the FACA question in particular, insiders attributed the concerns to either overly cautious agency lawyers or those who wanted to see collaboration fail. When a stakeholder group is not appointed or directed by federal agency personnel, and their advice is simply one more input to decision-making, FACA restrictions should not apply.

6 Somewhat to my surprise, the impact of climate change on forests was mentioned only seven times in passing over hundreds of pages of interview transcripts, despite several questions that asked specifically about threats for the future. As one community member said, "Then there's climate change and how that's going to affect watershed and forest health … That's a whole different ballgame!"

6

AN EASTERN FOREST

Case Study #2

My second case study was of the Croatan National Forest, located in the coastal plain of Eastern North Carolina (see Figure 6.1). This forest provides a stark contrast to the Western Oregon forests. Despite being managed under the same set of laws, regulations, and agency procedures, the Croatan was created decades later under different legal mandates, displays a unique set of physical, biological, and social characteristics, and faces its own management challenges. Nevertheless, a number of overlapping themes emerge—most notably the never-ending struggle to balance multiple-use objectives on public spaces. And once again, readers with experience in the ocean setting should keep their eyes open for some very familiar voices and debates.

History and setting

Current-day Eastern North Carolina was most likely occupied by Native Americans as long as 14,000 years ago, although physical evidence of human occupation only dates to around 3,000 years ago (USFS 2002). European settlers began to occupy the area in the 18th century, gradually increasing in numbers and pushing out the native inhabitants. In 1764 there were 40 water-operated sawmills along the Cape Fear River in coastal North Carolina sending timber to Northern states. By 100 years later, the state's pine forests were being clearcut to produce turpentine, primarily for military use (Frost 1993).

In the boom years at the start of the 20th century, large areas of coastal North Carolina were cleared for development, agriculture, commercial forestry, and industry, leaving little of the original ecosystem intact. Then, in 1936, President Franklin Roosevelt authorized purchases of 113,000 acres from private landowners, the first pieces of the patchwork that now comprises the Croatan National Forest. These purchases, greatly facilitated by Depression-era foreclosures and bankruptcy proceedings, were allowed under the Weeks and Clarke-McNary Acts (see Chapter 4), which encouraged conversion of marginal areas,

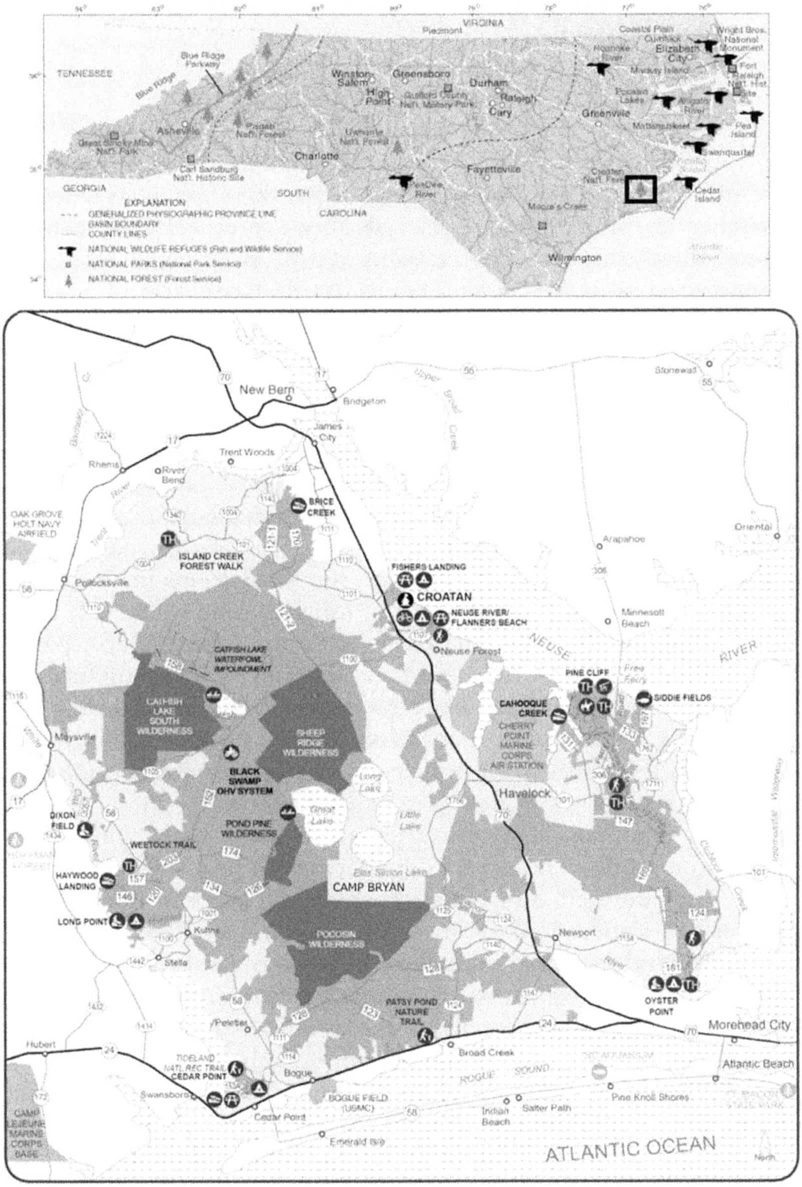

Figure 6.1 Map of the Croatan National Forest

Notes: Map of North Carolina (top) shows location of Croatan. Wilderness areas in dark gray, other Forest Service lands in medium gray, private lands in light gray and white.

Source: Adapted from USDA Forest Service map, accessed October 15, 2011 at http://www.fs.usda.gov/Internet/FSE_DOCUMENTS/stelprdb5403940.pdf.

primarily on the East Coast, back to forestland to be added to the National Forest System.

Since then, additional parcels of land have been purchased or swapped, resulting in the Croatan's current total of 161,000 acres. (For comparison, this is one-quarter the size of the Siuslaw National Forest and one-tenth the size of the Willamette, but by no means the smallest forest in the system.) As a result of its opportunistic establishment, the Croatan is interwoven with patches of commercial timber operations, private lands,[1] urbanized areas, and the 29,000-acre Cherry Point Marine Base, which was built on land transferred from the Croatan Forest during World War II.

Two facts are essential to understanding the Croatan landscape: The ground is low, reaching only 33 feet above sea-level at its highest; and it is wet, surrounded on three sides by Bogue Sound, the White Oak River, and the Neuse River. As one Forest Service employee told me, "The Croatan is an entirely unique National Forest because … [it] can almost be circumnavigated on rivers that are tidally influenced … The Croatan is not a coastal *plain* National Forest; [it] is a *coastal* National Forest!"

Prior to widespread European occupation, the slightly elevated areas (referred to locally as "ridges," although the word seems inapt to an outsider) consisted of large, open stands of longleaf pine trees, with a dense herbaceous groundcover dominated by wiregrass. These almost park-like habitats were sustained by frequent fires, sparked by lightning or deliberately managed by Native Americans for ease of travel and hunting. Local lore has it that: "[When] the first Europeans got here … they could ride down through this country on horseback, riding four abreast. [Now you] can't hardly get a horse through here in some places."

The other dominant ecosystem type is "pocosin," the Algonquin word for "swamp on a hill." These are boggy areas with peat soils and very slow drainage. The saturated, nutrient-poor, acidic soil supports dense, shrubby evergreens and scattered pond pines. The combination of wet ground with almost impenetrable vegetation makes the pocosin landscape inhospitable to humans, but provides excellent habitat for many other species. In the transition area between the longleaf pine savannahs and pocosin wetlands, fascinating and unusual species can be found, such as the carnivorous sundew, pitcher plant, and Venus flytrap (the only National Forest where this species is found). Additional habitat types exist in the brackish and saltwater marshes associated with the surrounding rivers. Although these niches are smaller in extent, they contribute greatly to the overall biodiversity of the forest (USFS 2002).

An important feature of the natural Croatan habitat was its adaptation to, and dependence on, fire. One state employee told me, "These ecosystems have evolved through fire. A lot of the species that exist in that type of ecosystem depend on fire to let them flourish." More specifically, a forest manager explained that "fire doesn't get to [the longleaf pine] … It *likes* fire—as a matter of fact *has* to have a fire to open the cones for the seed to drop ... [and] have some bare soil for it to seed." The original short wiregrass undergrowth carried fire along the ground at low temperatures, although this ecosystem process was not understood until relatively recently. On the contrary, foresters in the late 1800s and early 1900s believed that fire was inherently destructive and should be eradicated: "The burnings of the present and future, if not soon discontinued, will mean the final extinction of the longleaf pine in [North Carolina]"; thus, "the people must be educated to a sentiment against fires" (quoted in Frost 1993). Unfortunately, where longleaf pine was later replaced by plantations of less fire-resistant loblolly pine, and a dense woody understory replaced wiregrass as a result of fire suppression, sudden wildfires could be catastrophic.

The wet pocosin areas were similarly well adapted to fire. Because the pond pine is long-lived and fire resistant, the trees in pocosin habitats were historically over 100 years old. More recently, due again to decades of fire suppression, flammable vegetation is building up in the understory, raising concerns that intense wildfires might sweep through, smoldering down into the thick peat soils and killing entire stands (NCWRC 2010).

As was typical in East Coast National Forests, the original landscape had been substantially altered by the time Croatan lands were purchased and they continue to be affected by adjacent agriculture, residential and commercial development, recreation, road-building, and industrial forestry. As recently as the 1970s, large areas of longleaf pine were still being clearcut and transformed into loblolly pine plantations in keeping with typical forestry practice at the time. Out of an original 74 million acres of longleaf pine habitat in the Southeastern U.S., by 1993 there were only 10,000 acres of old growth left (Means 1996), with an additional 2 million acres of young longleaf areas, many of them almost unrecognizable as a result of active fire suppression (Frost 1993). Some of the wetter areas were drained and filled to create more profitable land. Although pocosins once covered over 2 million acres of the North Carolina coastal plain, the Croatan National Forest and Camp Lejeune Marine Corps Base now harbor most of the few remaining pocosin wetlands in the U.S.

Wildlife

As might be expected, the diverse habitats found in the Croatan are home to a wide variety of mammals, birds, fish, and reptiles. Deer, black bear, squirrel, rabbit, raccoon, turkey, and quail are all hunted for food and sport. The streams and estuaries harbor dozens of desirable fresh and saltwater fish species. Salt marshes provide important nursery areas for oysters, shrimp, and crabs. Even the elusive American alligator can be found in the deeper swamps and waterways of the Croatan. With its numerous water elements, the Croatan is a haven for birdlife. The swampy pocosin habitat provides nesting areas for egrets, herons, woodcocks, owls, osprey, and many other species. The forest is also located on the Atlantic flyway for migratory birds such as ducks and geese. Several species of rare birds have been sighted, including the bald eagle, the peregrine falcon, and, perhaps most notably, the endangered Red-cockaded Woodpecker, or RCW. Because the continued survival of this small bird drives many of the management decisions on the Croatan to this day, its habits and history merit a closer look.

Unlike other woodpeckers that nest in the rotted softwood of dead trees, the RCW creates its nesting cavities exclusively in living pine trees. The original longleaf pine savannahs were the preferred RCW habitat, although other types of old-growth southern pine also harbor them. For a pine tree to be suitable for RCW nesting, it must be alive, over 75 years old, and in an open stand with little woody understory (USFS 2002). The original range of the RCW extended throughout the Southeastern United States, from New Jersey down to Florida and as far west as Oklahoma. The 20th century, however, saw these birds rendered locally extinct in New Jersey, Maryland, Missouri, Tennessee, and Kentucky as their habitat disappeared.

By 1973, the RCW was declared an endangered species under the ESA, with formal recovery plans issued in 1979 and 1985. Despite these actions, almost all monitored populations continued to decline throughout the 1970s and into the 1980s. After decades of litigation and repeated injunctions against Forest Service logging practices, a RCW recovery plan was finally accepted by the courts in 2003. Although the litigation, initiated in 1985 by the Texas Committee on Natural Resources with backing from the Sierra Club and Wilderness Society, was originally targeted at halting clearcutting on National Forests in Texas, its impacts were felt throughout the range of the RCW. One recreational user of the Croatan forest observed that "the war over the Red-cockaded Woodpecker might well have been fought here—maybe should have been fought here! ... The upside of [the Texas] lawsuit was that it changed the management on the Croatan immediately." This observation was echoed by Forest Service staff, with a touch of defensiveness:

> What brought [the timber harvest] to a screeching halt was the Red-cockaded Woodpecker recovery. The Croatan was in violation and it wasn't the Croatan's fault ... There was nobody at the Croatan at that time in the seventies and eighties to evaluate effects on endangered species.

Despite ongoing recovery efforts, described further below, as of 2008 only 12,500 RCWs remain nationwide, representing about 1 percent of their original population (USFWS 2008). In the Croatan, the RCW population has stabilized at around fifty-four potential breeding groups in the western part of the forest, much lower than the 101 called for in the 2003 RCW Recovery Plan (USFS 2010).

Timber harvest

Starting in the 1920s and continuing through the 1970s, "scientific forestry" (see Chapter 4) dictated that North Carolina's longleaf forests should be clearcut and then replanted in dense, even-age stands with faster-growing, more economically desirable loblolly pines. These plantations were to be periodically thinned, until they reached optimal commercial size, then clearcut once more to start the process anew. Fires were to be closely monitored and quickly extinguished. This approach to forest management and timber harvest was virtually the same on private and public lands in the region. Timber harvests steadily increased, peaking in the 1970s (Figure 6.2), although the maximum harvests on the Croatan, even adjusting for its smaller area, never approached the quantities of wood being extracted at that time from the Western forests (Table 6.1).

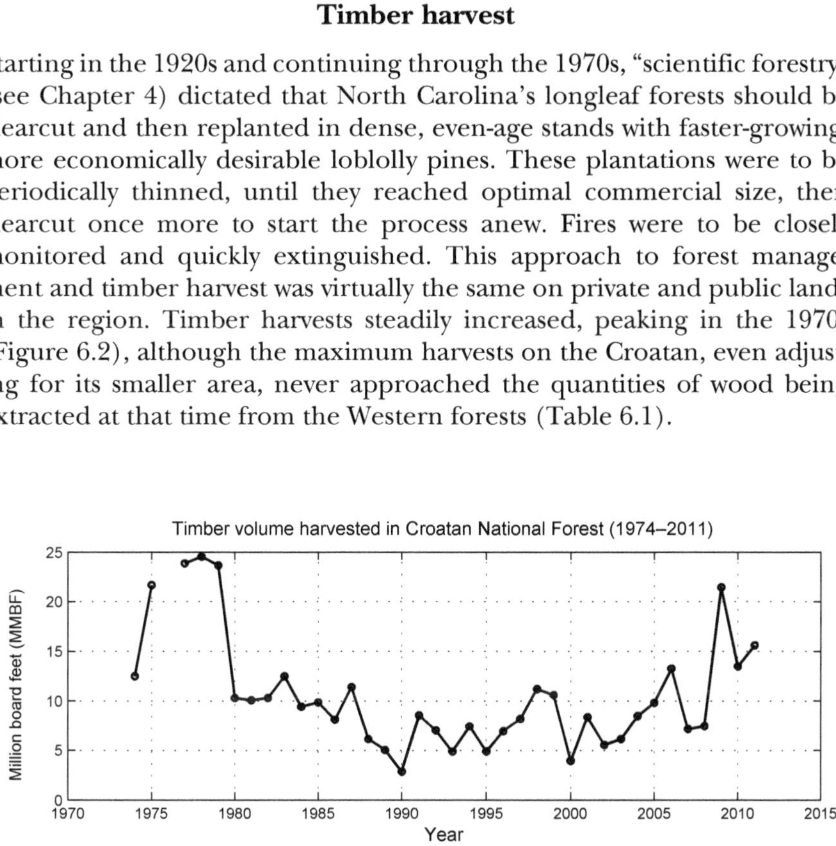

Figure 6.2 Timber harvest on the Croatan National Forest

Source: Created by author based on USDA Forest Service data; annual harvest figures not available prior to 1974.

Table 6.1 Basic facts about the Croatan National Forest (Western Oregon forest data shown for comparison)

	Croatan	*Siuslaw*	*Willamette*
Year established	1936	*1908*	*1933*
Total area (acres)	160,000	*630,000*	*1,675,000*
Highest elevation (ft)	33	*4,097*	*10,495*
Wilderness area (acres) (proportion of total area)	31,000 (19%)	*16,000 (3%)*	*381,000 (23%)*
1978 timber harvest (MMBF)	25	*315*	*693*
1978 harvest intensity (BF per non-wilderness acre)	194	*513*	*536*
2008 timber harvest (MMBF)	7	*28*	*31*
2008 harvest intensity (BF per non-wilderness acre)	54	*46*	*24*
Decrease in harvest, 1978–2008	72%	*91%*	*96%*

Source: Compiled by author from various sources.

Another departure from Oregon's experience, although seemingly a matter of simple administrative convenience, had important consequences for the Croatan. Because all four National Forests in North Carolina are relatively small, they are grouped under one Forest Supervisor rather than the usual practice of assigning a Supervisor to each forest. That person is based in Asheville, in the far Western region of the state. Mandates from the Washington office go directly to Asheville, where the four North Carolina forests are treated as Districts within the same forest management unit. But the Croatan is fundamentally different from its sister forests in mountainous Western North Carolina which include more classic forested landscapes and attract more recreational users and greater public support. According to one Croatan community member, "[The Croatan] was, among the National Forests of North Carolina, the stepchild. The headquarters have been in Asheville forever; [the Croatan] was (a) a long way away, and (b) it was swampy, and (c) who cared?"

As a result of this perception—combined with good growing conditions and easy access to rail lines, roads, and a port—the Croatan was fated to be the production-oriented unit within the broader multiple-use paradigm for all North Carolina Forests. As one old-timer who lived near the Croatan told me:

> If we got an administration in D.C. who was pro-development, and they wanted to up the commercial timber production out in the National Forests—which is a recurrent thing [that] happens under some administrations—they'd pass it down to the headquarters in Asheville and Asheville would say, "Hey, we can cut these steep hillsides and really tick off a bunch of environmentalists and tree huggers or we [can] just throw the whole cut into the Croatan. Who cares if they cut another acre?"

Another issue that was frequently raised by those I spoke with—although with less agreement among them—was the relative importance of public vs. private timber to the economy. Although there is less timber in the National Forest, it has a significant impact on local jobs and welfare.

> The Croatan is a nickel and dime operation in terms of timber production. Weyerhauser owns … 550,000 [acres] … The whole Croatan is 165, about half in wilderness that can't be touched.[2] So it really does nothing in terms of the regional timber economy, or very little. (COMM)[3]
>
> A lot of [loggers], a fair amount of their annual income is derived from logging on the National Forest system lands … We cut that back, we're going to be putting people out of work, just like what happened in the Western forest. It's [also] going to reduce the amount of wood going to the mill … It has a ripple effect. (FS)

One Forest Service staff member, grappling with his personal conflicts about the role of the Croatan, encapsulated a broader national schizophrenia about the role of National Forests:

> My belief is that timber production in the United States should probably be done on private land. I don't think it should come off National Forest land. [*pause*] Although you *can* take it off National Forest land. We are a land of multiple use. So, if there is a viable option, and it's biologically sound, and it doesn't harm the environment … then I don't think there's any reason *not* to take timber off National Forest land. (FS)

The most recent Croatan Forest Plan (USFS 2002) designates only 26,000 acres (16 percent of the full 160,000) as "suitable for sustained timber production" and directs that this area be managed "for high-quality pine sawtimber … by maintaining growth and development through intermediate harvests [i.e., periodic thinning]." Predictably, a local logger was less than pleased with these restrictions, while a community member welcomed them:

> In the mid to early eighties … there was a big kibosh: no more clearcutting on the Croatan, none, zero … And now everything since the early eighties has been all thinning … I'm not for thousand-acre clearcuts or anything of the kind. But I think they could have 20, 30, 40-acre clearcuts and it wouldn't hurt a thing in the world … The difference between a National Forest, to me, and a national refuge or a National Park is … the existence of this forest is to put money in the U.S. treasury. (IND)
>
> Gradually we started to see big changes, and some of these changes were morphing out of D.C. where "ecosystem management" and "biodiversity" … was the big deal … Another huge change came when Clinton appointed one of my heroes as Chief of the Forest Service [Jack Ward Thomas, in 1993]. He came in with a different philosophy of what the forest should be like—that they should be *forests* as opposed to fiber production factories. (COMM)

Ecosystem restoration

As noted above, a major turning point in management of the Croatan was the need to accelerate the recovery of the RCW. The Croatan's 2003 Forest Plan addressed this primarily through a focus on restoration of the longleaf pine ecosystem that had been decimated through fire suppression and dense planting of loblolly pine. The vision for the Croatan, as articulated in the Plan, is to "manage for healthy natural communities and processes, and provide for human uses and values within the context of sustainability." It goes on to say that the Croatan "will increasingly be a special place where natural landscapes and natural processes dominate." A little over ten years later, this vision is deeply ingrained in Forest Service staff:

> The overriding ecological thing that we are trying to achieve is longleaf pine … large-scale ecosystem restoration … I believe in that, I think that it's a good thing … It was what was here prior to the Europeans coming here and it was a very efficient, very good ecosystem. It worked well, had a good amount of wildlife, Red-cockaded Woodpeckers … The trees were spaced further apart. Timber guys, it drives them nuts if you don't have a tree every eight foot. (FS)

This change in direction is reminiscent of events in Oregon's Siuslaw Forest, where the court-supervised recovery of an endangered species led to a complete turnaround in forest management, from optimization of timber removal to restoration of native habitats. As in the Siuslaw, the new restoration focus also allowed for—in fact required—some continued logging. However, managers and stakeholders on the Croatan were dealing with a different physical and social setting, which created different challenges. First of all, the landscape had long ago been profoundly altered. Could the planned transition from dense loblolly plantations to functioning longleaf savannahs be accomplished without causing further damage to the ecosystem? Second, the forest is surrounded and interwoven with highways, private landholdings, and developed areas. How could the frequent fires needed to maintain the ecosystem be reconciled with this human presence? These biological and social dilemmas remain central to today's conversation.

Answers to the first question are complicated by incomplete biological understanding and uncertainty about goals. Initial restoration efforts simply attempted to replace one kind of tree plantation (the loblolly) with another (the longleaf).

> On this National Forest ... eventually we would like to do away with the loblolly pine and put the longleaf pine in there ... The reason that loblolly [was planted] is 'cause when you stick a seed in the ground, it ... grows fast. Longleaf pine ... takes sometimes ten or twelve years to get up out of the ground. (FS)

In one stand that I toured with a local community member, foresters had clearcut loblolly pines in 2001, tilled the soil, and then replanted longleaf pine seedlings in straight, bedded rows, following an agricultural paradigm. That site fared very poorly in subsequent years. Many young trees died and the artificial ridges and furrows were entirely unsuited to the native wiregrass understory and plant communities. Subsequent monitoring has found no rare plant species (such as the Venus flytrap) in that stand, and the site remains highly disturbed. Foresters are now adopting a more holistic approach to restoring the full suite of species, functions, and processes that make up a longleaf pine/pocosin ecosystem, although it is a difficult and uncertain task.

> How can you take something where you have mostly large loblolly and *gradually* shift it over to being mostly longleaf without a wholesale clearcut and start from scratch? ... The woodpecker is the driver under the Endangered Species Act ... If you can [recover] it sooner rather than later with the "wrong" kind of pine trees, but move gradually to the right kind of pine tree, then I'm fine with that. (ENGO)

One essential element of the desired landscape-scale restoration is fire. These forests evolved with periodic fires, and fire is necessary to maintain the natural ecosystem. A state government wildlife expert explained that "the longleaf pine's so important to ... the Red-cockaded Woodpecker, but also that whole assemblage of species associated with the longleaf ... Fire is really important in how you manage that system." But fire can also be difficult to control and potentially destructive to life and property, and is thus feared by surrounding communities. The risk is amplified as more public roads crisscross the area and development expands in and near the forest.

As recently as June 2012, a 200-acre prescribed fire on the Croatan burned out of control, eventually consuming 21,000 acres. Fortunately, there were no injuries or damage to buildings. The Croatan's District Ranger told a local news source that the event did not make him regret doing controlled burns since they are necessary to reduce fuel loads that would otherwise exacerbate the fire risk to nearby communities. (He chose not to mention that they are also needed to improve the health of the ecosystem and create improved habitat for the RCW.) Nevertheless, the vast majority of public comments posted on the website in response to the news story expressed outrage that government agents would knowingly start any fire.

More involved and knowledgeable forest stakeholders were acutely aware of the delicacy of this issue. Every one of them emphasized the value of "fuels reduction" (i.e., elimination of woody mid-story growth through both thinning and regular, controlled burning) to surrounding communities.

> If this forest was just left alone … you'd have wildfires like what's going on in California … There is not nearly the wildfires that there used to be, again because they're doing good prescribed burning. (IND)
>
> We know we want to try to manage fire as much as we can … to get the habitat benefits out of it and at the same time protect property … A good prescribed burning program is the best insurance policy you can have to protect your property from fire. (ST)

With regular prescribed burning to encourage longleaf pine seedlings, wiregrass groundcover, and RCW nest building, periodic thinning of dense loblolly stands, and ongoing monitoring and research, it may be possible to re-establish something akin to the native ecosystem. But is that the right goal? Who should decide? And how will the forest's future be affected by external forces such as urbanization, security concerns at nearby military installations, and climate change? The next section looks at how those involved view some of these challenges.

Issues and challenges

Balancing and planning for multiple uses

The Croatan National Forest, like its counterparts across the country, was always intended to provide for multiple uses. This particular forest no longer provides fodder for livestock (although it once did), but the MUSY

Act's other elements, "wood, water, wildlife, and recreation," are very much present. MUSY requires Forest Service staff to balance these "in the combination that will best meet the needs of the American people," and they are acutely aware of that responsibility:

> My job is to ... interpret the policies and direction from the Washington Office that come down through the Supervisor's office, as to what our priorities should be. And also ... look at the biological and ecological priorities that we have on an area, as well as the socio-economic, the people, and the politics of an area, and try to combine all that into a program that manages the land in the best interests of the people of the United States, who are the owners of the land and ultimately my supervisors and my clientele. (FS)
>
> It's easy to simplify into good guys and bad guys. And then there is the real world. I don't think you can really appreciate that until you have to try to balance ... [between] recreation or competitive bass fishing or an endangered plant or a watershed or archaeology. Until you've had to balance all that. (FS)

At various times different stakeholders have felt that their priorities were being given short shrift, since the absence of specific guidelines in MUSY gives the agency enormous discretion, and national priorities have changed over time. Many ENGOs believe that conservation is undervalued, hunters complain that hiking and other forms of recreation are given preference, and loggers perceive that environmentalists' demands dictate policy.

> I would love to sit in and be a mouse [in the corner] in some of [the Croatan] staff meetings ... to see if the timber beasts are still ruling the roost. (COMM)
>
> In my opinion the forest industry has been too silent for too long ... Environmentalists didn't build that road, timber built that road that they're gonna ride on and go hunting on. The bird watchers who are gonna look, or the wildlife ramp that they're gonna use, there was something that happened that paid for that. (IND)

Some policy analysts believe that widespread discontent—and potential negative consequences on the ground—are inevitable under a multiple-use framework, concluding that single-use mandates for public land would be more efficient and effective (e.g., Curtis 1973; also, see additional discussion in Chapter 7). That solution seemed unthinkable to those most familiar with the Croatan, even those who recognized the difficulties of multiple-use management and would have preferred a greater emphasis on their favorite use.

> I think [those who oppose multiple use], their arguments defy reality. The current National Forest is a prime example of multiple use—and pretty successful multiple use! ... As far as I can tell, it's working, and we have recreation, we have timber harvest, we have hunting, we have ... preservation of endangered species. It all happens simultaneously in the little 165,000-acre postage stamp Croatan. (COMM)
>
> Part of the job of this forest is to have a resource ready and to also provide money for the treasury and then multiple use, all kinds of water conservation, wildlife conservation. And all that can be happening simultaneously. (IND)

As discussed in Chapter 4, another controversial aspect of multiple-use management is the role of *planning* in creating a blueprint for project-level decisions, as required under NFMA. Although some form of strategic or operational planning guides virtually any large project or organization, forest planning has never provided the clarity expected, perhaps unrealistically, by NFMA proponents. With regard to the Croatan, comments were approximately evenly divided between the pro- and anti-planning camps, with those outside the Forest Service often reluctant to offer opinions about what they viewed as an internal, bureaucratic exercise. Typical comments in support of planning recognized its ability to even the playing field:

> Without some sort of planning, it's just chaos. Then it becomes whoever has the most money, whoever has the most political clout are the ones that get the things done that they want. (FS)
>
> NFMA was wonderful. It was a gift! It pretty much had the capacity to level the playing field among the resources, including recreation ... The second round of planning [in 1992] was just a much more complete idea of what the public wanted, and the timber harvest associations were in there too, what the NGOs wanted, what the congressional delegation wanted, and what law, regulation, and policy was, and how that could be met and what couldn't be met. (FS)

On the other side, comments critical of forest planning emphasized the difficulty of making actions on the ground match the plans:

> [The Forest Plan] does guide us, some of the activities and things we do, because it is a legal document ... But right now, where we are, it probably doesn't guide as much as it should. It's eight years old. A lot of things have changed in eight years. (FS)

> Inevitably, ad hoc-ism whips long-range planning every time. (COMM)
>
> The Plan does a pretty good job setting *goals*, but the Forest Service doesn't know how to get there. [It] doesn't have enough trained biologists to restore the ecosystem cautiously and with a long-term perspective. (COMM)

Coordinating multiple authorities

Because of the disconnected pattern of lands that make up the Croatan, as well as its close proximity to urbanized areas and a major military installation, this forest is particularly reliant on cooperation with other federal, state, local, and private landowners and managers. It is virtually impossible for the Forest Service staff to make a decision that does not affect their neighbors and vice-versa.

> Natural resources coordination [took place] primarily through collaboration with all of the local, state, and national agencies. [Also] lots of collaboration through research that we funded or assisted at a number of universities within and outside of North Carolina … And of course the ever-present support and coordination [with] the Marine Corps and the Navy … We coordinated so that [private] harvest would coordinate with the woodpecker [recovery plan]. We did that with prescribed burning as well, and with fire suppression. (FS)
>
> If we were going to propose a regulation, we would talk to the National Forest, we would all agree that's what we wanted, and then we would propose it as a rule … If the Forest Service said no, we do not want it—I speak for myself and I would think the agency—we would never pursue it. That would not be a very good relationship with your partner. (ST)

Of course, interactions between government agencies with different mandates are rarely simple. I heard stories of conflicts over military incursions into wilderness areas and widespread concerns about how disputes over road development through and around the forest would be resolved. The U.S. Department of Transportation has plans for significant expansion of the U.S. 70 highway to bypass urban areas in Havelock, Newport, and Morehead City (see map in Figure 6.1). All the proposed options require road construction within the Croatan's boundaries. One community member expressed little confidence in the Forest Service's ability to fight back to defend the forest's interests:

> Say the county wants some land to build a fire department … the Forest Service just [says], "Okay, you can have 3 acres or so." The bigger it gets and the more parties get involved, the more cantankerous everybody gets, the more the Forest Service hems and haws and hopes it all goes away. (COMM)

Even within the walls of the District office, different resource specialists (foresters, ecologists, archaeologists, planners, fire managers, etc.) must overcome the tensions of competing for staff and budgets and the prejudices of their training to create mutually beneficial solutions. One manager said:

> I'm trying to push my people to change, to give me ideas of how to do things differently. Here's our piece of land. You have this piece, you have this silo of information, you have this silo … My job is to blend all those together so that we're taking this piece of land in one direction. (FS)

Echoing this sentiment, a retired staff member told me:

> Integration of uses is a good thing, but it can't work if any one discipline dominates—whether for harvest as in the past, or conservation, or wildlife [for hunters]. By having various disciplines within the Forest Service staff, they can negotiate a balance that doesn't degrade overall forest quality. (FS)

Coordination between private and public landowners may be the most difficult challenge of all. One recent study (Weinberg 2012) documents the challenges of retaining "working" forests, which they define as the ability to "provide income, recreational opportunities, and ecosystem services, while maintaining biodiversity," in the face of growing urbanization. Many large forested areas of Eastern North Carolina, once owned by private timber and paper companies, have been sold to investment holding companies (such as the tax-favored Timber Investment Management Organizations or Real Estate Investment Trusts) whose foremost goal is to produce returns for investors. Increasingly these companies are finding that real-estate development can achieve that end as well as, or better than, commercial forestry. Between 2005 and 2011, over 200,000 acres of forestland in seven Eastern North Carolina counties were sold for development. Although the 2003 Croatan Forest Plan targeted 44,000 acres of adjacent private lands as "desirable for acquisition," these additions have still not been authorized or funded by Congress, and their purchase price is likely to continue increasing.

Engaging the public

By now, no Forest Service manager in the country can have escaped the hard-won lesson that stakeholders must be consulted before decisions are made. "Public engagement" is as much a Forest Service mantra now as "sustainable yield" once was.

> I don't think we can actually manage National Forests without [the stakeholders] and maintain objectivity and multiple use ... Those stakeholders, whether it's a deer hunting club, or the Sierra Club, or a Chamber of Commerce, or individuals, will see the value of the National Forests from whatever their standpoints are ... The great challenge for line officers and ethical staff officers is to fully integrate those stakeholders into decision-making. When you work on forest plans (and forgive me for this), if everybody's pissed off at us, then I guess we did OK. (FS)

But, as illustrated in the Oregon case study, public engagement can take many forms, with greater and lesser impact on decisions and greater or lesser satisfaction among participants. The "social analysis" provided as part of the Croatan Forest Plan identifies three types of community members:

> *Long-term residents* tend to view the [Croatan] as "common" land where they can hunt, fish, and recreate without many restrictions. [To them] timber harvesting and other traditional land uses are accepted practices ... *Newcomers* view the National Forest as a place for recreation [with] rules and regulations necessary to ensure a quality experience. Timber harvesting, road construction, or other activities that can alter the landscape ... are generally not accepted. *The transient segment of the population* generally holds fewer strong beliefs about activities on the forest and sees the effects of management in a much shorter timeframe.
>
> (USFS 2002, emphasis added)

Although these general characterizations were borne out in my interviews, the cultural differences did not lead to the kinds of bitter clashes and endless litigation experienced in Oregon—nor did they precipitate the experiments in multi-party collaboration seen there. Despite disagreements over specific projects, most agreed that management of the Croatan has generated little overt conflict, let alone legal action,[4] and that a lack of broad public interest leads to sparse attendance at public meetings beyond those immediately affected by a proposal.

> [When] you start talking wildlife, you're going to get the hunters out there. If you start talking [about] the travel management plan that came out recently, then you get ATV clubs and people in four-wheel-drive vehicles ... If we made the decision that we're going to reduce [the timber target] or do away with it ... that's going to have an economic effect on the loggers ... on the mills, on the port. (FS)

> This area doesn't have ... the big groups. That Center for Biological Diversity doesn't have an eyeball on the Croatan National Forest, thank goodness. We just don't rise up to that level ... We wanted to do a "Friends of the Croatan" [group] ... We needed one of the NGOs or an individual to step up and help us but, generally, they were pretty happy with us. There would be certain resource issues that somebody would be unhappy with, we made mistakes, but they were pretty happy with us. (FS)

As a result of this low level of concern, the approach to public engagement remains very traditional: a notice in the local paper, a public meeting, presentation of a Forest Service generated proposal, and time for brief public comments. Asked whether community members had experience with more interactive, multi-stakeholder dialogue, this answer from a logger was typical: "No, not at all, never had one, never seen one, never heard of one. That would probably be good. There's an environmentalist, retired guy ... he rides around, he has a small car, and he checks on us when we're logging ... it would be interesting to hear his perspective."

The future

As in Oregon, all respondents were asked to share their parting thoughts about threats to the forest and what they envisioned as a successful future. The answers revealed marked differences from those heard in the Western forests. On the Croatan, no one, including environmentalists, mentioned logging as the most significant threat, and no one, including community members, mentioned collaboration and dialogue as keys to success. All sectors seemed largely happy with the overall direction being pursued on this forest, namely periodic thinning, prescribed burning, and gradual restoration of the native longleaf/pocosin ecosystem.

> [I'd be happy] if we continued simply doing the things we're doing now: kept our cuts the same; take out our loblolly pine; depending on the weather, burn about 10,000–25,000 acres a year. [The] Red-cockaded Woodpecker ... if we left it strictly alone at this point, we'd be in twenty years at about where we are right now ... We're at a stable point, a relatively stable point. (FS)

Loggers would prefer to see more wood removed: "In my perspective, they're doing a great job, they're just not doing enough of it. They could probably do [i.e., cut] twice or three times what they're doing now." Environmentalists would prefer to see less: "Real success would be the conversion of all of it to ... a natural system with most of all of the natural processes in place." But the perceived threats are primarily external:

- falling budgets for prescribed burning, land acquisition, and recreational facilities;
- encroaching development which constrains the ability to burn forest land and puts additional pressure on trails and other facilities;
- further fragmentation caused by new and expanded roads and sales of private forest lands to developers;
- climate change, which was mentioned by several North Carolina respondents, perhaps due to the immediate and obvious impact of sea-level rise on the forest; and
- fears of additional land transfers from the National Forest to the military, justified by growing security concerns.

The closing comment from one state employee hints at the inevitability of change and the poignancy felt by those who see it coming.

> We're a rural landscape here for the most part ... Just imagine if it was like, oh shoot, Richmond, Virginia! ... When you start cramming people everywhere, that changes everything. You have more nuisance complaints, species can't move like they need to. [If] you add more people ... you add more roads ... But development improves the tax base ... It never will sit well with a poor county to tell them they don't need to develop ... People don't appreciate what they have when they have it. They only appreciate what they don't have after they've lost it. (ST)

Notes

1 One interesting story situated at the heart of the Croatan Forest involves Camp Bryan (see Figure 6.1). As recounted to me by a long-time resident and Croatan-watcher: "Camp Bryan [is] an old-time private hunting club that dates back probably post-civil war. Principally Kinston people, the upper middle class, the attorneys, the M.D.s, etc. They formed this exclusive hunting club, with a lodge and all this good stuff, and when the Croatan was being formed [in 1936] they just made sure that that chunk of woods did not become part of it. Basically, that's why it's still out there, surrounded by the Croatan. [It's] the play place for the same family descendants."

2 As shown in Table 6.1, only 19 percent of the Croatan is actually congressionally designated wilderness. This speaker was probably referring to the fact that significant areas of the Croatan are not available for timber harvesting for other

reasons, including unsuitable soil conditions or set-asides for RCW recovery. Tellingly, the mistaken belief that half of the Croatan forest is "wilderness" was repeated by several people.

3 As in Chapter 5, quotes are identified by category to maintain confidentiality, where FS = Forest Service staff, ST = state government, ENGO = environmental non-governmental organization, COMM = community member, and IND = industry representative.

4 No one with whom I spoke could recall any lawsuits against the Croatan National Forest; a May 2013 search of the Westlaw legal database also returned no results.

7

LEARNING FROM FOREST EXPERIENCES

While reading the previous three chapters on forest history, I hope that those more familiar with ocean and coastal policy issues experienced some eye-opening moments—as I did while researching and writing them—noticing surprising echoes of the ocean community's characteristics and struggles. In this chapter, I summarize findings from my exploration of National Forests, highlighting themes that reappeared throughout that account and suggesting how they might translate into lessons for the ocean management community.

The promise and pitfalls of "lesson-drawing"

Before attempting to use forest lessons as models for the EEZ, it is instructive to review the research on what is variously referred to as "policy transfer" (Dolowitz and Marsh 1996), "policy learning" (Bennett and Howlett 1992), "lesson-drawing" (Rose 1991), or "institutional transplantation" (de Jong et al. 2002). Each of these terms covers slightly different territory, but all look at the practice of drawing on successful policy efforts in one context—or avoiding unsuccessful ones—to improve policy elsewhere. The identification of successful programs and best practices can serve as a useful strategy for lowering the real and perceived costs of change, as long as certain caveats are heeded.

Most policy transfer research comes out of the international development field and focuses on trans-national learning; that is, national governments choosing, and sometimes being compelled, to adopt programs employed in other countries. Richard Rose, a leader in this area, begins his seminal article (Rose 1991) by stating that: "Every country has problems, and each thinks that its problems are unique to its place and time ... However, problems that are unique to one country ... are abnormal." Later work by Rose and others (e.g., de Jong et al. 2002) demonstrates that the subject "every country" in the quote above could easily be replaced by "every state," "every agency," "every manager," or, more broadly, "every policy setting." Drawing on his international consulting work, Rose concludes that policy makers are often more comfortable following models adopted elsewhere than relying on theoretical findings, noting that "public officials have little interest in discussing measures that have never been put into effect" (1991).

Rose (1991, 1993) distinguishes five types of lesson-drawing—Copying, Emulation, Hybridization, Synthesis, and Inspiration—which involve more or less faithful replications of a single policy model, combinations of multiple models, or purpose-built innovations that draw only loosely on existing models. The two central questions in this inquiry are: (1) What constitutes a successful model? and (2) Under what circumstances are successes and failures in one time, place, or policy context applicable in a new setting? Drawing on the work of Bennett and Howlett (1992), de Jong (2009), de Jong et al. (2002), Evans and Davies (1999), Rose (1991, 1993), and others, it is possible to identify several factors generally associated with successful policy transfer. Each of these conditions, to varying extents, is present in the context of National Forest to EEZ lesson-transfer.

The adopting community is sufficiently dissatisfied with the status quo that they are willing to take on the transaction costs associated with change.
As documented in Chapter 1, a raft of recent reports and articles have trumpeted the failure of the status quo in ocean policy. Vituperative and never-ending arguments and lawsuits concerning the impacts of fishing or the appropriate siting of offshore energy facilities highlight the failures. Thus many in the ocean management community may be primed for change, despite reluctance on the part of Congress and several established user groups to alter the status quo.

A sense of familiarity exists between the two settings—due to geographic proximity, shared culture, or institutional parallels.
Chapter 3 highlighted a number of intriguing similarities between the ecosystems, cultures, and institutions in the ocean and public lands settings. That comparison is revisited later in this chapter, supplemented by findings from Chapters 4–6.

A range of different, but related, policy approaches are available to draw from as potential prototypes—a common situation within the "quasi-laboratory of federalism" (Rose 1991).
As documented in Chapter 4, there has been wide variation in forest policies over time and between regions, thus offering a number of prospective models for ocean managers to consider.

Key actors in the adopting setting ("champions") are enlisted as supporters.
A small but committed circle of champions for change in ocean policy have already stepped forward in government, academia, the private sector, and civil society (Merrie and Olsson 2014).

Models are adapted to the realities of the new setting rather than precisely copied, making it easier to transfer broad policy lessons and concepts than specific laws or rules. Ironically, very strong similarities between the source and receiving settings can actually hinder transfer if those similarities mask the need for context-specific adaptation. As articulated by de Jong (2009), "cultural features, also known as 'informal institutions,' are vital to the way in which new lessons will be embedded into existing regulatory frameworks."

Although sufficient *differences* remain between the settings to negate any temptation to import forest laws and regulations wholesale, broad forest policy ideas and practices may well be adaptable to the ocean context as long as local and regional variations are allowed.

All researchers emphasize the importance of beginning any policy transfer exercise with a *retrospective* evaluation of the policies under consideration for adoption, then conducting a *prospective* evaluation of the likelihood of success in the new setting (i.e., evaluating the technical and political feasibility of the proposed policy, in light of existing formal and informal institutions in the adopter setting), and finally committing to *ongoing* evaluation and adaptation of any newly introduced policy. Following that guidance, the retrospective analysis in Chapters 4–6 looked at the track records of different approaches to National Forest management, while this chapter looks ahead to determine whether and how those policies might be translated to the ocean setting, relying on the "policy frameworks" presented in Chapter 3.

Comparing the U.S. EEZ and National Forests: an expanded analysis

In what meaningful ways are National Forests and the EEZ alike and different? Which elements in these two policy settings are most likely to facilitate or deter lesson-transfer? Table 3.2 first presented a broad comparison of the major institutional features that characterize National Forests and the EEZ, identifying a number of overlapping attributes. In this section, that comparison is expanded, drawing on the more detailed forest history developed in Chapters 4–6 and the policy transfer research discussed above, with a focus on the subset of contextual and institutional elements where similarities or differences in the two settings are most likely to significantly affect the prospects for successful policy transfer (Table 7.1). The highlights from Table 7.1 are discussed below.

Ecological setting

- Both locations are home to diverse ecosystems that include both sedentary and highly migratory species. However, species mobility and

Table 7.1 Major policy-relevant similarities and differences between National Forests and the EEZ (differences are highlighted in bold italics) (*Note*: This table expands on Table 3.2.)

Framework element	*Public land*	*Ocean*
Scope	A U.S. National Forest, plus closely linked human communities and ecosystem components	An ecosystem-based region of the U.S. EEZ (3–200 nm from shore), plus closely linked human communities and ecosystem components
Ecological setting	***Some animal species can range over long distances*** ***Frequent presence of threatened or endangered species*** Threats from habitat modification, overharvesting, invasive species, disease, climate change, ***and fire*** ***Monitoring and mapping are extensive. Ecological understanding has improved greatly over time***	***Higher mobility and connectivity for most species*** ***Fewer marine endangered species*** Threats from habitat modification, overharvesting, invasive species, disease, and climate change ***Monitoring is patchy at best; mapping is limited to coastal areas. Ecological understanding is limited, but growing***
Goods and services	Goods: Timber, forage, wildlife, other natural products, fossil fuels, hard rock minerals. Most goods managed by federal agencies but produced by private parties Combination of natural and human-created services: Non-extractive recreation, water and climate services, renewable energy, transportation (resource-related and thruways), wilderness and existence value	Goods: Fish, seafood, marine plants, other natural products, fossil fuels, minerals and aggregates. Most goods managed by federal agencies but produced by private parties Combination of natural and human-created services: Non-extractive recreation, water and climate services, renewable energy, transportation, wilderness and existence value
Social setting	***Humans live at forest boundaries*** ***Long history of human habitation and use throughout the area***	***Humans live far from EEZ (>3 nm)*** ***Long history of human uses near the coast, extending further offshore over last 50 years***

Framework element	*Public land*	*Ocean*
Social setting (*continued*)	Historically small, resource-dependent communities have undergone population growth and economic diversification over time	Ocean-dependent coastal populations increasingly displaced by urban/suburban and tourism-related communities
	Variable and complex narratives concerning forest resources and related communities; conflicting conceptions of problems and solutions	Variable and complex narratives concerning ocean resources and related communities; conflicting conceptions of problems and solutions
	Longstanding interest in forest policy among the general public and distant communities	***Relatively recent interest in ocean policy among the general public and distant communities***
	Incentives for collaboration due to agency interdependence, motivated leaders, scientific and policy uncertainties, plus "hurting stalemates" in many locations	***Few direct conflicts and relatively independent agencies provide little incentive for collaboration***
Governance setting	***Forest Service has primary authority, but other state and federal agencies have jurisdiction over specific activities, issues, or regulatory requirements***	***Sector-specific authorities dispersed among many parallel federal agencies. States have input via "consistency." Complex rights and international authorities beyond 12 nm***
	Dozens of independent and overlapping laws in operation	Dozens of independent and overlapping laws and conventions in operation
	Royalties to nearby jurisdictions based on harvest sales	Royalties to coastal states from oil and gas leasing fees
	Explicit multiple-use mandate in law	***Unclear statutory mandate for accommodating multiple uses***
	Privately owned lands often interspersed with federal lands	***No private ownership of space within the EEZ***
	Long-term leases can create complex property claims	Long-term leases and fishing quotas can create complex property claims

Continued

Table 7.1 Major policy-relevant similarities and differences between National Forests and the EEZ, *continued*

Framework element	*Public land*	*Ocean*
Governance setting (*continued*)	Primary venues for influence include the media, courts, elections and lobbying, administrative proceedings, ***and occasional collaborative settings***	Primary venues for influence include the media, courts, elections and lobbying, administrative proceedings, ***and international bodies***
	Management includes technocratic/regulatory and limited participatory approaches	Management primarily technocratic/regulatory with limited market-based approaches
	Major emphasis on area-wide, multiple-use planning	***No area-wide planning in EEZ; 2010 Executive Order calls for multiple-use MSP***
Participants	National, state, and ***local*** legislators	National and state legislators; ***selected international bodies***
	State and federal courts	State and federal courts; ***international adjudication***
	Agency staff	Agency staff
	Indian tribes	Indian tribes
	Local and national media	Local and national media
	Large, established, and engaged scientific community	***Smaller, less activist scientific community, but growing***
	Longtime and recent residents, frequently of different socio-economic status	Longtime and recent coastal residents, frequently of different socio-economic status
	Owners and workers related to forestry, agriculture, recreation (extractive and non-extractive), energy/mineral industries, and many special uses (such as lodges, ski areas, roads, telecommunications)	Owners and workers related to fishing, aquaculture, recreation (extractive and non-extractive), energy/mineral industries, commercial shipping, and renewable energy
	Environmental NGOs	Environmental NGOs
	Collaborative dynamics historically poor but growing, with leadership from agencies and communities, an emphasis on trust building, shared discovery, joint deliberation, and multi-agency decision-making	***Collaborative dynamics generally poor. Some fishery councils, coastal communities, and regions have demonstrated elements of engagement and shared motivation***

Framework element	*Public land*	*Ocean*
Coalitions	Organized advocates for: • commercial timber • recreational fishing and hunting • oil and gas extraction • conservation/sustainable use • wilderness preservation • market mechanisms and states-rights • local and state economic development • national security/military priorities • active fire management/suppression to protect surrounding development • ***water allocation*** • ***traditional native claims***	Organized advocates for: • commercial fishing • recreational fishing • offshore oil and gas extraction • conservation/sustainable use • no-take marine reserves • small government/“freedom of the seas” (anti-regulation) • coastal economic development • national security/military priorities • active erosion control to protect coastal development • ***international interests***

Source: Author’s work.

connectivity are higher in the ocean, making human-drawn boundaries even less meaningful than on land. The frequent invocation of the ESA has been a major driver in the National Forests that is not as prominent in the ocean setting. A number of marine species are endangered, with corresponding plans and litigation aiming to protect them, but these issues have not played as pivotal a role in EEZ management as they have in National Forests.

- Major, regime-changing natural events can occur in both settings, primarily through fire and disease in the forest and through storms and oceanographic changes in the ocean, as well as via climate change in both settings. But the ocean disturbances have not yet become a driving force in the way that fire management preoccupies forest stakeholders.
- The remoteness and difficulty of accessing the EEZ has delayed scientific understanding of ocean ecosystems relative to land-based systems.

Goods and services

- The two settings provide remarkably similar sets of goods and services—commercially exploitable living resources, renewable and non-renewable energy sources, extractive and non-extractive recreation, and climate control, among others—although the greater accessibility of forests allowed intensive resource exploitation and wide-ranging recreation to develop earlier in time.

Social setting

- The most obvious difference between land and water is that humans live on the former and only intermittently venture into the latter. Some argue (e.g., Shackeroff et al. 2009) that this profoundly affects human attitudes toward and relationships with these two locales, which is undoubtedly true. Few people other than scientists and scuba divers are able to truly experience ocean ecosystems and monitor changes in their health in the way any hiker can observe forest conditions. However, for the purposes of a governance comparison, that difference is not as important as it might seem. With rare exceptions,[1] people do *not* currently live within the National Forests; rather, they access the space temporarily for work and recreation and then return to their homes, as they do in the ocean.
- Forest-dependent and coastal communities share many features, including a historic dependence on resource extraction that has shifted over time toward urbanization, recreation, vacation homes, and retirement living, and has led to similar clashes over goals and values between old and new residents.

- Somewhat lower levels of public awareness, political attention, and user-conflict are present in ocean settings relative to forests, due in part to the time lag in recognizing marine resource declines, developing robust scientific and advocacy communities, and achieving widespread access to the ocean.

Governance setting

- One frequently noted distinction is that National Forests have one primary owner and manager, the Forest Service, charged with balancing multiple uses throughout its domain, while more than a dozen ocean agencies manage specific uses or activities in the EEZ. In theory, this should make it easier to document tradeoffs in the forest and achieve a satisfactory balance. This difference too is less definitive than it seems. As the case study respondents in Chapters 5 and 6 made clear, many competing statutes, regulations, and agencies continue to operate within a single forest, and a complex mosaic of land ownership types remains, creating a potential for conflict and requiring the same kind of cooperation and compromise called for in the ocean setting.
- Because of traditional freedom-of-navigation principles (see Chapter 2), the international community and its governance bodies play a larger role in ocean policy, although cross-boundary forest issues have required bi-national cooperation with Canada and Mexico.
- Although both settings experienced shifts over time from open access, "free-for-all" conditions to well-specified government regulation, these changes took place more recently in the ocean and many long-time users assert precedence for their traditional patterns of access and use.
- Management in both venues follows a largely traditional, regulatory model, with occasional experiments into alternatives such as collaboration, community-based management, or market mechanisms.
- Although both areas are seen as public-trust resources (de facto, if not de jure), established traditional users and the presence of private activities and structures permitted under long-term leases or agreements (e.g., drilling operations, dams, windfarms, cattle grazing, recreational facilities, fishing quotas) create expectations that are hard to reverse.
- Another important difference between the two governance approaches arises as a result of the National Forests' longstanding emphasis on multiple-use, area-wide, prospective planning, an idea which has just recently been introduced, and not yet implemented, in the EEZ. Extensive planning has occurred in connection with *specific* ocean uses, most notably oil and gas extraction and fishing and, to a lesser extent, marine protected areas, but multiple-use ocean planning is in its infancy.

Participants and coalitions

- The main protagonists in the two settings overlap to a great extent, as shown in Table 7.1, including elected officials, agency leaders and professionals, courts, the science community, the media, non-profit advocacy groups, industry associations, and nearby communities.
- In both places, disputes arise between individuals and groups with different interests, different values, and different histories. Some recurring divides occur between economic and environmental interests, individual and corporate interests, locals and "outsiders," extractive and non-extractive approaches to recreation, and proponents of nature-for-man and nature-for-itself.
- Environmental NGOs are active in both settings, although those advocating for land conservation are generally older, larger, more numerous, and better funded. For example, two major groups focused on forest issues are the Sierra Club, founded by John Muir in 1892 with an annual budget today of around $100 million, and the Wilderness Society, founded by John Marshall in 1935 with a budget today of $30 million. In contrast, the two largest U.S. ocean advocacy groups are the Ocean Conservancy, founded in 1972 with a current budget of $15 million, and Oceana, founded in 2001, also with a budget of around $15 million.[2] A 1999 study commissioned by the Pew Charitable Trusts, Oak Foundation, Marisla Foundation, Turner Foundation, and Rockefeller Brothers Fund found that less than one-half of 1 percent of resources spent by environmental groups in the United States went to ocean advocacy, although that number has probably increased somewhat over the last fifteen years.[3]
- The main extractive industries, timber in forests and fishing in the ocean, make similar arguments about their historic roles, economic importance, and ability to achieve sustainable harvest levels. Unlike the commercial fishing industry which is made up of many widely dispersed participants who must be organized to have an impact on policy, the timber industry included a few very large companies (in addition to smaller local operators) which may have given it greater influence in the political process.
- Another important contrast between participants in the two settings involves their approach to collaborative processes. Many National Forest communities meet the pre-conditions for negotiated agreement described in Chapter 3 (i.e., existence of a "hurting stalemate,"

> motivated leadership, incentives for participation, uncertainty, and perceived interdependence) and are already implementing many of the process elements associated with success (i.e., trust building, transparency, and development of shared understanding). The case study of the Siuslaw Forest in Oregon in Chapter 5 showed how these conditions enabled collaborative engagement among participants. The ocean community, however, is only beginning to experience many of the pre-conditions for collaboration. There are increasingly intractable conflicts between commercial and recreational fishermen, fishermen and environmentalists, the energy industry and many coastal communities, etc. There is also considerable uncertainty for "new" ocean users looking for permits, such as renewable energy and offshore aquaculture. But elements such as trust and shared understanding among stakeholders remain rare commodities (see Gopnik et al. 2012).

Keeping these comparisons in mind, the next section discusses some of the challenges and tradeoffs that have been experienced by National Forest managers and suggests how they might assist in resolving ongoing ocean management debates.

National Forest management challenges, potential responses, and ocean counterparts

Revisiting an article introduced in Chapter 3, Kidd and Ellis (2012) remind us that "many of MSP's core concepts, assumptions and institutional arrangements have not been subject to rigorous intellectual debate." Their review of the long history of theoretical and practical critiques of planning on land produced some cautionary advice for would-be planners, including thoughts about improving dialogue, respecting local context, and ensuring equitable participation by a wide range of stakeholders. Many of these lessons are echoed by the findings in this chapter.

The drawbacks of a multiple-use mandate

As discussed in detail in Chapter 4, the multiple-use approach has been a part of Forest Service practice since its earliest days, with all five major uses (wood, water, wildlife, range, and recreation) in place as early as 1916. Forest Service leaders and managers at all levels accepted and promoted the idea that their mission required "the management of … the national forests so that they are utilized in the combination that will best meet the needs of the American people," although those words were not actually put into law until 1960 when Congress passed the MUSY Act at the urging of the Forest Service. MUSY called for "harmonious and coordinated management … with consideration being given to the relative values of the various resources and not necessarily the combination of uses that will give the greatest dollar return or the greatest unit output." Multiple-use management has been central to the training, values, and culture of the Forest Service ever since (Wilkinson and Anderson 1987) and has been reinforced by Congress and the courts over time as the guiding principle for National Forest management. Where Congress wished to exclude multiple uses, they did so explicitly, for example in creating National Parks or Wilderness Areas.

Many participants and observers have endorsed the multiple-use approach (e.g., Hall 1963; Martin 1969; Fedkiw 1999). MacCleery (1992) finds that multiple use "(1) provides administrative flexibility to shift management over time in response to changing public demands and preferences on public lands; and (2) sets the stage for significant debates over preferred use, especially as competing demands become intense." However, the underlying assumption that impartial natural resource professionals will be able to implement a range of complementary uses on public land, based on objective analyses of sound data and science, in a way that maximizes public welfare, remains on shaky ground (Mortimer 2002).

Impediments to such a rosy scenario have been traced to many causes. Some relate to attributes of nature, such as finite resources and ecosystem complexity. Others are a function of institutional characteristics: imprecise, complex, and conflicting laws; complex, multi-level governance; short time horizons associated with electoral politics; the adversarial structure of the U.S. legal system; and incentives for advocates to advance extreme positions in anticipation of later compromise. Still others are the result of human cognitive and behavioral traits such as high discount rates, focus on self- or small group interest, limited knowledge and understanding, adherence to simplified narratives in the face of complex problems (e.g., "owls" vs. "jobs"), and other "predictably irrational" (Ariely 2008) behaviors. But at the heart of much of the criticism of multiple-use forest management are fundamental disagreements about appropriate forest *goals* (ecological, economic, and social) and the appropriate *locus* for decision-making (McKinney and Harmon 2004).

A number of critiques, written by academics, lawyers, advocates, and foresters, have been leveled against the multiple-use paradigm for National Forests. Shortly after the passage of MUSY, Zivnuska (1961) summarized many of its potential problems—the difficulty of comparing economic and non-economic uses, the impacts of lobbying on decisions, the pressure of congressional budget targets, local vs. national values, etc.—but concluded that the professional forester "through education and experience is qualified to judge the complex interactions of ... the several uses of forests and wild lands and is aware of the various values resulting from management," and thus "has a more valid base for contributing to management decisions than any individual or group." Others have been less convinced that foresters possess such Solomonic skills (e.g., Curtis 1973; Mortimer 2002).

In some circumstances, the goal of "balancing" conflicting uses within a given area will simply be unachievable: "Many resource uses are truly incompatible ... It is impossible ... to enjoy a wilderness experience in the middle of a forest clear-cut. An agency can 'balance' these ... uses only by distributing them across space" (Eagle 2006). As an alternative, many analysts have suggested the creation of single- or dominant-use zones, like National Parks, to minimize conflicts. Writing in 1967, Behan concluded that multiple use had become a convenient buzzword and a panacea, admonishing Forest Service staff to take greater advantage of MUSY's acknowledgment that "some land will be used for less than all of the resources." This view was echoed and strengthened in two important related documents, a 1970 report from the Public Land Law Review Commission (USPLLRC 1970) and a 1973 article in the *Yale Law Journal* (Curtis 1973), both of which call for dominant-use zones to be created on public lands: "Management of public lands should recognize the highest and best use of particular areas of land as dominant over other authorized uses" (USPLLRC 1970). The main difference between the two publications is that the Commission urges *Congress* to establish priorities among uses and set guidelines for choosing amongst them, leaving the *Forest Service* to establish the actual zones, while *Yale Law* would assign the zoning process directly to Congress, which they assert would ensure "full representation of all users and interests regardless of their location," revealing a faith in Congress's impartiality that rivals Zivnuska's faith in the wisdom of foresters.

Like a National Forest, the EEZ is a fundamentally multiple-use space.[4] Although the governing structure in the ocean is different than on land—with most agencies managing specific uses throughout the EEZ rather than coordinating many uses within a specific area—debates about priorities and interactions among uses are still central. A recent group of articles (Eagle 2006, 2008; Eagle and Kuker 2010; Sanchirico et al. 2010) extends the public lands debate discussed above into the ocean. Starting with the acknowledgment that the EEZ is a multiple-use space, they then analyze how different possible governance approaches might address associated problems, coming down in favor of a single- or dominant-use approach.

A 2010 Presidential Executive Order (EO #13547, analyzed in detail in Chapter 8) also addresses the multiple-use challenge in federal waters, calling on all ocean-related agencies to work together to develop regional plans that "enable a more integrated, comprehensive, ecosystem-based, flexible, and proactive approach to planning and managing *sustainable multiple uses* across sectors and improve the conservation of the ocean, our coasts, and the Great Lakes" (emphasis added). The Order goes on to state that the planning effort should "identify areas most suitable for various types or classes of activities in order to reduce conflicts among uses, reduce environmental impacts, facilitate compatible uses, and preserve critical ecosystem services to meet economic, environmental, security, and social objectives." Like MUSY, this guidance is inspiring, ambitious, and fiendishly difficult to implement.

In light of the current divisive political climate, and considering the massive government reorganization that would be required to establish single-use ocean zones and corresponding agencies, it seems most likely that the EEZ will continue to be managed as a multiple-use space for the foreseeable future. If that is true, how can the downsides of that approach be minimized?

Accepting tradeoffs

What, if anything, have we learned about balancing multiple uses on public space, and what options might be available for the future? In 1905, Gifford Pinchot, first Chief of the U.S. Forest Service, drafted a letter for his new boss, the Secretary of Agriculture, in which he wrote that, "where conflicting interests must be reconciled, the question will always be decided from the standpoint of the greatest good of the greatest number in the long run" (recounted in Behan 1967).[5] His inclusion of the words "in the long run" foreshadowed modern-day calls for sustainability but, in both time periods, the question remains: sustainability *of* what and *for* what purpose (Gale and Cordray 1994)? Generations of Forest Supervisors have striven to implement Pinchot's vision by implicitly or explicitly answering these questions, while outside participants applauded, excoriated, and second-guessed their efforts.

Accepting that multiple-use management built on the presumption of equal priorities for all permitted uses cannot deliver all desired policy outcomes while meeting the competing goals of economic and administrative efficiency, equity, accountability, and adaptability (Imperial 2005), tradeoffs must be made, and these tradeoffs will require value judgments. As echoed by USCOP (2004a), "in any system with multiple competing objectives, it will not be possible to meet every one." The question then arises as to *how* choices will be made, and by *whom*.

In the upcoming subsections, I explore three different axes along which choices must be made in any multiple-use setting: (1) the scale of decision-making, from national to local; (2) the decision-making *process*, from electoral politics to local collaboration; and (3) the degree of uniformity imposed, from standardization to flexibility. Where a management approach lies along these three axes will profoundly affect the kinds of decisions likely to be reached and the participants most likely to benefit.

Choices about scale: national, regional, state, or local focus

Selecting an appropriate scale for policy attention involves both ecological and institutional considerations. In forests and in the ocean, important *ecosystem processes* take place at scales from organismal to planetary. Likewise, the *institutions* that affect these spaces range from informal interactions among neighbors to global, inter-governmental treaties. Different analysts have made forceful, often mutually contradictory arguments for and against control at various levels, but all agree that choices will need to be made: "Thorny issues ... do not get any easier through delay or by forcing local managers to attempt to resolve national controversies" (Dombeck et al. 2003).

The fact that National Forests are under federal ownership creates "a *perceived* right and interest among all citizens on how these lands should be managed" (MacCleery 1992; emphasis added), namely a presumption of pre-eminent federal control, accompanied by a large body of federal law, an assortment of responsible federal agencies, and a "forest policy-making structure heavily concentrated in Washington." A similar picture can be drawn of the current state of ocean management in the EEZ. Those in favor of national-level policymaking argue that it ensures greater consistency, better expresses national values (to the extent they can be discerned), and prevents parochial concerns from influencing the use of public trust resources.[6]

This is not to say that the federal focus has gone unchallenged in either setting. Western states have never been happy with the preponderance of federally controlled lands within their borders. As an extension of the so-called "Sagebrush Rebellion,"[7] advocacy groups and elected officials annually promote national legislation calling for the return of federal land to the states (O'Toole 1997). Even dispassionate analysts have identified potential advantages to this idea, based on the value of decentralization in promoting diversity and innovation (Nelson 1995). In fact, federal forest management does accord a special status to surrounding jurisdictions, giving local governments opportunities to review forest plans for consistency with their own land-use plans (Brick and Cawley 1996).

With respect to ocean management, state and federal roles in the EEZ have been negotiated through similar "consistency" provisions in the Coastal Zone Management Act (USCOP 2004b), with periodic dissatisfaction on both sides (Salcido 2007). Since virtually any activity in the EEZ must be mediated through a coastal port, processing plant, or other transfer station, and the environmental impacts of offshore pursuits will be felt along the shoreline, this relationship continues to be tested. States and multi-state regions have already been given strong roles in fisheries through the Regional Fishery Management Councils, have taken the lead in promoting offshore renewable energy, and are central players in the Regional Planning Bodies being convened under the new National Ocean Policy discussed in Chapter 8. The U.S. courts have played a major role in partitioning public land responsibilities between federal and state authorities, as discussed by Leshy (1987) and Salcido (2007), but both authors conclude that greater *cooperation* between state and federal regulators, particularly from the earliest stages of the forest planning process, would be preferable to the minutely parsed outcomes of continued legal battles. Salcido extends this conclusion to the ocean context, urging the ocean community to work together in blurring, rather than reinforcing, the boundaries between state and federal waters and decisions.

A large body of theoretical and case study-based research, combined with the work of many active practitioners, makes a case for strong *local* participation as key to guiding public land management (e.g., Wondolleck and Yaffee 2000; Beierle and Cayford 2002; Yaffee and Wondolleck 2003; Marshall 2005; Kemmis and McKinney 2011; and many more). Not surprisingly, many of the community members interviewed and quoted in Chapters 5 and 6 also expressed a preference for more local control.

Arguments in favor of this position range from those based on the foundations of American democracy—Kemmis and McKinney (2011) look to the writings of 18th-century philosophers such as Montesquieu and U.S. constitutional framers Hamilton and Madison for support—to those based on personal involvement in successful locally led efforts over the last two decades (e.g., Gray et al. 2001; Wondolleck and Yaffee 2000; also see the Pacific Northwest case studies presented in Chapter 5). Supporters contend that cross-sectoral, community-level engagement, with local leadership, can transcend seemingly intractable disputes by: (1) building trust among those with shared connections to a particular place; (2) allowing community-based collective action to experiment with new approaches (such as restoration forestry); and (3) fostering seemingly small agreements that can contribute to a virtuous cycle of success. Although few of these authors appear to recognize it, many of their conclusions echo research findings from the wider fields of game theory and institutional analysis (e.g., Ostrom et al. 1994; Ostrom 2005).

Opponents of local control reply that such an approach excludes distant citizens who may have equally strong feelings and deserve an equal voice as beneficiaries of the public trust. Coggins (1999) states this unequivocally: "When the subject is every American's natural heritage, devolved local collaborationism is entirely inappropriate," and makes a legal case for why it should not be allowed. Unfortunately, he supports his thesis by advancing two debatable and inflammatory claims, proposing that "federal bureaucrats are enthusiastic about [local collaboration] because it is an all-purpose method of passing the buck on difficult and controversial allocations issues" and asserting that "the theoretical ... premises underlying local superiority are false or unproven." Many national environmental advocates—often the most vocal critics of giving communities a primary role in national forest management—believe that local residents will neither understand nor care sufficiently about ecosystem protection and will be willing to sacrifice environmental protection for local economic gain (e.g., McCloskey 1999).

To date, local coastal communities have not had a strong say in management of the EEZ, although recent work by St. Martin and Hall-Arber (2008), which documents and maps the connections between specific fishing ports and distinct offshore areas, may help policymakers recognize the importance of local perspectives to ocean planning. A report on MSP to the U.N.'s Global Environment Facility concludes, "The optimal approach seems to be of nested institutions in which local level institutional policies are supported by national institutions, while local institutional actions are in agreement with national priorities" (GEF 2012).

A thoughtful paper by Kagan (1999) reviews the many pros and cons of implementing environmental protection at different levels of government, including comparisons to outcomes in other federalist systems abroad. He concludes that intractable disagreements persist in the U.S. to a greater degree than elsewhere because "interest groups and politicians—and perhaps the electorate at large—want to have it both ways." He goes on: "They prize local democracy [and] want to allow local and state governments discretion to make difficult tradeoffs," but do not necessarily trust these decision-makers to protect broader national values. Kagan's solution is to rely on the legal system to arbitrate disputes between local, state, and federal goals, shifting the debate from being about the appropriate *scale* of decision-making to the appropriate *manner* of decision-making, a different set of tradeoffs.

Choices about process: political, technocratic, judicial, or participatory decision-making

The U.S. Constitution and its subsequent 225 years of accreted interpretation allow for a number of different bodies, operating under different mandates, to make overlapping and even contradictory decisions. Over time, strong claims have been made in favor of each as being the best venue for making management decisions regarding public space and resources. Some point to elected officials as the true representatives of citizens' interests (e.g., Curtis 1973; Mortimer 2002). Some put their faith in a combination of scientists and agency professional staff as the most impartial and objective decision-makers (e.g., Pinchot 1947 and his philosophical followers). Others—generally lawyers—favor a more central role for the courts in interpreting often-ambiguous statutory language and steering presumptively partial agency leaders (e.g., Coggins 1981). A more recent, but growing, cadre of participants and scholars promote the value of place-based collaborative decision-making, which emphasizes broad citizen participation, facilitated dialogue, and a preference for compromise (e.g.,

Wondolleck and Yaffee 2000). This section looks briefly at each of these decision-making options in the forest and ocean contexts.

Political decision-making: Because multiple-use management requires difficult, value-laden choices to be made, many have suggested that elected officials must take the lead (e.g., Bryner 1998; Mortimer 2002; Nie 2008). According to Nie, laws should express clear policy choices and specify desired outcomes, to then be implemented by agencies. Coggins (1981) goes so far as to accuse legislators of "embracing the multiple-use philosophy in part because it enabled them to avoid the inevitable, and politically volatile, hard choices." Howard Zahniser, a high-profile environmental advocate in the 1950s and 1960s who played a major role in advancing the Wilderness Act, explained that enacting legislation is a huge undertaking, "not because it goes so far, but because it must be taken by so many. A whole nation steps forward with … such legislation, and it marches only when so many are ready to go that the others must move too. Nor in our great government do we disregard the reluctant ones. Rather, we persuade, we confer, we try to understand, we cooperate" (Zahniser 1961). It is hard to imagine that Zahniser would observe the same level of comity today; nevertheless, because of the hurdles he cites, laws in the U.S. have generally been more stable, and accepted as having greater legitimacy, than agency regulations.

Since the 1960s, environmental advocates have often looked to Congress as a better champion for non-economic goals on public lands, such as wilderness preservation and ecosystem services, believing that economic interests would continue to dominate any agency-led multiple-use process. This perspective is central to Eagle's (2006, 2008) calls for congressional designation of single- or dominant-use zones in the ocean whereby some areas could be dedicated to marine ecosystem protection. With respect to fisheries management in particular, a 2002 study from the National Academy of Public Administration finds that

> NMFS' ability to reconcile [its] varied mandates—to conserve fisheries, preserve protected species, protect the environment, promote U.S. economic interests, encourage recreational fishing, and address socio-economic issues—would be enhanced if Congress were to clarify their relative priority … Congress—with help from the Administration, states, and parties representing the environment, conservation, and U.S. commercial and recreational fishing—should begin to discuss U.S. fisheries objectives and priorities with a view toward providing legislative guidance.
>
> (NAPA 2002)

Elected officials can also influence policy through tools other than legislation. By setting agency appropriations, often with attached policy-related riders, Congress has exerted a major influence over natural resource policies. For example, each forest plan created by Forest Supervisors pursuant to NFMA regulations must specify the maximum quantity of timber to be sold during the plan period. However, that target can be, and frequently has been, overridden by higher timber sale levels mandated in congressional appropriations. In the ocean setting, text attached to the 2012 NOAA budget appropriation precluded that agency from spending any funds on implementation of the previous year's Executive Order on MSP.

Of course, Presidents are also elected officials, although they cannot create new laws without cooperation from Congress. They can however represent their constituents (i.e., exert political power) in other ways, for example through executive and judicial appointments, executive orders, and influence within the Office of Management and Budget (Davis 2001). One presidential prerogative that has been used to protect natural resources on land and in the ocean is the creation of National Monuments. Motivated by the rapid destruction of archaeological sites in the West, the Antiquities Act of 1906 authorized presidents to proclaim "historic landmarks, historic and prehistoric structures, and other objects of historic or scientific interest" as National Monuments, "the limits of which in all cases shall be confined to the smallest area compatible with the proper care and management of the objects to be protected." Presidents have greatly stretched the original intent of the Act, creating extensive protected areas on land and in the ocean, over the objections of many resource users and members of Congress.

Technocratic decision-making: Progressive conservationists dominated forest management from the start of the 20th century, spearheaded by Gifford Pinchot. Their faith in the value of science, professionalism, and rational decision-making provided a welcome contrast to the previous era's combination of "first in time, first in right" land grabs and the influence of a small number of wealthy landowners and industrialists on politics (McKinney and Harmon 2004). The impartial, efficient, forward-looking management they envisioned would be housed in newly established professional agencies such as the Forest Service, the Bureau of Reclamation, and the Park Service. An important component of the progressive approach was their reliance on *planning*, based on estimates of forest growth and timber demand, calculations of sustainable harvest levels, and forecasts of demand from recreational hunters and visitors.

For decades this approach was accepted and applauded. Marshall (1933) found that "the U.S. Forest Service does an excellent, scientific job." In his treatise on "The Forest Ranger," Kaufman (1960) praised the organizational cohesion, respect, and success of the Forest Service. But he was also prescient in noting that an organization as smoothly functioning, unified, and well adapted to its milieu as the Forest Service might have difficulties navigating social change—social change that was just around the corner.

In support of the pre-eminent role of foresters, Zivnuska (1963) commented that "forestry involves the management of forests and related wild lands for *the various ends of society*" (emphasis added), a goal he believed could be best achieved by trained professionals. Three years later, Behan (1966) responded sharply that "when the professional forester arbitrarily determines those ends [of society] ... he most seriously violates ... our democratic politics ... 'Goodness' and 'badness' in our society are collective value judgments and land expertise is no better a qualification than many others for making them."

When competing groups possess unequal power and agencies retain considerable discretion, they become susceptible to charges of "capture"—in other words, inappropriate bias in favor of particular interests.[8] The Forest Service has been frequently accused of capture by the timber industry (see discussion in Chapter 4), the Minerals Management Service (recently renamed the Bureau of Ocean Energy Management) of capture by the oil industry, and NMFS of capture by the fishing industry. However, except in cases of blatant illegal collusion, it can be very difficult to distinguish between *capture*—an agency ignoring its public obligations in order to favor its friends—and *judgment*, whereby an agency makes legitimate choices within a multiple-use context in response to a wide range of constituent voices. DeShazo and Freeman (2005) state flatly that there is almost no evidence of significant agency capture. One author—who levels plenty of other criticism at the Forest Service—concludes on this question that foresters were "responding in variable and locally appropriate ways to heterogeneous communities" (Coggins 1981). He goes on to note:

> Timber companies ... were staunch supporters of [multiple-use management] as it was practiced. But as the agencies have begun to give higher priority to formerly ignored values ... their enthusiasm has waned ... More recently, conservationists, environmentalists, and preservationists have used ... multiple-use planning mechanisms to ... [shift priorities toward] noneconomic resources. To the extent they succeed ... they are becoming proponents.

Most agency staff, including all those with whom I spoke, vociferously defend their choices as reflections of the directions provided by Congress and the public—either directly or through elected representatives—as they understand them at any given time. Even if this is true, it highlights one of the drawbacks to agency discretion: professional staff members may become insulated from politics and public discourse, be slow to perceive changes in public opinion over time, and thus fail to adapt their practices accordingly.

Through the 1970s and 1980s, many observers continued to believe that land agencies could make multiple use work if only they had more data, better analytic methods, and new decision tools to calculate the optimum mix of uses. The task, according to some, could be boiled down to "evaluating the costs and benefits from alternative decisions" (Hall 1963). Describing a 1956 controversy that ended in cancellation of a proposed dam in Echo Park, Colorado, Hall concludes that the disagreement was resolved thanks to improved scientific analysis. Significantly, a review of the same events by Scott (2001) in his history of wilderness activism attributes the very same outcome not to scientific findings, but to vigorous grassroots lobbying. The 1970 Public Land Law Review Commission also recommended improved analytical tools (USPLLRC 1970), and two new laws from that time, NEPA (passed in 1970) and NFMA (passed in 1976), exhorted agencies to rely on the latest physical, biological, economic, and other scientific information in their planning and decision-making (Applegate 1977). To put these trends in context, this was also the era of the space race, the first mainframe computers, futuristic pavilions at the New York World's Fair, the War on Poverty, and major U.S. investments—and faith—in the power of science and engineering to change society.

The Forest Service developed a sophisticated computer program called FORPLAN (a clever mash-up of FORTRAN, the computer program it is based on, and Forest Planning) to handle its new duties under NFMA. A 1986 evaluation of FORPLAN describes it as a computer-based method of "using linear programming to simultaneously determine the land allocations and activity schedules that maximize present net value subject to such other goals as might be prescribed by the constraints," and which "embodies procedures for analyzing the economic efficiency and environmental consequences of alternative forest plans" (Teeguarden 1986). After reviewing all the embedded assumptions and operator choices needed to make such a program produce meaningful results, Teeguarden praises Congress for leaving plenty of leeway for the agency to "exercise professional judgment to separate applications of benefit-cost analysis that are reasonable and valid from those that are not"—fodder for those who question just how "scientific" these approaches really are.

Forest planners, operations research experts, and computer programmers continued to tweak and refine the FORPLAN model and its application (see, e.g., Iverson and Alston 1986) but soon realized it could not provide the answers everyone sought. Johnson's article "Reflections on the Development of FORPLAN" (1987) comments that "[planning models] are not predictive of what will happen in the future ... These models are not meant to dominate the process or drive out aspects of the thinking by planners or decision makers that cannot be quantified." Echoing this thought a few years later, Kent et al. (1991) conclude that "more emphasis should be placed on using [FORPLAN] to seek *insights* instead of *answers* ... It is as important to understand what FORPLAN can and cannot do, as it is to understand how to use it." Various forms of computer-assisted analyses continue to this day, but changing views of science and society were leading many to question the omnipotence—or even competence—of the technocracy: "Untrammeled expertise has had its day, and it did not work" (Coggins and Evans 1981).

By the late 1980s, even forest scientists were rejecting simplified linear models in favor of concepts such as ecosystem complexity, uncertainty, adaptability, and resilience, all of which were difficult to quantify and model. The prospect of including even less well-understood factors, such as economic, sociological, and cultural impacts, where data are limited and forecasts notoriously unreliable (Justus et al. 2009), raised the bar even higher. But the progressive movement really began to lose its legitimacy as the public realized there simply is no such thing as an "optimal solution," just different possible balances between varied, and often divergent, interests (Yaffee and Wondolleck 2003).

Ocean managers went through similar phases of reliance on science to guide decisions, focused first on quantitative modeling, followed by broader attention to ecosystem concerns. Once again, these stages lagged behind those on the land by years or decades. Starting with the Stratton Commission's exhortations to increase U.S. exploitation of offshore fisheries resources (CMSER 1969), stock assessment scientists have been at the heart of NOAA's effort to achieve maximum sustainable yields. Reports from the National Research Council (e.g., NRC 1994, 1998, 1999, 2000) are filled with advice for refining and improving stock assessments. In one study, the NRC concluded that "a substantial fraction of the litigation that NMFS faces is a consequence of real or perceived deficiencies in data or science" (NRC 2002a). Marine ecologists are called on to identify essential fish habitat and provide technical support for broad EBM (NRC 2001, 2002b, 2004).

However, like MUSY for the forests, fisheries laws leave room for the Regional Councils to balance ecological considerations with economic and social goals, with similar fights over the results. USCOP (2004a) found that "accurate, reliable science is critical to the successful management of fisheries," and decried the fact that "social, economic, and political considerations have often led the Councils to downplay the best available scientific information." Although this phrase seems to imply that "science" does not play a role in the latter areas, other reports do stress the importance of using social and economic analyses to inform marine fisheries management (NRC 2002b).

No one doubts that scientific analyses, forecasting, and planning remain necessary components of any strategy for managing public space and resources. One eloquent statement concerning the National Forests could apply just as well to the EEZ:

> The public wants beauty, recreation, and wildlife, ... we have reached a national commitment to preserve endangered and threatened species, ... [and] the public also wants [commercial products] from these same [areas] ... How can we possibly address

> issues of that magnitude, and achieve an acceptable mix of all the many commodity and non-commodity values, without extensive planning?
>
> (Wilkinson 1997)

Recent calls for marine spatial planning make much the same argument. But the era of primary reliance on agency decisions based on "objective" numerical analyses has waned. "Scientific research can define the biological and physical decision space for ecosystem decision-making, but it cannot determine decisions that must also reflect the values of society, its interest groups, landowners, and managers" (Fedkiw 1999).

Judicial decision-making: In the U.S. system, the federal courts play an important role in resolving conflicts by interpreting often unclear statutory language and applying fundamental constitutional principles, thereby creating a widely accepted body of law. But judges are also people, with personal histories, perspectives, and political allegiances that inform their analyses. Clever lawyers and advocates proudly practice "venue shopping" to identify courts most likely to be receptive to their positions (Scott 2001). The history of litigation over management decisions in both National Forest and ocean settings has been amply documented and analyzed (see, e.g., Wilkinson and Anderson 1987; Wilkinson 1997; Bryner 1998; NAPA 2002; USCOP 2004b; Baur et al. 2008), but several findings from these studies are worth highlighting in the context of considering the tradeoffs between different approaches to decision-making.

Proponents of the legal approach, often attorneys and law professors (e.g., Coggins 1981; Kagan 1999; Davis 2001), point to a number of benefits in relying on courts to resolve conflicts over public resource management, including arguments that:

1 at the end of a full round of court proceedings and appeals, an issue is resolved in a fairly durable way;
2 as secure, lifetime appointees, federal judges may be more independent and objective than elected officials or agency staff; and
3 courts can consider the validity of both the *process* and *outcomes* of agency decision-making, either of which may be at the heart of a dispute.

Coggins (1981) believes that forest ecosystems would be better protected if courts were more willing to review the agency's discretionary decisions, decisions that he presumes to be overly influenced by industry. In the ocean setting, Sanchirico et al. (2010) and Eagle and Kuker (2010) also look to the relatively orderly process associated with the legal system's adjudication of property rights as a more definitive way to resolve marine use conflicts than the current system.

But there are also many downsides to relying on the courts: delays of months, years, and even decades in reaching a decision; significant costs, which disadvantage individual or small group interests; and a focus on adversarial interactions and win–lose outcomes that can tear communities apart and poison the atmosphere for compromise. As Yaffee and Wondolleck (2003) remind us, the legal system may work well for dispute resolution, but not for relationship building.

Kagan (1999) acknowledges those critiques, but finds that

> hyperpluralism and high legal transaction costs are better than too little pluralism and too little responsiveness to environmental concerns ... That is the substantial price Americans pay for a brand of federalism that tries to guarantee ... local responsiveness and central control.

In a similar vein, Coggins (1981) concedes that "management and improvement of the public lands will likely be delayed and perhaps retarded by lengthy and expensive judicial oversight," but then concludes that "such a development is healthy and overdue," a statement that would certainly be disputed by many of those interviewed in communities close to National Forests.

Legal challenges to agency decisions have also played a central role in ocean management, primarily in the area of fisheries. Similar to the situation described above in the public lands context, advocates for any given position—primarily commercial fishermen, recreational fishermen, conservationists, and those who aspire to represent them—tend to praise or decry intervention by the courts depending on how a particular ruling has affected their interests. A report from the NRC (NRC 2002a) looked in detail at the history of litigation against NMFS, primarily cases arising either from fishing industry resistance to reductions in allowed catch or environmental groups' desire for greater protection of fish populations and ecosystems. The report finds that, since the mid-1990s, environmental plaintiffs have successfully used MSFCMA, NEPA, and the ESA to increase judicial review of federal fishery management, citing environmental and social goals not given priority when Congress first crafted comprehensive fisheries legislation in 1976. Challenges to the agency's failure to prepare adequate EISs, as required under NEPA, have been a successful approach in blocking or delaying NMFS decisions. A companion report from the National Academy of Public Administration (NAPA 2002) agreed that fisheries management "is increasingly exercised by the courts through litigation ... and by constituencies that seek redress through these forums," with rulings that sometimes favor increased emphasis on conservation, sometimes lean toward maintaining catch levels, and sometimes simply defer to agency judgment.

An important difference between the role of courts in National Forests and the EEZ occurs because the single-sector approach to ocean management does not involve an integrated planning process that can be reviewed. A court adjudicating a dispute about an offshore windfarm will not—and cannot—simultaneously consider ongoing plans for oil lease sales under the OCSLA, or review related fishing regulations under MSFCMA. For more than ten years, various parties have been fighting Cape Wind's proposal to site a 130-turbine windfarm in federal waters between Cape Cod and Nantucket. Problems first arose when the permit application, filed in 2001, was looked on favorably by the Army Corps of Engineers, based on relatively narrow provisions in the Rivers and Harbors Act of 1899. By broadening the debate to include factors such as effects on threatened seabirds, interference with commercial fishing, disruption of prized viewsheds, and impacts on Native American sacred sites, opponents were able to find support for reconsideration of the permit in Congress and the courts. In April 2010, Interior Secretary Ken Salazar, relying on new authority over offshore energy development granted to the Department of the Interior under the Energy Act of 2005, announced his approval of the Cape Wind project, but lawsuits are still pending (Horgan 2011). A similar proposal to site a windfarm off the coast of Rhode Island has progressed much more rapidly, due in part to its reliance on a broader ocean planning process that brought stakeholders together before a facility was proposed (Disavino 2012).

McKinney and Harmon (2004) believe that many litigants are turning to courts to resolve essentially non-legal disputes. They document a history of participants attempting to re-frame fundamental values questions under cover of rights and legal mandates, going all the way back to the Eurocentric and cavalier, but court-enforced, "first in time, first in right" property claims to lands already occupied by Native Americans. The only way they see to avoid this misdirected emphasis, and thus honestly address differences in goals and values, is through greater public dialogue.

Participatory decision-making: As public faith in technocratic decision-making waned and the realization emerged that multiple-use management required someone to define "the public good," many observers suggested that the public itself might be the best source of guidance (Reich 1962). Since then, there has been an explosion of experiments, case studies, analyses, and theory building regarding the most effective role for the public in public policy.

Starting with statutory requirements to facilitate public participation, such as those in the Administrative Procedure Act (passed in 1946), FOIA (passed in 1966), and NEPA (passed in 1970) that led to standardized, formal opportunities for public comment on agency proposals through the 1970s and 1980s, the trend on public lands over the last twenty years has been toward increasingly flexible, participatory efforts, referred to alternatively as place-based collaboration, community-based ecosystem management, interest-based negotiation, grass-roots ecosystem management, environmental conflict resolution, or collaborative governance (see Gray 1985; Susskind et al. 1999; Weber 2000; Wondolleck and Yaffee 2000; Gray et al. 2001; Hibbard and Madsen 2003; Lane and McDonald 2005; Emerson et al. 2012). New communities of knowledge and practice have emerged, drawing on the latest research in political science, behavioral economics, sociology, psychology, communications, and education. Where managers previously focused on isolated land units, "relying on technical models to maximize production of a narrow set of goods," now "management is moving toward an ecosystem-scale perspective where agency officials collaborate with a range of groups to manage for a broad set of values across a fragmented landscape" (Yaffee and Wondolleck 2003).

Steelman (2001) articulates some of the major distinctions between "elite" (referred to in this chapter as technocratic) and "participatory" approaches, differences that reflect shifting views about government authority, the role of science, the attributes of the individual, and the nature of democracy (see Table 7.2). The "periodic," "limited," and "passive" opportunities for participation found in the traditional model often mean that "crucial decisions

Table 7.2 Distinctions between elite (or technocratic) and participatory approaches

	Elite/technocratic decision-making	*Participatory decision-making*
Opportunities to participate	Periodic	Continuous
Style of participation	Limited/passive	Promoted/active
Locus of decision-making	Elites	Public
Value of democracy	Instrumental, procedural, the means to an end	Intrinsic, the goal itself
View of bureaucracy	Trustworthy, competent	Distant, not representative
Primary concerns	Efficiency, stability, rationality	Responsiveness, individual growth
Main form of participation	Voting	Multiple venues
View of the public	Uninformed, easily manipulated	Knowledgeable, discerning, active

Source: Adapted from Steelman 2001.

have already been made and citizen involvement becomes a formality leading to small changes" (Smith and McDonough 2001).

If indeed the new locus of decision-making power is to be the public, then legitimate questions follow about what that implies. If the public means *all* citizens, elections are the traditional tools for gauging their views. But if, as many have suggested (e.g., Daniels and Walker 2001; O'Leary and Bingham 2003), truly meaningful participation requires face-to-face, collaborative dialogue, who should be at the table and who decides? Some possibilities include the following distinct, but often overlapping, groups: communities of *place*—those who share a connection to a specific location; communities of *interest*, similar to "advocacy coalitions"—those who share goals; and communities of *expertise*—those who focus on a specific issue, such as timber management or recreational fishing. Each of these groups will have legitimate interests in virtually any disputed issue but, where the aim is to agree on an appropriate mix of uses in a federally owned or managed space, public participation experts generally look to communities of *place* as the preferred forum. This is where the drivers for collaboration are most intense and where the prospects for enduring trust and relationship building are greatest.

Extensive case-study research has identified features commonly associated with the successful initiation, maintenance, and success of collaborative public participation in natural resource management (Yaffee and Wondelleck 2003; Leach 2006; Emerson et al. 2012):

- participants must have the capacity (i.e., skills, training, and information) for joint action;
- there must be a shared problem to be solved which provides the incentive to overcome the costs of continued dialogue;
- leaders and facilitators must allow for relationship and trust building apart from direct problem-solving efforts; and
- the process should be inclusive, transparent, negotiation-based, and consensus-seeking, while accepting that full consensus may not be achieved.

When they work well, collaborative efforts can break through long-standing gridlock (see examples in Chapters 4 and 5), result in greater stakeholder satisfaction with the process and subsequent decisions (Steelman and DuMond 2009), and decrease time spent in administrative appeals (Gericke and Sullivan 1994). Based on their detailed history of public lands management in the West, McKinney and Harmon (2004) conclude that the way to "produce wise, durable decisions over the use of natural resources is to bring together the right people with the best available information in constructive forums that focus on the places and issues people care about."

Nevertheless, serious and sometimes profound philosophical and practical concerns about collaboration have also been raised. Most critics complain that highly participatory processes, by their nature, will exclude some perspectives, either because those individuals are not aware of the proceedings or cannot be present (Manring 2005). Large national ENGOs have been some of the strongest opponents, believing that "the shift toward local control disenfranchises distant stakeholders ... Most of those who own the public forests are excluded from the process" (McCloskey 1999). Critics frequently assume that local communities will inevitably be more focused on economic concerns than on environmental protection (Bryner 1998; McCloskey 1999; Manring 2005). Community members reply that large, well-funded groups have chosen to concentrate their resources and power in Washington, D.C. and have become disconnected from the realities on the ground, a common complaint expressed in the case study interviews discussed in Chapter 5. Wondolleck and Yaffee (2000) found that the resource-dependent communities they studied did include "vocal environmentalists, many of whom were at least as strident as the national groups" in advocating preservation.

The criticism of locally led efforts is also couched in more philosophical terms, decrying the devolution of federal government responsibilities as out of keeping with the American form of government. For example, Manring (2005) fears that "the focus on the community of place ... [will] undermine the democratic accountability of the forest planning processes." Others look to the PTD and the need to allow *all* its beneficiaries to assert their legal rights. Unfortunately, many of these seemingly theoretical critiques of local decision-making are advanced by individuals with clearly expressed policy preferences—whether for increased environmental protection or fewer restrictions on extraction—whose desired outcomes may not be the overriding priority at the local level.

Another challenge arises in trying to merge the benefits of a flexible collaborative approach into the existing highly structured legal and political system. Although Nie (2008) considers full delegation to local processes to be an "abdication of congressional, executive, and judicial responsibility," he supports collaboration as a useful supplement to traditional decision-making processes. Even strong believers in the added benefits of collaboration (e.g., Wondolleck and Yaffee 2000; McKinney and Harmon 2004) believe that its outcomes must be used as one input to established administrative processes.

A particular mismatch occurs between collaborative approaches and application of the 1972 FACA. The purpose of that law was to limit the influence of special interests by requiring that government agencies follow more transparent procedures for assembling advisory committees, but they may also have "created a number of chilling effects on public participation," due to excessive procedural requirements and ambiguities in the law and regulations that discourage procedural innovation (Long and Beierle 1999).

To date, federal ocean managers have not really experimented with, let alone embraced, inclusive, collaborative governance. The processes for regulating ocean activities—from leasing offshore sites, to issuing shipping regulations, to regulating fishing—generally follow a traditional "notice and comment" approach to public participation.[9] NAPA's 2002 review of fisheries litigation revealed that:

> The view of many of NMFS' partners and constituents is that it does not reach out to involve them in meaningful participation in its activities. NMFS, from their standpoint, does not engage them in designing policies and programs, implementing projects, and evaluating results. Fishers question NMFS science and its motivation, just as environmentalists challenge its willingness to adopt restrictions.

NAPA's resulting recommendation suggests that: "The NMFS Assistant Administrator [should] issue a policy requiring responses to constituents' and partners' concerns ... [to be provided] as part of the decision process"—an approach that is very unlikely to appease a dissatisfied public.

The 2010 Executive Order regarding marine spatial planning (analyzed further in Chapter 8) calls for "cohesive actions across the Federal Government, as well as participation of State, tribal, and local authorities, regional governance structures, nongovernmental organizations, the public, and the private sector." However, implementation of the order so far has employed very traditional outreach mechanisms, such as public hearings during which agency leaders make presentations and allow short statements from the public, and publication of draft documents in the Federal Register with the opportunity for outsiders to provide written comments. Given the similarities between the National Forests and the EEZ in their mix of stakeholders, types of uses present, and relevant authorities, it is reasonable to believe that more collaborative approaches may also prove useful in the ocean setting.

One astute observation about the motivations behind collaborative efforts reminds us that, ultimately, "People act collaboratively as a strategy for achieving their own interests, including their interest in [achieving] a creative and durable solution" (Yaffee and Wondolleck 2003).

Mixed approaches: In the real world, electoral, technocratic, judicial, and participatory approaches are usually operating simultaneously within the broader context of social and economic forces. Sabatier envisions "advocacy coalitions"—which typically include representatives from all sectors—using their resources, influence, and connections to take advantage of any opportunity to advance their cause. Perhaps without fully realizing it, each group then tends to praise whichever venue is best suited to achieving their ends at any given time.

For example, after boasting of the environmental movement's successful use of grassroots organizing, media campaigns, public demonstrations, and Congressional lobbying to finally gain passage of the Wilderness Act—all quintessentially political levers—Scott (2001) goes on to say, "A law ... represents a national social consensus [...] The bicameral legislature and the gauntlet of Congressional procedures ... [produce laws that] are not susceptible to willy-nilly change with the ebbs and flows of American politics." Moreover, the "social consensus" supposedly represented in the Act, which instructed the agencies to assess their lands for wilderness potential according to certain criteria and then make recommendations to Congress, was actively circumvented by the environmental community when the outcomes were not what they preferred. Scott proudly discusses how wilderness advocates side-stepped the agencies by lobbying sympathetic Members of Congress to designate areas as wilderness that would never have met the statutory definitions that guided the agencies' review.

Not surprisingly, timber, mining, and oil interests employed similar tactics, praising the durability of legislation, the scientific impartiality of agency decisions, the wisdom of the courts, or the power of the people, depending on which of these bodies was most in tune with their interests at that moment. In a similar vein, NAPA's 2002 study of fisheries management found that both "major constituencies—fishers and environmental and conservationist groups—regard the system as primarily serving the interests of the other."

Elected officials from Alderman to President, staffs of many different agencies, courts from municipal to Supreme, and the public from near and far will continue to play central roles in debates about natural resource policy. Adding this assortment of actors to the ecological, institutional, and cultural variability found in National Forest and ocean communities is likely to result in both decision-making *processes* and *results* that look different from place to place. The next section considers the implications of such variability.

Choices about uniformity: standardized or flexible implementation

A third difficult set of tradeoffs must be made between the desire for harmonization—with the certainty and predictability that accompany such standardization—and the search for more flexible approaches, generally associated with greater adaptability and innovation. Views about this tradeoff often go hand in hand with attitudes about the previous two regarding the correct *scale* and *locus* of decision-making. Although many different combinations along these three decision axes are certainly possible, it seems that individual scholars and advocates often lean toward either:

1 nationalized, statute-driven, legally enforceable, standardized approaches (e.g., Coggins 1981; Eagle and Kuker 2010); or
2 localized, participatory, flexible approaches (e.g., Yaffee and Wondolleck 2003; Ostrom 2005).

As discussed below, this may be as much the result of varied philosophical stances as it is of divergent analytical conclusions.

There is a definite appeal to notions of standardization, rulemaking, coordination, and adjudication, all of which connote a degree of order and provide predictability to leaders, businesses, and the public. These concepts are very much in tune with Progressive ideals (Pinchot 1947) and the related "modernist" perspective (Scott 2001): through science, the rule of law, proactive planning, functional design, and rational analysis, society would be able to transcend the "messiness" of human behavior and maximize human welfare. Wherever there are multiple, overlapping jurisdictions, statutes, offices, and agencies, all tasked with some aspect of resource management, you are likely to find reports calling for standards, coordination, planning, or functional consolidation, to be back-stopped by court adjudication (e.g., Curtis 1973; Coggins 1981; Wilkinson 1997; Pew Oceans Commission 2003; USCOP 2004a; Sanchirico et al. 2010). Scientists and engineers are enlisted to forecast sustainable harvest levels, model optimum-use profiles, and predict maximum sustainable yields, while mapmakers are relied on to create orderly spatial representations of ecosystems and activities—at least those they care about.[10]

One obvious advantage to such enforced uniformity is the assurance that high-priority national goals cannot be ignored in favor of parochial local or regional interests. Good examples can be seen in the creation and maintenance of wilderness areas or the protection of endangered species. Both of these goals involve one-way ratchets—once wilderness is destroyed or a species is lost, there is little hope of reversing course—thus a heightened level of precaution may be warranted that limits flexibility.

To achieve greater consistency and uniformity, the suggestion is often made to enforce tighter links between offices and agencies, mandating coordination so that all arms of government are pulling in the same direction. MacCleery (1992) observes that as forest management moved toward more ecosystem-based goals, the former divisions of responsibility no longer functioned well:

> A timber sale, formally the responsibility of the timber staff (and funded by a timber sale budget line item), may now be the mechanism to reduce forest fuels—a task which was previously the responsibility of the fire staff (funded by the fire budget line item). The same activity may also advance the objectives of restoring watershed conditions or enhancing wildlife habitat (under the

> purview of the watershed and wildlife staffs, respectively). It has sometimes been difficult for the existing functional disciplines—with their traditional budget line funding from Congress—to rationalize and clarify their roles under the new mission focus.

Although this observation describes disconnects *internal* to the Forest Service, Chapters 4–6 showed that similar problems occur across agencies with overlapping missions, including the FWS, NMFS, state fish and game departments, etc.

The report from the U.S. Ocean Commission (USCOP 2004a) repeatedly decries the lack of coordination among ocean agencies and ties it to the nation's failure to achieve environmental and economic goals. Entire chapters are devoted to topics such as "Coordinating Management in Federal Waters" and "Strengthening the Federal Agency Structure." The Commission also makes a number of recommendations for new overarching federal bodies[11] and proposes a long-term goal of "consolidation of all natural resource functions, including those applicable to oceans and coasts, [to] enable the federal government to move toward true ecosystem-based management."

However, attempts to coordinate, centralize, or merge authorities also have critics who argue, for philosophical and practical reasons, that resource management will actually fare better by maintaining greater diversity among agencies and allowing more flexible, place-based solutions to develop. In his 1989 study of the San Francisco area public transit system—at that time a crazy-quilt of buses, metrorail, light rail, and trolleys, all run by different agencies—Chisholm begins by summarizing the then widely touted view that the system was "uncoordinated and in disarray [with] inefficient use of resources, lost opportunities, useless conflict," and "multiorganizational suboptimality." He then presents the generally recommended cure that came out of the accepted diagnosis: "central control and vertical integration."

However, following extensive interviews and hundreds of hours of onsite observation, Chisholm discovered that widespread and effective coordination was in fact occurring, through "informal channels, behavioral norms, and personal agreements," all prompted by perceived interdependence, joint challenges, and mutual needs. What's more, the study found that these informal agreements and adaptations were often more stable and reliable than formal mechanisms.

Whereas forced coordination can become an end in itself, displacing substantive goals, Chisholm saw how decentralized systems could "increase innovation, encourage public participation, and strengthen local government capacity." He proposes that most interagency disconnects are more likely due to genuinely different interests, uneven costs and benefits, and poorly structured incentives than to the common diagnosis of "structural defects." Although informal channels of coordination can seem "messy" to outsiders, Chisholm finds that the drive for "superficial consistency, neatness, and elimination of redundancy [is] badly misplaced." Most suggestions for reorganization, he concludes, are not based on close study of the existing institutions, but reflect instead a kind of moral judgment about what a "good" organization should look like.

Two later works reach many of the same conclusions. In Bardach's (1998) study of interagency collaboration, he contrasts "the bureaucratic ethos [that] venerates hierarchy, stability, obedience, and procedures," with real, effective interagency cooperation that thrives on equality, adaptability, and discretion, supports flexibility of thought and action, and is focused on results. Likewise, Thomas (2003) finds that "politically imposed interagency committees typically provide little more than the appearance of coordination." Instead, "individuals work together to achieve things they cannot achieve individually," and true interagency cooperation is "shaped by the potential for joint gains." DeShazo and Freeman (2005) go a step further, finding that interagency conflict can actually be a *constructive* force in implementing multiple-use mandates. Looking carefully at agency decision-making, they find "not lone agencies making isolated decisions in a cocoon of bureaucratic insularity, but collections of agencies intervening in each other's decision-making processes" as needed. These observations echo a study from thirty-five years earlier (Martin 1969) which concluded that, at that time, the Forest Service's multiple-use mandate was fostering strong, diverse, internal, conflict resolution mechanisms within the Forest Service, causing "basically cooperative groups to manifest some healthy competition among their members."

Related to the tradeoffs between coordination and diversity are debates about how natural resource managers can enhance system resilience and facilitate adaptive management. From the 1970s on, a new generation of ecologists was discovering that single-species, linear models do not accurately describe ecosystem processes, especially when humans and their activities are included. Instead, they turned to new concepts such as complexity, networks, cycles of growth and reorganization, multiple equilibria, diversity, and resilience to explain the world (e.g., Holling 1986; Gunderson et al. 1995; and many more). Social scientists were also updating older client-agent, cause-and-effect models of policy change, looking instead to public choice theory, institutional analysis, behavioral psychology, and political ecology (Sabatier 2007a).

These new views of ecology and human institutions both support the importance of flexible, context-specific, multiple-scale governance in increasing resilience to unexpected events and promoting nimbleness in adapting to changes in economic, ecological, social, or political conditions over time. Nie (2008) concludes that, by their very nature, EBM and adaptive management preclude prescriptive approaches and compel flexibility. If EBM is to be attempted, agencies will have to be empowered to make some fairly subjective decisions and to change course more frequently than legislative change would allow. Like many others, Nie calls for the use of "management experiments," wherein each decision is treated as a hypothesis and each outcome a data point, followed by careful monitoring and evaluation to revise approaches over time.

Unfortunately, flexible, adaptive management does not mesh well with traditional political, regulatory, and legal structures due to "short-term risk intolerance" (MacCleery 1992), "inherent cultural and institutional barriers ... [within] management and regulatory agencies, including the Council on Environmental Quality" (Thomas 2003), and conflict with the legal system's "mission ... to provide social stability" (Ruhl 2012). The Northwest Forest Plan, discussed in Chapter 5, included ten innovative "adaptive management areas," covering about 1.5 million acres. These were specifically intended to be laboratories for testing new management ideas, but the inflexibility of existing bureaucracy made that goal virtually impossible to implement on the ground (Stankey et al. 2003).

Summary

This chapter built on findings from the fields of institutional analysis, policy development, collaborative governance, and policy transplantation to identify those similarities and differences between the National Forest and the EEZ that are most likely to affect policy transfer and lesson-learning between these two public spaces. Striking overlaps are found in the mix of activities pursued, the types of parties involved, and ongoing tensions between resource exploitation and conservation. However, important differences also emerge that must be accounted for, such as species mobility, allocation of authority, and very different human histories in the two settings. The chapter then looked back to the National Forest analysis developed in Chapters 4–6 to evaluate how various policies and management approaches employed in the National Forests might apply in the ocean setting.

As experienced managers and scholars might predict, there is no simple, one-size-fits-all, "best" approach for managing public space and resources in the interests of all citizens. It is a challenge that requires choices to be made and tradeoffs to be accepted. Moreover, the outcomes of a given policy choice will not be the same in every place or in different time periods. Ecosystem-based management, where the ecosystem is understood to include all the related human communities, is complex, uncertain, and deeply context-dependent. But this does not mean that policy analysis has nothing to add, or that the results of particular policy options are completely unforeseeable.

In this chapter, three different areas were identified where tradeoffs have been particularly visible—and widely analyzed—over the course of U.S. National Forest history: (1) the scale of problem definition; (2) the "who" and "how" of decision-making; and (3) the extent of flexibility allowed.

The ocean management community—defined in keeping with the ACF to include all the politicians, agency personnel, scientists and scholars, media, advocacy groups, ocean industries, coastal communities, workers and visitors with an interest in ocean management—should be acutely aware of these tradeoffs and well informed about the kinds of results likely to accompany different choices. Possible metrics for evaluating outcomes include: durable resolution of conflicts, participant satisfaction, cost in time and money, and effect on ongoing stakeholder relationships (McKinney and Harmon 2004); efficiency, equity, accountability, and adaptability (Ostrom et al. 1994); compliance, feasibility, effectiveness, level of effort, and quality of outcomes (Imperial 1999, p. 455, citing others); or the sum of information, coordination, and strategic transaction costs (Ostrom et al. 1994; Imperial 1999). Each of these methods for weighing results itself embodies value judgments, and will be seen as more or less important by different participants.

In the end, everyone involved will need to accept that managing the vast expanse of the U.S. EEZ in a way that benefits current and future generations is as important and complex as any human endeavor. There are no panaceas. There can be no single decision-maker. If a solution seems simple, it is certainly neglecting something. Any workable approach will involve nested authorities at multiple scales, operating under varying degrees of coordination, with a diverse public participating in every step. The next chapter looks at how these take-away lessons compare to the approach taken over the last few years to advance marine spatial planning.

Notes

1 Some vacation homes built some time ago in National Forests have been allowed to remain under grandfathering provisions.

2 All founding dates and budget figures are based on the organizations' annual reports and audited financial statements.

3 Figures obtained from http://oceana.org/en/about-us/history. Accessed March 20, 2014.

4 Both settings include some Presidential, agency, or Congressionally approved limited-use areas—such as wilderness in forests and marine sanctuaries in the ocean—but they constitute a small percent of the total area and have not resolved the broader spatial conflicts.

5 Pinchot was borrowing from the utilitarian philosopher Jeremy Bentham who first wrote that: "It is the greatest good to the greatest number of people that is the foundation of morals and legislation." (Bentham 1789).

6 This phrase is used here based on its common understanding, not as a legal term. For more in-depth discussion of the PTD as it applies to public lands see Wilkinson (1980), and as it applies to the EEZ, Turnipseed et al. (2010).

7 The Sagebrush Rebellion refers to a movement started in the 1960s in the Western United States which sought to have federally owned lands returned to the states. The "Sagebrush Rebellion" bill, passed in the 1979 Nevada Legislature with similar versions passed in other Western states, was designed to create a process for state control of lands within their boundaries, in hopes of such a

transfer being authorized at the national level. The movement reflected a feeling that federal land policies were catering to a national audience while ignoring Western concerns (Brick and Cawley 1996; McKinney and Harmon 2004).

8 The concept of agency capture was originally developed by Bernstein (1955) but is discussed extensively in the context of public lands by Culhane (1981), Feller (1995), Davis (2001), Nie (2008), and others.

9 There have been some exceptions. For example, NMFS has experimented with cooperative fishery research, which brings fishermen directly into the stock assessment process, and many National Marine Sanctuaries do a good job engaging their stakeholder advisory groups.

10 Many scholars have noted that maps tend only to include those features deemed important by the maps' creators (Monmonier 1996). For example, National Forest maps do not reveal areas whose ownership is disputed by prior inhabitants (Kosek 2006), and ocean maps are typically spotty in their spatial coverage (NRC 2004) and limited in what information they depict (St. Martin and Hall-Arber 2008).

11 Proposed new federal bodies recommended by USCOP included a National Ocean Council Committee on Ocean Science, Education, Technology, and Operations, Office on Ocean Education, Office on Ocean Information, Committee on Ocean Resource Management, International Committee, and Presidential Council of Advisors on Ocean Policy (USCOP 2004a, pp. 475–476).

8

BACK AT THE SHORE

Lessons for the ocean community

In 2008, I embarked on this research project based on a hunch—a gut feeling that those of us promoting marine spatial planning (MSP) at the time may have been glossing over some of the challenges it would pose. I searched the literature for similar situations where managers were required to balance multiple interests in a common-pool resource and emerged with three broad questions:

1. Are U.S. public lands and the U.S. EEZ sufficiently similar that successes and failures in one arena might be expected to be relevant to the other?
2. Has over 100 years of active public lands management in the U.S. produced any "lessons" that might be applicable to the more recently developing field of ocean management, particularly when it comes to multiple-use planning and management?
3. If these settings are similar in meaningful ways, and if interesting themes do emerge in examining public lands management, how might these be adapted to inform the current drive for more integrated ocean management, particularly through the tool of marine spatial planning?

Chapters 1–3 demonstrated that, by using the tools and analytic frameworks of policy analysis, ocean and public lands settings can be shown to share many fundamental governance features. Chapters 4–7 then looked at over 100 years of National Forest history to uncover certain recurring themes and "lessons learned." In this chapter, the spotlight returns to the sea as I revisit recent developments in ocean management—particularly those related to the implementation of marine spatial planning—and hold them up against the suggested forest management lessons.

International developments in marine spatial planning

Since the first UNESCO-hosted International Workshop on MSP was held in 2006, significant advances in marine planning have been made in a number of countries and the academic scholarship on MSP prospects and implementation has exploded (Merrie and Olsson 2014). Norway, China, Belgium, the Netherlands, and Germany have completed marine plans, Canada, the United Kingdom, Portugal, Sweden, and six countries surrounding the Baltic Sea have planning processes underway, and the European Commission has a number of policies and directives in place that are likely to influence the development of MSP in its 28 member countries. These include the Integrated Maritime Policy, Marine Strategy Framework Directive, Common Fisheries Policy, Water Framework Directive, Renewable Energy Directive, and others (Qiu and Jones 2013). One optimistic assessment projects that 33 percent of the world's EEZs will have approved marine spatial plans in place by 2025 (Ehler 2013).

The narrative surrounding all these initiatives reflects that found in the academic literature and practical guides to MSP (e.g., Gilliland and Laffoley 2008; Beck et al. 2009; Ehler and Douvere 2009). Planners expect benefits such as coordination, streamlining, regulatory effectiveness, and ecosystem protection to be achieved through a structured, deliberate approach that moves from setting a vision, through articulating goals and objectives, to reviewing and adapting plans over time. However, the few careful evaluations of MSP conducted to date reveal that these idealized processes rarely correspond to the realities on the ground. According to Merrie and Olsson (2014), "there is a clear implementation gap between the 'idea' of MSP that has been developed internationally and how it is implemented in individual country contexts." Actual *outcomes*—whether measured as economic development, ecosystem protection, or reduced conflict—are even harder to demonstrate at this early stage.

Collie et al. (2013) compare the process and results of sixteen marine spatial plans to the steps recommended in four expert guides to MSP. The only recommended elements found in all the plans were the existence of a high-level government mandate and the presence of one or more institutions with authority to implement the plan. Stakeholders were included in some way in every process other than China's, but the definition and selection process varied widely and most programs did not include the public at every stage of the process. When it comes to other commonly recommended measures, such as the use of decision-support tools, alternate-use scenarios, metrics of success, monitoring benchmarks, and adaptive management, there was considerable inconsistency, with many plans omitting these steps altogether. Another recent review of nine MSP projects in Europe (Jones et al. 2014) found a similar disconnect between actual planning exercises and recommended practices, noting that "marine spatial planning processes are actually more complex and dynamic than the step-wise, reductive and deterministic processes that were anticipated and on which many concepts are based." The projects they looked at turned out to be driven primarily by national priorities, "focus[ing] on the development of certain strategically and economically important sectors, rather than on implementing an integrated and ecosystem-based approach."

Many of the findings from these careful retrospective studies echo National Forest experiences, including:

- the acceptance of an underlying technocratic rhetoric, "a discourse of modernization and administrative decision making … driven from a top-down perspective … [where] decision making is a managerial function given over to expert knowledge rather than political discussion" (Ritchie 2014);
- the marginalization of many stakeholders when "participation is … limited, with key sectors having the most influence on decisions" (Jones et al. 2014);
- the inherent conundrums of multiple-use management where "conflicts cannot be 'planned away' … trade-offs are often required, and there are losers as well as winners" (Jones et al. 2014); and
- the difficulty of measuring effectiveness along the many axes people care about, including economic growth, environmental health, community tradition, and others. Ritchie (2014) found that too often the "big issues of reconciling environment and economy" were put aside, assuming that scientific expertise could guarantee sound policies.

Marine spatial planning in U.S. waters

As introduced briefly in Chapter 1, the idea of marine spatial planning (MSP)[1] in U.S. waters moved quickly from relative obscurity to its current prominence on the national scene (see Table 8.1).[2] A small number of environmental NGOs with ocean agendas (notably the Ocean Conservancy, SeaWeb, Marine Conservation Institute, Nature Conservancy, and Conservation Law Foundation), private funders (led by the California-based Packard and Moore foundations), and academics prodded the issue forward through the mid-2000s. Their methods included prominent scientific publications (e.g., Norse 2005; Crowder et al. 2006; Douvere and Ehler 2008), grassroots education and lobbying campaigns particularly in supportive regions such as the Northeast, and multi-sector workshops (e.g., Gopnik et al. 2012).

Table 8.1 Timeline of marine spatial planning implementation in the U.S.

Date	*Event*
2004	USCOP report released; Pres. Bush establishes cabinet-level, interagency Committee on Ocean Policy
2005–2006	National Center for Ecological Analysis and Synthesis (NCEAS) Working Group on Ocean Zoning meets
2006	First International Workshop on MSP hosted by UNESCO
2008	Special Issue of *Marine Policy* journal dedicated to MSP
2009	"Step-by-Step" guide to MSP published by UNESCO
	Presidential Memorandum creates Interagency Task Force and requests report on MSP; Task Force holds a series of public meetings and releases Interim MSP Framework for public comment
2010	Massachusetts Ocean Plan released
	Final Task Force recommendations released
	Executive Order accepts Task Force recommendations, including the NOP and NOC, and calls for MSP in 9 designated regions
	Rhode Island Special Area Management Plan released
	NOC meets
2011	MSP Legal Analysis released
	NOC Governance Coordinating Committee appointed
	NOC Strategic Action Plan outlines released
	National MSP workshop and 12 regional listening sessions held
	Federal leads announced for each region
2012	Draft NOC Implementation Plan released for public comment
	First Northeast Regional Planning Body (RPB) meeting
2013	NOP Implementation Plan released
	NOC Marine Planning Handbook released
	First Pacific Islands RPB meeting
	First Mid-Atlantic RPB meeting
	First Caribbean RPB meeting
	Mid-Atlantic RPB releases draft Planning Framework for public comment
2014	Second Northeast RPB meeting
	Northeast RPB releases Planning Framework

Source: Compiled by author.

Because international MSP efforts had been initiated earlier and many other countries had plans in place, overviews of MSP developments (e.g., Agardy 2010) and UNESCO's timely and influential "Step-by-Step" guide to MSP (Ehler and Douvere 2009) were based primarily on experiences in Australia, China, Vietnam, Canada, and Europe. Logically, as U.S. proponents moved forward, they embraced these guidelines, particularly in the early adopting, historically progressive Northeastern states of Massachusetts and Rhode Island where MSP was rapidly completed in state waters. However, this approach proved less successful as efforts moved to the national stage where the significant differences in U.S. history, politics, and culture proved a barrier to the largely top-down, highly structured, technocratic approaches advanced in the UNESCO guide.

Executive action

Marine planning efforts at the national level were set in motion by President Obama in June 2009—just six months into his first term—when he sent a memorandum to cabinet members and agency heads creating an Interagency Ocean Policy Task Force (the Task Force) and charged it with developing "a national policy for our oceans, coasts and the Great Lakes, a framework for improved Federal policy coordination, ... and a recommended framework for effective coastal and marine spatial planning" (White House 2009). One year later, two documents were released simultaneously: (1) the final recommendations of the Presidentially mandated Task Force (CEQ 2010), including its Framework for coastal and marine spatial planning (CMSP) (the Framework, discussed in detail below); and (2) an Executive Order that formally accepted the Task Force recommendations, established a new National Ocean Policy (NOP), created a cabinet-level interagency National Ocean Council (NOC) with associated advisory bodies, and called for development of "coastal and marine spatial plans that ... enable a more integrated, comprehensive, ecosystem-based, flexible, and proactive approach to *planning and managing sustainable multiple uses* across sectors and [that] improve the conservation of the ocean, our coasts, and the Great Lakes" (Executive Order #13547, July 2010, emphasis added). The Order goes on to say that marine plans will be "certified by the National Ocean Council and developed in accordance with the definition, goals, principles, and process described in the [Task Force] Final Recommendations." To the extent that this order is implemented, it will mark the dawn of deliberate, integrated, multiple-use management of U.S. ocean territory.

Whether it is viewed as a positive development or not, this approach raises some red flags relative to the "lessons" summarized in the previous chapter by implementing a significant change in the management of a public space through a Presidential directive, with little debate and no action in Congress. Although a bill had twice been introduced in the House of Representatives to achieve much the same goals (H.R. 21, or OCEANS 21, introduced in January 2007 and January 2009), it was strongly opposed by ocean industries, received only two hearings in subcommittee, and was never voted out of the House Resources Committee. As a result, frustrated environmental supporters of these bills (see, e.g., Mann 2009) looked to the new Democratic president and his recently appointed NOAA Administrator, a long-time environmental advocate, to advance H.R. 21's goals through executive action.

Of course a President has the authority and responsibility to instruct Executive branch agencies to improve their coordination, to establish subject-specific Task Forces within the Council on Environmental Quality (CEQ), and to set up interagency committees. In fact, one of the newly established NOC's first tasks was to prepare a 50-page review of *Legal Authorities*

Relating to the Implementation of Coastal and Marine Spatial Planning (NOC 2011) to show that ocean planning efforts are congruent with existing law. Nevertheless, opponents of the new approach, including those who had successfully derailed H.R. 21, quickly attacked the new developments as an end-run around Congress. A press release from the Recreational Fishing Alliance (RFA 2009) labeled the newly appointed Task Force "an attempt by the Executive branch to circumvent the established legislative process and enact policy that failed as legislation 5 years in a row … RFA believes enacting laws through Executive order and proclamation sets a dangerous precedence [*sic*]."

One can legitimately question whether the RFA would have been as worried about overriding legislative prerogatives if the Executive Order had been to their liking, but their charge does echo recurring concerns raised in the public lands context. First, under the Task Force's approach, national goals and objectives for marine planning would be set by unelected professional agency staff, a frequent criticism of multiple-use planning on land. Second, no matter how sensible, well thought-out, and thoroughly vetted the eventual plans might turn out to be, the absence of congressional buy-in for this new direction in ocean management is likely to weaken implementation and threaten future budgetary support. As one industry representative told me, "Without a legal requirement, people just won't take MSP seriously," while another pointed out that "nothing gets done if there's no funds […] The way I understand it, there is no money attached to this. Somehow it's got to get into legislation to be appropriately funded." Even from one environmentalist's perspective, agency-led MSP "doesn't guarantee ecosystem protection. Unless there are specific, legal requirements for protected areas, resource users will keep chipping away at ocean space." As discussed in Chapter 4, the requirement for multiple-use planning in National Forests was enshrined in the 1976 NFMA, which itself amended existing forest management laws *and* conformed in many ways with ongoing Forest Service practice. By contrast, the launch of MSP did not involve congressional action, exists outside the established statutory structure, and represents a significant departure from current practice.

National guidelines for marine spatial planning

The Task Force on which the President relied included not only the obvious natural resource agencies (e.g., the NOAA, Environmental Protection Agency, Department of the Interior, and the CEQ) but also representatives from entities as diverse as the National Aeronautics and Space Administration, the National Security Council, and the Office of the U.S. military's Joint Chiefs of Staff—in short, any agency with any authority, interest, or connection with ocean and coastal research, use, or protection. The MSP Framework drafted by this group sets out to justify the need for marine planning and convey the benefits expected to flow from its implementation, including:

- sustainable economic growth;
- promotion of national objectives, such as enhanced energy security and trade;
- improvements in ecosystem health and services;
- a more complete evaluation of cumulative effects;
- greater opportunities for community and citizen participation;
- stronger and more diverse ocean economies and communities; and
- preservation of cultural and recreational uses, human health and safety, and the continued security of the United States.

This responds directly to criticisms from the public, documented in comments on the CEQ website and articulated in my interviews with industry representatives, that marine planning is, at best, an unnecessary bureaucratic exercise—a "solution in search of a problem"—and, at worst, an attempt to drastically restrict activities in the ocean.[3]

Because the practice of MSP is still quite new and careful retrospective evaluations have not yet been published, it is extremely difficult to assess the likelihood of achieving these benefits. However, their breadth and generality are reminiscent of the aspirations once held for planning and EBM in the National Forests, both of which fell short of the lofty goal of resolving multiple-use conflicts to the satisfaction of all parties.

Implementation of the Framework relies on a regional approach, proposing nine regions that coincide roughly with LMEs in U.S. waters, as was recommended by USCOP (2004a). Although federal responsibilities lie mainly beyond the three-mile band of state waters, the Framework establishes planning regions that "extend landward to the mean high-water line ... [and] include inland bays and estuaries." Regional planners are also allowed, but not required, to include inland areas as needed to account for the influences of land-based activities on coastal and ocean waters. The potentially continent-wide reach of this guidance was quickly targeted as a sign of Executive overreach by opponents.

Each region is to establish a Regional Planning Body (RPB) which would consist of "Federal, State, and tribal authorities relevant to CMSP for that area ... with an appropriate level of responsibility to be able to make decisions and commitments." The members of the RPB are further instructed to "coordinate" with other relevant authorities, whether local jurisdictions, other regional entities (e.g., Fishery Management Councils, existing Regional Ocean Councils, Watershed Councils), or bordering states, regions, and nations. The regional approach requires RPBs to "define local and regional objectives ... and implement CMSP in a way that is meaningful to regionally specific concerns." Although this verbiage seems to acknowledge the particularities of place so central to institutional analysis and common-pool resource theory, the actual extent of devolution of decision-making—from federal agencies to large regional compacts of state and federal representatives—is quite limited.

Many policy analysts have struggled with the issues of reconciling multiple scales for decision-making (e.g., Young 2006; Marshall 2007), promoting subsidiarity (i.e., moving decisions to the lowest level possible), and "nesting" of successively larger scales of action. These themes were also very evident in the forest lessons explored in Chapter 7. As one environmental advocate asked me: "How can we reconcile the scale of ecosystems ... with the smaller scale needed for practical planning and inclusive stakeholder involvement?" One sentence within the Task Force's 30-page Framework does imply that RPBs have the "flexibility to develop sub-regional plans, provided that these plans are encompassed in an overarching regional plan and overseen by the regional planning body," but the idea of nested, sub-regional planning is not mentioned again in any of the more detailed implementation steps despite substantial research and National Forest experience that validates such an approach. This worried one industry representative, who said: "I just think [the timeline] is too fast ... It doesn't really allow for local and sub-regional input. That's the biggest concern; we need to have a more iterative dialogue along the way."

Increased public participation in ocean decisions, highlighted by the Task Force as one of the expected benefits of marine planning, is mentioned repeatedly throughout the Framework. Broad participation is justified in part "to strengthen mutual and shared understanding"—a phrase that hints at a more collaborative approach—but other details in the Framework indicate that the process envisioned will rely on fairly traditional participation techniques. Activities mentioned include informational workshops, public hearings, public comment processes, document availability, educational materials, webinars, and manuals "to better inform all participants." These fall far short of the methods recommended when the goal is to help a wide range of potentially competing or conflicting partners reach a shared vision, as has been done successfully in some National Forest settings (Wondolleck and Yaffee 2000; Daniels and Walker 2001) and certain ocean programs such as the National Estuary Program (Korfmacher 1998) and the Florida Keys National Marine Sanctuary (Delaney 2003).

Another indication that national ocean leaders have not yet embraced the latest findings of public participation experts was evident at three official MSP events I observed, all of which were billed as opportunities for stakeholder input. In every case, more than half the available time was filled by statements and presentations from agency representatives, with very limited windows for brief comments from the public, and no meaningful attempt at cross-sector dialogue. This viewpoint was poignantly expressed in a newspaper article written by a Maine fisherman (Nelson 2012). After attending the first Northeast RPB meeting, he says he "felt disheartened and disenfranchised," feeling that "my community, and others like mine, are not well represented … [A]n involved and informed citizen has to beg for inclusion into this process."

The importance of gathering and continually improving data and science is also strongly emphasized throughout the Framework, which states that "CMSP is fundamentally science based" and suggests that plans be adapted "in response to new evidence, technology, and understanding." The section on "Scientific Data and Knowledge" (CEQ 2010, pp. 66–69) talks in broad terms about the need to understand "human uses, ecosystem conditions, [and] management alternatives … [in] the context of changing environmental conditions and societal needs," all critical elements. However, the proposed approach for assembling such data and creating decision-support products seems to then be heavily oriented toward large, existing natural sciences databases. Unfortunately, such large databases, associated data standards, and spatially referenced data representations are not possible for most of the critical social science information that—to the extent it exists—tends to be qualitative (based on case studies and interviews) and somewhat idiosyncratic based on the disciplinary roots of the researcher.[4]

The contributions of the natural sciences to resource management are undeniable, and their impacts on forest management were evident throughout Chapters 4–6. For example, advances in forest ecology allowed managers to move away from the inadequate "trees as crops" paradigm toward a more nuanced view of EBM, and understanding of the role of habitat in species survival fundamentally changed the approach to forest planning. However, at their core, multiple-use management challenges revolve around tradeoffs among human goals and values. A focus on physical and biological data, without a good understanding of the communities who value and rely on the ocean, will limit long-term success in marine planning. As one fisherman told me, "[Government] needs better knowledge about biological, economic, *and* social factors. They really need business experts and psychologists more than traditional economists!"

In further response to its charge from the President, the Interagency Task Force developed seven goals and twelve guiding principles for CMSP in the U.S. (listed in Boxes 8.1 and 8.2 respectively), where the goals are intended to "define the desired outcomes" and the principles to provide the means "to achieve the national goals." The crucial unanswered question, in the ocean setting as it was in the National Forests, is how these potentially conflicting goals are intended to be weighed against each other, and who will decide. Would the creation of an efficient, predictable process (Goals 5 and 6) be worth some level of economic or environmental sacrifice (Goals 1 and 2)? What level of reduced public access to the ocean (Goal 3) could be justified to achieve more robust ecosystem resilience (Goal 2)? These are not scientific questions amenable to quantitative modeling, and their resolution affects all subsequent decisions.

Box 8.1 The national goals of CMSP

1 Support sustainable, safe, secure, efficient, and productive uses of the ocean, our coasts, and the Great Lakes, including those that contribute to the economy, commerce, recreation, conservation, homeland and national security, human health, safety, and welfare;
2 Protect, maintain, and restore the Nation's ocean, coastal, and Great Lakes resources and ensure resilient ecosystems and their ability to provide sustained delivery of ecosystem services;
3 Provide for and maintain public access to the ocean, coasts, and Great Lakes;
4 Promote compatibility among uses and reduce user conflicts and environmental impacts;
5 Improve the rigor, coherence, efficiency, and consistency of decision-making and regulatory processes;
6 Increase certainty and predictability in planning for and implementing new investments for ocean, coastal, and Great Lakes uses; and
7 Enhance interagency, intergovernmental, and international communication and collaboration.

Source: CEQ 2010, p. 47.

Box 8.2 The national guiding principles for CMSP

1 CMSP would use an EBM approach that addresses cumulative effects to ensure the protection, integrity, maintenance, resilience, and restoration of ocean, coastal, and Great Lakes ecosystems, while promoting multiple sustainable uses.
2 Multiple existing uses (e.g., commercial fishing, recreational fishing and boating, subsistence uses, marine transportation, sand and gravel mining, and oil and gas operations) and emerging uses (e.g., off-shore renewable energy and aquaculture) would be managed in a manner that reduces conflict, enhances compatibility among uses and with sustained ecosystem functions and services, provides for public access, and increases certainty and predictability for economic investments.

3 CMSP development and implementation would ensure frequent and transparent broad-based, inclusive engagement of partners, the public, and stakeholders, including with those most impacted (or potentially impacted) by the planning process and with underserved communities.
4 CMSP would take into account and build upon the existing marine spatial planning efforts at the regional, state, tribal, and local level.
5 CMS Plans and the standards and methods used to evaluate alternatives, tradeoffs, cumulative effects, and sustainable uses in the planning process would be based on clearly stated objectives.
6 Development, implementation, and evaluation of CMS Plans would be informed by sound science and the best available information, including the natural and social sciences, and relevant local and traditional knowledge.
7 CMSP would be guided by the precautionary approach as reflected in Principle 15 of the Rio Declaration, "Where there are threats of serious or irreversible damage, lack of full scientific certainty shall not be used as a reason for postponing cost-effective measures to prevent environmental degradation."
8 CMSP would be adaptive and flexible to accommodate changing environmental conditions and impacts, including those associated with global climate change, sea level rise, and ocean acidification; and new and emerging uses, advances in science and technology, and policy changes.
9 CMSP objectives and progress toward those objectives would be evaluated in a regular and systematic manner, with public input, and adapted to ensure that the desired environmental, economic, and societal outcomes are achieved.
10 The development of CMS Plans would be coordinated and compatible with homeland and national security interests, energy needs, foreign policy interests, emergency response and preparedness plans and frameworks, and other national strategies, including the flexibility to meet current and future needs.
11 CMS Plans would be implemented in accordance with customary international law, including as reflected in the Law of the Sea Convention, and with treaties and other international agreements to which the U.S. is a party.
12 CMS Plans would be implemented in accordance with applicable federal and state laws, regulations, and Executive Orders.

Source: CEQ 2010, p. 48.

Further guidance is also needed on the question of whether all uses must be accommodated everywhere or whether some areas can be set aside for single or limited use. This issue was addressed for National Forests by the 1960 MUSY Act, which required foresters to manage forest resources

> in the combination that will best meet the needs of the American people; making the most judicious use of the land for some or all of these resources or related services [and so] that some land will be used for less than all of the resources. (See discussion in Chapter 4.)

Virtually all those I interviewed worried about how an appropriate balance could be found among different ocean uses and between use and conservation. One individual promoting offshore renewable energy feared that "existing users—like shipping lanes, the military, even fishing—will always get priority over new users." Speaking more generally, an industry executive suggested that "[environmentalists] see businesses as annoying threats to the environment, not valuable contributors to society." Fishermen feared that "MSP is just a Trojan horse for bringing in more MPAs [marine protected areas]," while environmental advocates felt quite differently: "Repeated references [in the Framework] to the need for 'balance' ... could be interpreted to suggest that conservation is just one of many objectives of the policy, rather than a central purpose."

The Framework then goes beyond declaring broad goals and principles to specify *how* regional planners should proceed with their task (the "Essential Elements of the CMSP Process," Box 8.3a) and what their final product should include (the "Essential Elements of a CMS Plan," Box 8.3b), as well as presenting a detailed sequence of steps to be followed by the NOC and RPBs in creating marine plans. The final step says that outcomes are to be monitored over time, using national and regional *performance measures* to evaluate progress toward *national and regional objectives*, with revisions to the marine plan implemented as needed. The importance of monitoring the outcomes of resource management and then adapting where appropriate is stressed throughout the literature on ecosystem-based MSP (e.g., Caldwell et al. 1994; Gilliland and Laffoley 2008; Kidd et al. 2011), as well as in several recent guides to MSP best practices (e.g., Beck et al. 2009; Ehler and Douvere 2009). However, as noted in the review of National Forest management, major challenges are likely to arise in balancing a plan's *flexibility*, needed to cope with uncertainty, against the *predictability* typically demanded by the regulated community. Many of those interviewed raised this dilemma:

> It's too soon for MSP because new uses are too untested ... We don't want to be "locked in" to certain areas when technologies are still changing. (Renewable energy industry)

> There shouldn't be uncertainty in the regulatory system ... Companies ... are capable of operating within highly structured review processes provided they can rely on getting a clear answer (even if it is a rejection!) in a predictable period of time. (Oil industry)
>
> How can we do "adaptive management" once there are hard structures in the water? That level of investment precludes frequent review, adaptation, or changes in location. (Fisherman)

In addition, one government source noted astutely, "Monitoring is expensive and lacks political support ... [If it] reveals a *failure* to reach objectives, the program will be open to criticism and funding cuts."

Box 8.3 Essential elements for marine planning (as specified by the Interagency Ocean Policy Task Force)

a) Essential Elements of the CMSP Process

- Identify Regional Objectives
- Identify Existing Efforts that Should Help Shape the Plan throughout the Process
- Engage Stakeholders and the Public at Key Points throughout the Process
- Consult Scientists and Technical and Other Experts
- Analyze Data, Uses, Services, and Impacts
- Develop and Evaluate Alternative Future Spatial Management Scenarios and Tradeoffs
- Prepare and Release for Public Comment a Draft CMS Plan with Supporting Environmental Impact Analysis Documentation
- Create a Final CMS Plan and Submit for NOC Review
- Implement, Monitor, Evaluate, and Modify (as needed) the NOC-certified CMS Plan

b) Essential Elements of a CMS Plan

- Regional Overview and Scope of Planning Area
- Regulatory Context
- Regional Assessment
- Objectives, Strategies, Methods, and Mechanisms for CMSP
- Compliance Mechanisms
- Monitoring and Evaluation Mechanisms
- Incorporation of the Dispute Resolution Process

Source: CEQ 2010.

Taken together, the Framework's goals, guiding principles, essential elements, planning steps, and other requirements—set forth by a Task Force composed exclusively of federal agency representatives—result in a more detailed, prescriptive, and centralized process than the research would suggest is desirable for such a large undertaking covering such diverse regions. This did not go unnoticed by one industry observer who told me:

> The release of the Framework represented the biggest setback in terms of being able to get behind [MSP] … When you look at its description of … how regional plans are supposed to be developed, it starts to read like the instructions to a complicated board game and it is of huge concern to me that it is so confused about where authority lies and who does what.

In addition to adopting the Task Force Framework outlined above, the July 2010 Executive Order created a new NOC with a number of its own assignments, foremost among them development of a detailed National Ocean Policy Implementation Plan to be released by April 2012. The draft plan was released for public comment in January 2012, followed by a wave of hostile hearings and press releases from the House Resources Committee[5] and vocal opposition from some industry interests (NOPC 2012). After seven months of speculation, a slightly revised version of the plan, labeled as a "Pre-decisional Draft," was provided to selected reviewers. It included an Action Plan for CMSP that adhered fairly closely to the Task Force's Framework. Figure 8.1 illustrates the sequence of steps that would have been required at the national and state levels based on the Framework and the pre-decisional draft of the NOC Action Plan.

Finally, in April 2013, almost two years after it was called for by Executive Order 13547, the NOC released its final Implementation Plan (the Plan, NOC 2013a), followed three months later by a Marine Planning Handbook (the Handbook, NOC 2013b). These documents were strikingly different in tone and content from all the Administration's previous MSP documents. The term "marine spatial planning" is gone entirely, as is any hint of national performance measures, NOC-run workshops, detailed instructions about how RPBs will be constituted and what they will do, requirements for RPBs to obtain NOC approval at each step of the process, or directions to RPB members that they conform their actions to the region's marine spatial plan. On the contrary, the new Plan states that:

> The scope, scale, and content of marine planning will be defined by the regions themselves, to solve problems that regions care about in ways that reflect their unique interests, capacity to participate, and ways of doing business … This approach balances regional and national interests and recognizes that actions commensurate with

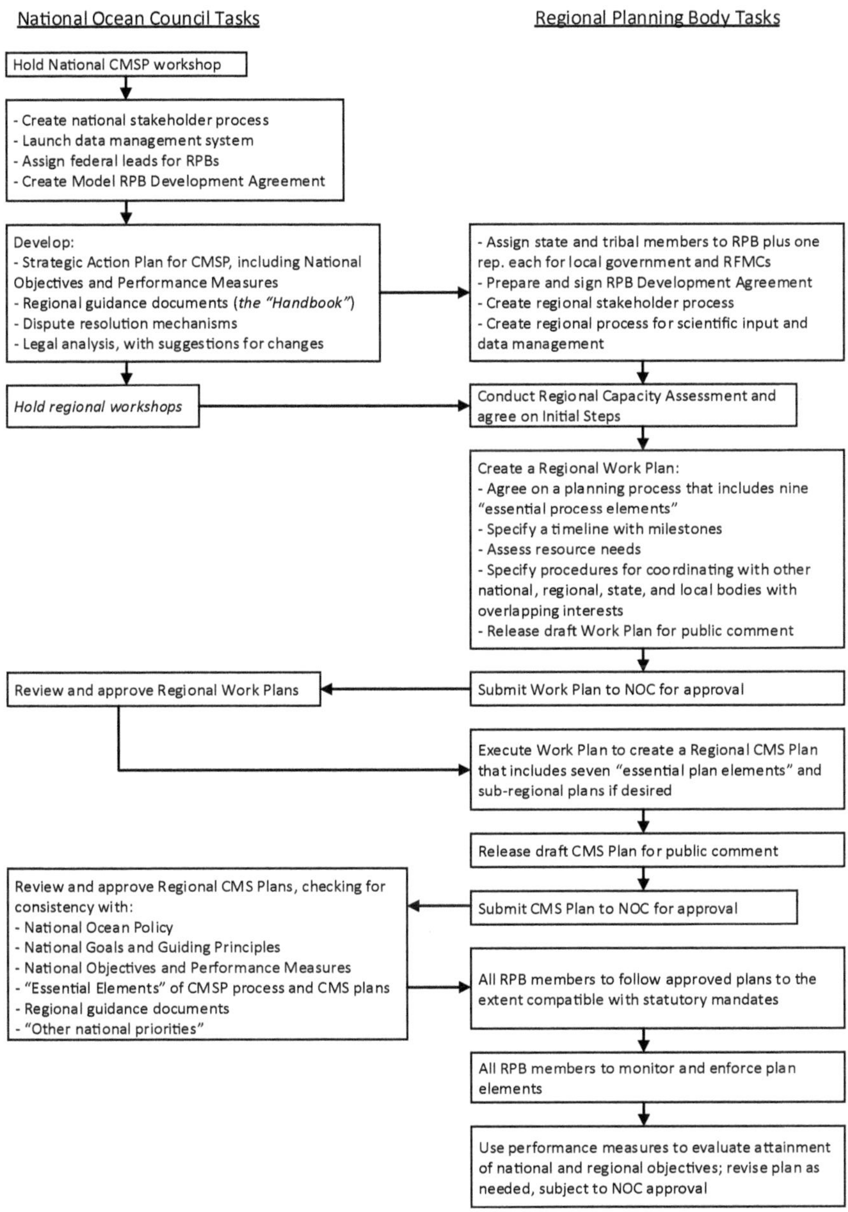

Figure 8.1 Proposed U.S. marine spatial planning implementation steps, as outlined in the Interagency Ocean Policy Task Force Framework (CEQ 2010) and the August 2012 pre-decisional draft of the NOC Action Plan

> regional interests and capacities will provide the most immediate regional benefits ... Each region has flexibility to build the elements of its plans over time in response to what the region wants to accomplish.

In fact, the Plan makes clear that participation in RPBs is strictly voluntary and that no RPB will be established in a region if those states are not interested. The reasons behind this major shift in approach are made clear in the introductory text: "This Plan ... reflects careful consideration of extensive public comments, particularly those that relate to the importance of incremental change, pilot projects, support for local and regional capacity and self-determination, and the fundamental need for more and better information."

The Handbook provides additional information about the proposed composition of RPBs and describes typical elements of MSP (referred to only as "marine planning"), generally repeating the guidance found in other MSP guides concerning capacity assessments, setting a vision, goals, and objectives, gathering data, inviting public participation, ensuring transparency, etc. But, unlike the earlier Task Force's MSP Framework, the Handbook emphasizes that these elements are set forth only as helpful guidance—not requirements—for those regions that choose to establish RPBs and wish to undertake a planning exercise. Finally, the notion of NOC "approval" of plans is also gone. Instead, if a region chooses to produce some sort of marine plan, the NOC will decide whether to "concur" with the plan, where concurrence means that "Federal agencies agree that they will use the marine plan to *inform* and *guide* their actions in the region" (NOC 2013b, emphasis added).

The increased flexibility provided in the Plan was well received by many stakeholders (see, e.g., Congressional Sportsmen's Foundation 2013) and adheres to the concept of subsidiarity. Whether it also means some regions will produce less robust plans, downplay certain national priorities or decline to engage in marine planning at all, remains to be seen. An issue still to be resolved involves the wide gap between the more laissez-faire approach found in the NOC Plan and the fairly prescriptive instructions found in the Task Force Framework. Because the latter were endorsed and incorporated by reference in the 2010 Executive Order, RPBs are left to wonder which elements they are actually intended, or even required, to implement (Eagle 2014).

Regional developments

Action at the regional level has varied, as might be expected. The Northeast RPB was established, held its first meeting, and began drafting its workplan and collecting data in 2012, before the final NOC Plan and Handbook had even been released (see Table 8.1). At that first meeting, RPB members asserted their independence from NOC requirements and guidance and were encouraged in this by a presentation from the Director of the NOC who did not mention the Task Force Framework, stating instead that:

> This is about ... the things that all of *you* identify and define as important to address ... The region will determine the scope, scale, and content of what comes out as the product from marine planning ... This is fundamentally a regional effort.

The Mid-Atlantic RPB began its work soon after, and RPBs have now been established in four of the nine regions. The direction and results of regional planning will continue to play out over the next few years, but a few forest lessons may be relevant as RPBs move forward with their work. First, RPBs should allow for and encourage sub-regional dialogue and planning. This will be particularly true in large regions, such as the West Coast, or dispersed regions such as the Pacific Islands. Issues of great local significance could be overlooked at the larger scale, while workable resolutions might be found through collaboration among directly affected parties at smaller scales. RPBs should allow such local ideas to emerge and then develop mechanisms for reconciling any disparities that arise between adjacent sub-regions.

Funding for new government programs is scarce at both federal and state levels. Absent congressional buy-in and appropriations, RPBs will need to consider other, possibly novel sources of support for their tasks, including grant funding, public–private partnerships, and in-kind contributions. However, public-land experiences warn that care must be taken to avoid letting funding considerations drive decision-making.

RPBs will also have to oversee significant new data collection, synthesis, analysis, and mapping efforts. Already, several regions have established regional data portals to begin these tasks. Looking at current data holdings in federal and regional ocean databases (e.g., http://ocean.data.gov, www.northeastoceandata.org, http://midatlanticocean.org/data-portal, and http://portal.westcoastoceans.org), it appears that significant efforts are still needed to incorporate social, cultural, and behavioral data, research approaches, and knowledge.

Comparing U.S. marine spatial planning efforts to lessons from the forest

Comparing the developing approach to marine planning in the U.S. (as described in the Interagency Ocean Policy Task Force MSP Framework, the NOC Final Implementation Plan and Marine Planning Handbook, and RPB documents) to the "lessons learned" from National Forest management summarized at the end of Chapter 7, several issues emerge.

- National and regional MSP efforts currently lack any legislative foundation, forcing agency staff to set national objectives (a quintessentially political task), providing no guidance as to priorities among uses, and threatening ongoing funding. Given other pressing national issues and a polarized Congress, this gap is unlikely to be filled in the near term, and will remain a weakness in the program.
- Based on the final NOC documents, the federal agencies evidently recognized some of the potential pitfalls of overly centralized planning and chose to emphasize the importance of regional leadership and stakeholder input, leaving room for experimentation and innovation. Nevertheless, the first two regions to take up marine planning, the Northeast and Mid-Atlantic, have so far followed fairly traditional models of organization and decision-making.
- By emphasizing the primacy of existing laws and regulations, the NOC acknowledged that even the best coordination, dialogue, and planning cannot trump legal requirements established by Congress and enforceable by the courts. However, a related assignment from the Task Force—an analysis of how the dozens of existing ocean-related laws might be deconflicted or better integrated—remains to be tackled. USCOP (2004a) made a number of recommendations in this area that could be revisited. Ideally such a task would be undertaken by a congressionally commissioned body whose recommendations about legislative changes might carry more weight than those from an interagency committee.
- Although the need to gather all available data and learn from both the scientific community and the public has been duly recognized, the importance of searching out and improving knowledge about the social, cultural, and behavioral aspects of ocean communities remains under-emphasized. The study of forest management showed that, while natural science findings are critical to understanding the ecosystems and resources involved, balanced, multiple-use management is a fundamentally social process. Fortunately, the costs of supporting investigators and acquiring data in these areas will be quite reasonable compared to the large investments in ship time, instrumentation, and personnel needed for traditional oceanographic data collection.

The existing academic structure provides few incentives for researchers to interact with policymakers, but the need for such exchanges is acute. Relevant findings must be translated into actionable policy options, in language that is accessible to managers. The ocean management community would benefit greatly from increased scholarly attention to policy-relevant questions such as the following: How can findings based on studies of small or relatively isolated communities be translated to more complex, formalized, highly interconnected policy settings? How can improved understanding about the management of specific resources (often fisheries) be extended to a multiple-resource, multiple-use context? How can the benefits of face-to-face collaborative governance be meshed with legal requirements for open processes and government duties toward public-trust resources?

- Both federal and state leaders have so far failed to transcend traditional, formalistic public participation models in ways that might foster genuine cross-sectoral dialogue and potentially break new ground. The distinction made in MSP documents between "stakeholders" (i.e., those presumed to have a direct interest in marine planning outcomes) and "the public" (i.e., everyone else) is unlikely to help achieve a lasting, unified vision for the future of ocean space. Documents, meeting agendas, and discussions to date also seem to be perpetuating a position-driven, potentially adversarial system rather than bringing all parties to the table as citizens with shared values and an equal interest in the disposition of their ocean heritage.
- Finally, although industry and foundation funding have been critical to progress on state-level marine plans and early regional collaborations, particularly in the Northeast, sustainable national funding mechanisms for this monumental undertaking remain elusive. Public–private partnerships and user fees have been suggested and should be evaluated, keeping in mind the conflicts that arose on public lands when communities came to rely heavily on income connected with resource use. Heavy reliance on private foundation funding, with its lack of transparency or accountability, also has the potential to distort decision-making (Fleishman 2009).

The notion of pursuing integrated, sustainable, multiple-use planning and management of U.S. ocean areas is in its infancy, with considerable promise and plenty of opportunities for mistakes. Participants from every sector—government, civil society, academia, and the business community—and at scales from local to national, will need to work together to avoid the most obvious pitfalls and to move forward when the process inevitably hits rough patches. In the words of one of the many observers who shared their hopes and concerns with me over the last four years:

> We need to get to a place where we have spatial planning in the oceans … I'm favorable to it because I think it will go a long way to protecting special places in the ocean, which I think is extremely important, but it will also go a long way to help protect ocean users and industries that we need and depend on … I still have a lot of questions about how it would be done and I really have some doubts about the ability of our government to do this in the right way to achieve either objective.

Wrap up

The original intent of this study was to explore ocean policy within a broader theoretical and historical context and, more specifically, to critically examine the relatively new concept of marine spatial planning (MSP). Although the spread of MSP has thus far been modeled primarily on implementation experiences in Europe and Australia, different political, legal, historical, and cultural realities in the United States may limit the applicability of those experiences. In searching for other potential models and analytic approaches on which to base U.S. ocean planning, the long record of U.S. public lands management emerged as a possible analogue and public policy research supplied a useful theoretical framework.

My analysis of forest history suggests that a complex, multi-dimensional decision-space exists, encompassing a wide array of plausible management choices, and that policymakers must be aware of the likely consequences of selecting alternatives at different points within this decision space. Some of the most significant axes along which ocean policymakers will need to make choices are:

1 *The scale of problem definition and resolution*—i.e., the selection of national, regional, state, or local focal points for different processes. National-level decision-making is more likely to express broad, majoritarian public values, provide greater consistency, and preclude narrow local concerns from dictating the use of federal public-trust resources. At the other end of the spectrum, local decision-making allows for stronger community engagement, greater diversity in policy solutions, and the emergence of innovative approaches. It is also more likely to foster trust among diverse stakeholders and promote small agreements that can overcome entrenched conflicts. Intermediate scales will provide a mix of large/national and small/local attributes.

2 *The "who" and "how" of decision-making*—i.e., determining which choices will be made through political, technocratic, judicial, or participatory approaches. Elected officials may be viewed as coming closest to representing the interests of all citizens and reflecting broad national values, thus imbuing their decisions with an inherent level of legitimacy. Acts of Congress also tend to be more stable than agency regulations. On the other hand, professional agency staff can be viewed as more objective decision-makers, relatively insulated from the fundraising and vote-getting pressures of politics, and trained to rely on science and technical skill to implement statutory requirements. The technocratic approach requires the availability of good scientific understanding, reliable data, and sound analytic methods and is ill-equipped to make value judgments or choose among equally defensible options. The U.S. courts have also played an important role in resource management

by interpreting often-ambiguous statutory language and adjudicating the validity of agency decisions. With lifetime appointments, federal judges may be more independent than elected officials or agency staff, although this also makes them less accountable. But judges can only rule on specific disputes, brought before them by interested parties with sufficient resources to access the legal system, and framed through an adversarial process. Direct citizen participation provides another avenue for decision-making. Many participants and scholars promote the value of face-to-face, collaborative dialogue with its emphasis on building trust and seeking compromise. Such settings have been able to arrive at solutions where traditional approaches encountered gridlock. But participatory processes by their very nature will exclude some interested parties, and thus cannot be given the ultimate say over the management of a public resource.

3 *The extent of flexibility allowed*—i.e., the need to balance harmonization and standardization against adaptability and innovation. By standardizing the procedures to be followed among a variety of agencies or regions, policymakers seek to establish greater consistency and predictability for participants. This approach can also guard against sub-units adopting policies that undermine or contradict broad programmatic goals. Moves toward functional consolidation and mandated coordination are often justified by similar logic. However, new insights into ecosystem functioning and human institutions highlight the value of diversified, context-specific actions that can increase resilience to unexpected events and foster nimbleness in adapting to changing conditions. Interagency cooperation may also be more effective where it is self-generated, task-oriented, and flexible.

Different choices among the range of options described above will result in different internal and external outcomes, with different levels of success with respect to resolving conflicts, satisfying participants, generating revenues, protecting ecosystems, increasing resilience, promoting civic engagement, facilitating monitoring and compliance, defending the interests of vulnerable minorities, or any of dozens of other worthy goals. By being informed and conscious of these tradeoffs, decision-makers can be intentional in their prioritization among conflicting goals and deliberate in their approach to meeting them. But first they must be willing to step back, question their own assumptions, re-examine accepted practices, and broaden their toolbox, whether that involves talking with different kinds of people, learning from unfamiliar disciplines, experimenting with new approaches, relinquishing some control, or accepting the validity of alternate worldviews. Fortunately, there is a storehouse of knowledge and experience developed in other policy arenas that can be tapped by those seeking to improve our stewardship of the ocean and its resources.

A parting vision

What might it look like if every member of the ocean community—broadly defined to include relevant elected officials, agency personnel, judges, ocean industry workers, scientists and scholars, the media, advocacy groups, private funders, and coastal communities—behaved in a way that remained true to their role while contributing constructively to broader social, economic, and environmental goals for the ocean? What would happen if each participant in the ocean policy arena was aware of the range of options available to them and mindful of the impacts of their choices? Perhaps they might take on some version of the roles and responsibilities described below, helping to achieve a workable balance between different branches of government, multiple users of public space, science and judgment, and order and flexibility.

Congress, as the elected representatives responsible for federal policy, would pass legislation that expresses a national consensus about broad goals and priorities for ocean use, examine the multiple, overlapping ocean laws and agencies to eliminate inconsistencies or contradictions, indicate priorities among goals/uses where possible, set broad standards that allow for flexibility and adaptation, refrain from pre-determining results, and set adequate agency budgets that reflect the national goals rather than advancing specific outcomes.

Regulatory agencies would have sufficient discretion to craft subnational goals and plans and issue necessary implementing regulations, recognizing that not all uses are compatible and that uses may have to be distributed over time and space. They would also provide opportunities for innovation and adaptation, while ensuring that their legal obligations are fulfilled. Agencies would work closely and collaboratively within their own organizations and with other federal, state, local, and tribal authorities, seeking areas of mutual gain rather than establishing rigid rules for cooperation. Government officials would actively reach out to the social science community, demonstrating a willingness to listen, to learn the unfamiliar vocabulary used in these fields, and possibly to see themselves in new ways.

Involvement of the public would extend well beyond the rote and formal public participation processes required by law, fostering genuine cross-sector learning and dialogue and following the principle of subsidiarity. For example, local input would be considered paramount for decisions with primarily local effects (e.g., allocation of nearshore space among a community of fishers), with increasingly broad regional to national input as the scale of potential impacts increases (e.g., climate change, endangered species).

State, local, and tribal authorities would actively participate in planning and goal-setting exercises for portions of the EEZ likely to affect their interests, clearly articulating their stake in policy outcomes while recognizing that the EEZ is a public-trust area of national importance.

Courts would ensure that agencies, whether under pressure from political leaders or other external influences, do not violate the goals and procedures established by Congress, while avoiding substituting their own judgments about results. Potential litigants would more carefully weigh the significant costs of litigation, not only financially but in terms of their impacts on ongoing relationships with other participants in the policy process.

Researchers from a wide variety of fields, including ocean sciences, marine ecology, resource economics, sociology, political science, geography, engineering, public policy, and others, would find ways to communicate important, policy-relevant findings to the public and decision-makers in a timely and accessible way, while acknowledging the sources and magnitude of uncertainties, and making honest distinctions between scientific results and personal values. Prominent policy scholars who have not previously considered the application of their work to ocean and coastal issues would be intrigued by this new opportunity to test their ideas.

Supporters and funders of issue advocacy, largely from the philanthropic and business communities, would be acutely conscious of tradeoffs between the use of heavily funded, rhetorical campaigns designed to achieve specific near-term objectives and the practice of patient diplomacy that focuses on building trust, fostering relationships, winning hearts and minds, and achieving long-term goals. They would use a portion of their resources to encourage increased research, training, and active experimentation in the art of meaningful collaborative processes.

Advocates of all persuasions would seek out novel ways to serve both their constituents' interests and the broader public good. They would continue to educate others about the basis for their views while remaining willing to listen to other perspectives, acknowledging the legitimate needs of others, and communicating respectfully. There may be rare occasions when a no-holds-barred battle is absolutely necessary to protect disempowered populations or fundamental values. More often, however, locked horns, inflammatory rhetoric, and scorched-earth legal clashes only make it harder to reach durable solutions.

I know all too well that current political, cultural, and economic realities make the scenario depicted above unlikely to be achieved in the near-term. But even small movements in this direction will go a long way toward the successful implementation of sustainable, multiple-use, integrated marine planning and management.

Notes

1 Early U.S. government documents favored the term "coastal and marine spatial planning" (CMSP), but more recent guidance (e.g., NOC 2013b) refers simply

to "marine planning," with no acronym. For consistency, I use the term marine spatial planning, or MSP, throughout.

2 An interesting analysis of the timeline, triggering events, and underlying causes for the global advance of MSP is presented in Merrie and Olsson (2014).

3 An anti-MSP opinion piece, originally posted as a news item on the ESPN Outdoors website on March 10, 2012, suggested that the new policy might "prohibit U.S. citizens from fishing." The claim quickly went viral and morphed into the widely repeated claim that President Obama intended to "ban father–son fishing trips." ESPN Outdoors' editors eventually took down the piece and apologized for the inaccuracy.

4 These issues were explored in depth at a forum on Social Science for Coastal Decision-Making held in February 2012 and archived at www.csc.noaa.gov/socialcoastforum.

5 Oversight Hearing on "Empty Hooks: The National Ocean Policy is the Latest Threat to Access for Recreational and Commercial Fishermen," March 22, 2012; Oversight Field Hearing on "Alaska's Sovereignty in Peril: The National Ocean Policy's Goal to Federalize Alaska," April 3, 2012. These were in addition to two previous hearings titled "The President's New National Ocean Policy: A Plan for Further Restrictions on Ocean, Coastal and Inland Activities," that had been held on October 4 and October 26, 2011.

REFERENCES

Agardy, T. (2010). *Ocean Zoning: Making Marine Management More Effective.* Oxford, Earthscan/Routledge.

Ansell, C., and Gash, A. (2008). Collaborative Governance in Theory and Practice. *Journal of Public Administration Research and Theory* 18(4): 543–571.

Applegate, R. (1977). The Multiple Use Planning Process: Descent into the Maelstrom. *Environmental Law* 8: 427–460.

Argow, K. (2009). From Omnipotence to Omnipresence: The Evolution of the American Forester. Presentation to the Society of American Foresters.

Ariely, D. (2008). *Predictably Irrational.* New York, Harper.

Arkema, K., Abramson, S., and Dewsbury, B. (2006). Marine Ecosystem-based Management: From Characterization to Implementation. *Frontiers in Ecology and the Environment* 4(10): 525–532.

Babcock, H. M. (2009). The Public Trust Doctrine: What a Tall Tale They Tell. *SCL Rev.* 61: 393–414.

Balogh, B. (2002). Scientific Forestry and the Roots of the Modern American State: Gifford Pinchot's path to progressive reform. *Environmental History* 7(2): 198–225.

Bardach, E. (1998). *Getting Agencies to Work Together: The Practice and Theory of Managerial Craftsmanship.* Washington, D.C., Brookings Institution Press.

Barr, B. W., and Lindholm, J. (2000). Conservation of the Sea Using Lessons from the Land. *The George Wright Forum* 17(3): 77–85.

Basurto, X., and Coleman, E. (2010). Institutional and Ecological Interplay for Successful Self-governance of Community-based Fisheries. *Ecological Economics* 69(5): 1094–1103.

Baumgartner, F. R., and Jones, B. D. (1993). *Agendas and Instability in American Politics.* Chicago, IL, University of Chicago Press.

Baur, D. C., Eichenberg, T., and Sutton, M. (2008). *Ocean and Coastal Law and Policy.* American Bar Association, Section of Environment, Energy, and Resources. Chicago, IL, ABA Publishing.

Beaufort Observer (2012). What you need to know about LOST (Law of the Sea Treaty). Beaufort Observer Online, June 26, 2012. Accessed August 1, 2014 at http://www.beaufortobserver.net/Articles-c-2012-06-25-261157.112112-What-you-need-to-know-about-LOST-Law-Of-the-Sea-Treaty.html.

Beck, M. W., Ferdana, Z., Kachmar, J., Morrison, K. K., and Taylor, P. (2009). *Best Practices for Marine Spatial Planning.* Arlington, VA, The Nature Conservancy.

Behan, R. W. (1966). The Myth of the Omnipotent Forester. *Journal of Forestry* 64(6): 398–407.

Behan, R. W. (1967). The Succotash Syndrome, or Multiple Use: A Heartfelt Approach to Forest Land Management. *Natural Resources Journal* 7: 473–484.

Beierle, T. C., and Cayford, J. (2002). *Democracy in Practice: Public Participation in Environmental Decisions.* Washington, D.C., Resources for the Future.

Bennett, C. J., and Howlett, M. (1992). The Lessons of Learning: Reconciling Theories of Policy Learning and Policy Change. *Policy Sciences* 25(3): 275–294.

Bentham, J. (1789). *An Introduction to the Principles of Morals and Legislation. Printed in the Year 1780, and Now First Published by Jeremy Bentham.* London, T. Payne, and Son.

Bernstein, M. H. (1955). *Regulating Business by Independent Commission.* Princeton, NJ, Princeton University Press.

Black, H. C., and Garner, B. A. (2009). *Black's Law Dictionary.* St. Paul, MN, West Publishing Company.

BLM (2010). Public Land Statistics 2010. Vol. 195, BLM/OC/ST-11/001+1165. Washington, D.C., U.S. Dept. of the Interior, Bureau of Land Management.

Blumberg, L., and Knuffke, D. (1998). Count Us Out: Why the Wilderness Society Opposed the Quincy Library Group Legislation. *Chronicle of Community* 2(2): 41–44.

Bolle, A. W., Pengelly, W. L., Wambach, R. F., Browder, G., Payne, T., and Shannon, R. E. (1970). A University View of the Forest Service. Prepared for the Committee on Interior and Insular Affairs, United States Senate. Washington, D.C., U.S. Government Printing Office.

Boyle, B., Shannon, M., Rose, R., Halvorsen, K., and Elway, H. S. (1994). *Policies and Mythologies of the US Forest Service.* A Research Report. Seattle, WA, University of Washington, College of Forest Resources, Institute for Resources in Society.

Braxton, J. (1995). The Quincy Library Group. *American Forests* 101: 21–23.

Brick, P. D., and Cawley, R. M. (1996). *A Wolf in the Garden: The Land Rights Movement and the New Environmental Debate.* Lanham, MD, Rowman & Littlefield.

Bryner, G. C. (1998). *U.S. Land and Natural Resources Policy: A Public Issues Handbook.* Westport, CT, Greenwood Press.

Bryson, J. M., Crosby, B. C., and Stone, M. M. (2006). The Design and Implementation of Cross-sector Collaborations: Propositions from the Literature. *Public Administration Review* 66(s1): 44–55.

Burns, S. (2001). A Civic Conversation about Public Lands: Developing Community Governance. *Journal of Sustainable Forestry* 13(1–2): 271–291.

Bushouse, B. K. (2011). Governance Structures: Using IAD to Understand Variation in Service Delivery for Club Goods with Information Asymmetry. *Policy Studies Journal* 39(1): 105–119.

Butler, K. F., and Koontz, T. M. (2005). Theory into Practice: Implementing Ecosystem Management Objectives in the USDA Forest Service. *Environmental Management* 35(2): 138–150.

Caldwell, L. K. (1970). Ecosystem as a Criterion for Public Land Policy. *Natural Resources Journal* 10(2): 203–221.

Caldwell, L. K., Wilkinson, C. F., and Shannon, M. A. (1994). Making Ecosystem Policy: Three Decades of Change. *Journal of Forestry* 92(4): 7–10.

Carr, M. H., Neigel, J. E., Estes, J. A., Andelman, S., Warner, R. R., and Largier, J. L. (2003). Comparing Marine and Terrestrial Ecosystems: Implications for the Design of Coastal Marine Reserves. *Ecological Applications* 13(1): S90–S107.

CCA (2012). Coastal Conservation Association comments on the Draft National Ocean Policy Implementation Plan. March 27, 2012 letter to CEQ and OSTP. Accessed August 1, 2014 at http://www.joincca.org/articles/38.

CEQ (Council on Environmental Quality) (2010). Final recommendations of the Interagency Ocean Policy Task Force. Washington, D.C.

Chisholm, D. (1989). *Coordination without Hierarchy: Informal Structures in Multiorganizational Systems.* Berkeley, CA, University of California Press.

Cicin-Sain, B., Knecht, R. W., Jang, D., and Fiske, G. W. (1998). *Integrated Coastal and Ocean Management: Concepts and Practices.* Washington, D.C., Island Press.

Clement, F. (2010). Analysing Decentralised Natural Resource Governance: Proposition for a Politicised Institutional Analysis and Development Framework. *Policy Sciences* 43(2): 129–156.

CMSER (Commission on Marine Science, Engineering and Resources) (1969). *Our Nation and the Sea.* Washington, D.C., U.S. Government Printing Office.

Coggins, G. C. (1981). Of Succotash Syndromes and Vacuous Platitudes: The Meaning of Multiple Use, Sustained Yield for Public Land Management. *University of Colorado Law Review* 53: 229.

Coggins, G. C. (1999). Regulating Federal Natural Resources: A Summary Case against Devolved Collaboration. *Ecology Law Quarterly* 25(4): 602–610.

Coggins, G. C., and Evans, P. B. (1981). Multiple Use, Sustained Yield Planning on the Public Lands. *University of Colorado Law Review* 53: 411–469.

Collie, J. S., Adamowicz, W. L., Beck, M. W., Craig, B., Essington, T. E., Fluharty, D., Rice, J., and Sanchirico, J. N. (2013). Marine Spatial Planning in Practice. *Estuarine, Coastal and Shelf Science* 117: 1–11.

Committee of Scientists (1999). *Sustaining the People's Lands.* Washington, D.C., USDA Forest Service.

COMPASS (2005). *Scientific Consensus Statement on Marine Ecosystem-based Management.* Accessed August 1, 2014 at www.compassonline.org/sites/all/files/document_files/ EBM_Consensus_Statement_v12.pdf.

Congressional Sportsmen's Foundation (2013). *Final National Ocean Policy Implementation Plan Released.* News release posted April 24, 2013. Accessed August 1, 2014 at http://www.sportsmenslink.org/the-media-room/news/final-national-ocean-policy-implementation-plan-released.

Crowder, L. B., Osherenko, G., Young, O. R., Airamé, S., Norse, E. A., Baron, N., Day, J. C., Douvere, F., Ehler, C. N., Halpern, B. S., Langdon, S. J., McLeod, K. L., Ogden, J. C., Peach, R. E., Rosenberg, A. A., and Wilson, J. A. (2006). Resolving Mismatches in U.S. Ocean Governance. *Science* 313(5787): 617.

Culhane, P. J. (1981). *Public Lands Politics: Interest Group Influence on the Forest Service and the Bureau of Land Management.* Baltimore, Published for Resources for the Future by Johns Hopkins University Press.

Curtis, C. (1973). Managing Federal Lands: Replacing the Multiple Use System. *Yale Law Journal* 82: 787–805.

Daniels, S. E., and Walker, G. B. (2001). *Working through Environmental Conflict: The Collaborative Learning Approach.* Westport, CT, Praeger.

David, P. (1985). Clio and the Economics of QWERTY. *American Economic Review* 75(2): 332–337.

Davis, C. E. (2001). *Western Public Lands and Environmental Politics.* Boulder, CO, Westview Press.

de Jong, W.M. (2009). Rose's "10 Steps": Why Process, Messiness, History and Culture are not Vague and Banal. *Policy & Politics* 37(1): 145–150.

de Jong, W. M., Lalenis, K., and Mamadouh, V. (2002). *The Theory and Practice of Institutional Transplantation: Experiences with the Transfer of Policy Institutions.* Dordrecht and Boston, Kluwer Academic Publishers.

Delaney, J. M. (2003). Community Capacity Building in the Designation of the Tortugas Ecological Reserve. *Gulf and Caribbean Research* 14(2): 163–170.

DeShazo, J. R., and Freeman, J. (2005). Public Agencies as Lobbyists. *Columbia Law Review*: 2217–2309.

Dietrich, W. (1992). *The Final Forest: The Battle for the Last Great Trees of the Pacific Northwest.* New York, Simon & Schuster.

Disavino, S. (2012). Deepwater to Build First U.S. Offshore Wind Farm. *Reuters*, U.S. Edition, Oct. 23, 2012. Accessed August 1, 2014 at http://www.reuters.com/article/2012/10/03/us-deepwater-wind-idUSBRE8920ZX20121003.

Dolowitz, D., and Marsh, D. (1996). Who Learns What from Whom: A Review of the Policy Transfer Literature. *Political Studies* 44(2): 343–357.

Dombeck, M. P., Wood, C. A., and Williams, J. E. (2003). *From Conquest to Conservation: Our Public Lands Legacy.* Washington, D.C., Island Press.

Douvere, F., and Ehler, C. N. (eds) (2008). Special Issue on the Role of Marine Spatial Planning in Implementing Ecosystem-based, Sea-use Management. *Marine Policy* 32(5).

Douvere, F., and Ehler, C. N. (2009). New Perspectives on Sea Use Management: Initial Findings from European Experience with Marine Spatial Planning. *Journal of Environmental Management* 90(1): 77–88.

Duff, J. A. (2004). Offshore Management Considerations: Law and Policy Questions Related to Fish, Oil, and Wind. *Boston College Environmental Affairs Law Review* 31: 385–402.

Eagle, J. (2006). Regional Ocean Governance: The Perils of Multiple-use Management and the Promise of Agency Diversity. *Duke Environmental Law & Policy Forum* 16: 143.

Eagle, J. (2008). The Practical Effects of Delegation: Agencies and the Zoning of Public Lands and Seas. *Pepperdine Law Review* 35: 835–894.

Eagle, J. (2014). Complex and Murky Spatial Planning. *Journal of Land Use & Environmental Law* 28(1): 35.

Eagle, J., and Kuker, A. (2010). Public Fisheries. *Ecology and Society* 15(1): 10.

Ehler, C. N. (2013). *The Present and Future of Marine Spatial Planning around the World.* OpenChannels Forum for Ocean Planning and Management, Jan. 1, 2013. Accessed April 2, 2014 at http://openchannels.org/blog/cehler/present-and-future-marine-spatial-planning-around-world

Ehler, C. N., and Douvere, F. (2007). *Visions for a Sea Change: Report of the First International Workshop on Marine Spatial Planning.* Intergovernmental Oceanographic Commission and Man and the Biosphere Programme. IOC Manual and Guides No. 48, IOCAM Dossier No. 4. Paris, UNESCO.

Ehler, C. N., and Douvere, F. (2009). *Marine Spatial Planning: A Step-by-step Approach toward Ecosystem-based Management.* IOC Manual and Guides No. 53, IOCAM Dossier No. 6. Paris, UNESCO.

Emerson, K., Nabatchi, T., and Balogh, S. (2012). An Integrative Framework for Collaborative Governance. *Journal of Public Administration Research and Theory* 22(1): 1–29.

Erlandson, J. M., Rick, T., Braje, T. J., Casperson, M., Culleton, B., Fulfrost, B., Garcia, T., Guthrie, D. A., Jew, N., Kennett, D. J., Moss, M. L., Reeder, L., Skinner, C., Watts, J., and Willis, L. (2011). Paleoindian Seafaring, Maritime Technologies, and Coastal Foraging on California's Channel Islands. *Science* 331(6021): 1181–1185.

Evans, M., and Davies, J. (1999). Understanding Policy Transfer: A Multi-level, Multi-disciplinary Perspective. *Public Administration* 77(2): 361–385.

Executive Order #13547 (2010). Stewardship of the Ocean, Our Coasts, and the Great Lakes. Washington, D.C. 75 FR 43023, July 19, 2010.

Farnham, T. J., and Mohai, P. (1995). National Forest Timber Management over the Past Decade: A Change in Emphasis for the Forest-Service? *Policy Studies Journal* 23(2): 268–280.

Fedkiw, J. (1999). *Managing Multiple Uses on National Forests, 1905–1995.* Washington, D.C., USDA Forest Service. FS–628.

Feller, J. (1995). Til the Cows Come Home: The Fatal Flaw in the Clinton Administration's Public Lands Grazing Policy. *Environmental Law* 25: 703–714.

FEMAT (1993). *Forest Ecosystem Management: An Ecological, Economic, and Social Assessment—Report of the Forest Ecosystem Management Assessment Team.* Portland, OR, USDA Forest Service.

Fleishman, J. L. (2009). *The Foundation: A Great American Secret; How Private Wealth is Changing the World.* Philadelphia, PA, PublicAffairs.

FLPMA (1976). Federal Land Policy and Management Act, P.L. 94–579. Franklin, J. (1989). Toward a New Forestry. *American Forests,* Nov–Dec.

Frost, C. (1993). Four Centuries of Changing Landscape Patterns in the Longleaf Pine Ecosystem. *Proceedings of the Tall Timbers Fire Ecology Conference* 18: 17–43.

Gale, R. P., and Cordray, S. M. (1994). Making Sense of Sustainability—9 Answers to What Should Be Sustained. *Rural Sociology* 59(2): 311–332.

Gale, R. P., and Miller, M. L. (1985). Professional and Public Natural-resource Management Arenas—Forests and Marine Fisheries. *Environment and Behavior* 17(6): 651–678.

GEF (2012). *Marine Spatial Planning in the Context of the Convention on Biological Diversity: A Study Carried Out in Response to CBD COP 10 Decision X/29.* Secretariat of the Convention on Biological Diversity and Technical Advisory Panel. Montreal, Technical Series No. 68.

Gericke, K. L., and Sullivan, J. (1994). Public-Participation and Appeals of Forest Service Plans—An Empirical-Examination. *Society & Natural Resources* 7(2): 125–135.

Germain, R. H., Floyd, D. W., and Stehman, S. V. (2001). Public Perceptions of the USDA Forest Service Public Participation Process. *Forest Policy and Economics* 3(3–4): 113–124.

Gilliland, P. M., and Laffoley, D. (2008). Key Elements and Steps in the Process of Developing Ecosystem-based Marine Spatial Planning. *Marine Policy* 32(5): 787–796.

Gillis, A. M. (1990). The New Forestry—An Ecosystem Approach to Land Management. *Bioscience* 40(8): 558–562.

Gopnik, M. (2008). *Integrated Marine Spatial Planning in U.S. Waters: The Path Forward.* Report to the Gordon and Betty Moore Foundation.

Gopnik, M., Fieseler, C., Cantral, L., McClellan, K., Pendleton, L., and Crowder, L. (2012). Coming to the Table: Early Stakeholder Engagement in Marine Spatial Planning. *Marine Policy* 36(5): 1139–1149.

Graham, B., and Reilly, W. K. (2011). *Deep Water: The Gulf Oil Disaster and the Future of Offshore Drilling.* Report to the President. U.S. National Commission on the BP Deepwater Horizon Spill and Offshore Drilling.

Gray, B. (1985). Conditions Facilitating Interorganizational Collaboration. *Human Relations* 38(10): 911–936.

Gray, G. J., Enzer, M. J., and Kusel, J. (2001). Understanding Community-based Forest Ecosystem Management: An Editorial Synthesis. *Journal of Sustainable Forestry* 12(3–4): 1–23.

Gray, J. S. (1997). Marine Biodiversity: Patterns, Threats and Conservation Needs. *Biodiversity & Conservation* 6(1): 153–175.

Gunderson, L. H., Holling, C. S., and Light, S. (1995). *Barriers and Bridges to Renewal of Ecosystems and Institutions.* New York, Columbia University Press.

Haeuber, R. (1996). Setting the Environmental Policy Agenda: The Case of Ecosystem Management. *Natural Resources Journal* 36(1): 1–28.

Hall, G. R. (1963). Myth and Reality of Multiple Use Forestry. *Natural Resources Journal* 3: 276.

Hanna, S., Folke, C., and Mäler, K-G. (1996). *Rights to Nature: Ecological, Economic, Cultural, and Political Principles of Institutions for the Environment.* Washington, D.C., Island Press.

Harvey, M. W. T. (2005). *Wilderness Forever: Howard Zahniser and the Path to the Wilderness Act.* Seattle, University of Washington Press.

Hennessey, T., and Juda, L. (2001). Governance Profiles and the Management of the Uses of Large Marine Ecosystems. *Ocean Development & International Law* 32(1): 43–69.

Hibbard, M., and Madsen, J. (2003). Environmental Resistance to Place-based Collaboration in the U.S. West. *Society & Natural Resources* 16(8): 703–718.

Hodgson, G. (2006). What Are Institutions? *Journal of Economic Issues* 40: 1–26.

Holling, C. S. (1986). The Resilience of Terrestrial Ecosystems: Local Surprise and Global Change. In W. C. Clark and R. E. Munn (eds), *Sustainable Development of the Biosphere.* Cambridge, Cambridge University Press.

Horgan, D. E. (2011). Reconciling the Past with the Future: The Cape Wind Project and the National Historic Preservation Act. *Vt. L. Rev.* 36: 409–1015.

House Resources Committee (2011). *Top 10 Things to Know About President Obama's Plan to Zone the Oceans.* Press release from the U.S. House of Representatives' Committee on Natural Resources, issued September 30, 2011. Accessed January 31, 2014 at http://naturalresources.house.gov/news/documentsingle.aspx? DocumentID=262435.

Hunt, Lee O. (1966). Points of View: Has the Society Lost Direction? *Journal of Forestry* 64(6): 407–408.

Imperial, M. T. (1999). Institutional Analysis and Ecosystem-based Management: The Institutional Analysis and Development Framework. *Environmental Management* 24(4): 449–465.

Imperial, M. T. (2005). Using Collaboration as a Governance Strategy: Lessons from Six Watershed Management Programs. *Administration & Society* 37(3): 281–320.

Imperial, M. T., and Yandle, T. (2005). Taking Institutions Seriously: Using the IAD Framework to Analyze Fisheries Policy. *Society and Natural Resources* 18(6): 493–509.

Ingram, H., Schneider, A., and deLeon, P. (2007). Social Construction and Policy Design. In P. Sabatier (ed.), *Theories of the Policy Process, Second Edition*. Boulder, CO, Westview Press.

IOPTF (Interagency Ocean Policy Task Force) (2009). *Interim Framework for Effective Coastal and Marine Spatial Planning*. Washington, D.C. Council on Environmental Quality.

Iverson, D., and Alston, R. (1986). *The Genesis of FORPLAN: A Historical and Analytical Review of Forest Service Planning Models*. USDA Forest Service, Intermountain Research Station, Technical Report INT–214.

Jentoft, S. (2000). The Community: A Missing Link of Fisheries Management. *Marine Policy* 24(1): 53–60.

Johnson, K. N. (1987). Reflections on the Development of FORPLAN. *Proceedings of a Symposium, Denver, CO, Nov. 4–6, 1986*. USDA Forest Service, General Technical Report RM–140.

Johnson, K. N., Agee, J., Beschta, R., Dale, V., Hardesty, L., Long, J., Nielsen, L., Noon, B., Sedjo, R., and Shannon, M. (1999). Sustaining the People's Lands —Recommendations for Stewardship of the National Forests and Grasslands into the Next Century. *Journal of Forestry* 97(5): 6–12.

Jones, P., Qiu, W., and Lieberknecht, L. (2014). Marine Spatial Planning in Reality: Outline and Key Points from Governance Research under the MESMA project. Accessed April 2, 2014 at www.homepages.ucl.ac.uk/~ucfwpej/pdf/MESMAGovernanceFindingsOutline.pdf.

Juda, L. (1996). *International Law and Ocean Use Management: The Evolution of Ocean Governance*. London and New York, Routledge.

Juda, L., and Burroughs, R. H. (1990). The Prospects for Comprehensive Ocean Management. *Marine Policy* 14(1): 23–35.

Justus, J., Colyvan, M., Regan, H., and Maguire, L. (2009). Buying into Conservation: Intrinsic versus Instrumental Value. *Trends in Ecology & Evolution* 24(4): 187–191.

Kagan, R. A. (1999). Trying to Have It Both Ways: Local Discretion, Central Control, and Adversarial Legalism in American Environmental Regulation. *Ecology Law Quarterly* 25(4): 718–732.

Kaufman, H. (1960). *The Forest Ranger: A Study in Administrative Behavior*. Baltimore, MD, Johns Hopkins Press.

Kearney, R., Farebrother, G., Buxton, C. D., and Goodsell, P. (2012). How Terrestrial Management Concepts Have Led to Unrealistic Expectations of Marine Protected Areas. *Marine Policy* 38: 304–311.

Keiter, R. B. (1994). Beyond the Boundary Line: Constructing a Law of Ecosystem Management. *University of Colorado Law Review* 65: 293–333.

Kelson, A. R. (1998). Integrating Wilderness within Broader Landscapes: The U.S. Public Land Experience. *Land Use Policy* 15(3): 181–189.

Kemmis, D., and McKinney, M. (2011). Collaboration as an Emerging Form of Democracy. *National Civic Review* 100(2): 2–12.

KenCairn, B. (1995). A Community-based Approach to Forest Management in the Pacific Northwest: A Profile of the Applegate Partnership. *Ecosystem Management of Natural Resources in the Intermountain West, Proceedings of the Symposium* 5: 43–52.

Kennedy, J. J., Dombeck, M. P., and Koch, N. E. (1998). Values, Beliefs and Management of Public Forests in the Western World at the Close of the Twentieth Century. *Unasylva-FAO* 49(192): 16–26.

Kent, B., Bare, B. B., Field, R. C., and Bradley, G. A. (1991). Natural Resource Land Management Planning Using Large-scale Linear Programs: The USDA Forest Service Experience with FORPLAN. *Operations Research* 39(1): 13–27.

Kidd, S., and Ellis, G. (2012). From the Land to Sea and Back Again? Using Terrestrial Planning to Understand the Process of Marine Spatial Planning. *Journal of Environmental Policy & Planning* 14(1): 49–66.

Kidd, S., Plater, A., and Frid, C. (2011). *The Ecosystem Approach to Marine Planning and Management.* Oxford, Earthscan/Routledge.

Kingdon, J. W. (1984). *Agendas, Alternatives, and Public Policies.* Boston, Little, Brown.

Kingdon, J. W. (1995). *Agendas, Alternatives, and Public Policies, Second Edition.* New York, HarperCollins.

Knecht, R., and Kitsos, T. (1984). Multiple-use Management in the EEZ. *OCEANUS*, Winter 1984/85.

Kohm, K. A., and Franklin, J. F. (1997). *Creating a Forestry for the 21st Century: The Science of Ecosystem Management.* Washington, D.C., Island Press.

Korfmacher, K. (1998). Invisible Successes, Visible Failures: Paradoxes of Ecosystem Management in the Albemarle-Pamlico Estuarine Study. *Coastal Management* 26(3): 191–211.

Kosek, J. (2006). *Understories: The Political Life of Forests in Northern New Mexico.* Durham, Duke University Press.

Lane, M. B., and McDonald, G. (2005). Community-based Environmental Planning: Operational Dilemmas, Planning Principles and Possible Remedies. *Journal of Environmental Planning and Management* 48(5): 709–731.

Leach, W. D. (2006). Public Involvement in USDA Forest Service Policymaking: A Literature Review. *Journal of Forestry* 104(1): 43–49.

Leach, W. D., and Sabatier, P. A. (2005). To Trust an Adversary: Integrating Rational and Psychological Models of Collaborative Policymaking. *American Political Science Review* 99(4): 491–503.

Leshy, J. D. (1987). Granite Rock and the States' Influence over Federal Land Use. *Environmental Law* 18: 99.

Liebowitz, S. J., and Margolis, S. E. (1995). Path Dependence, Lock-in and History. *Journal of Law, Economics, and Organization* 11: 205–226.

Long, R. J., and Beierle, T. C. (1999). *The Federal Advisory Committee Act and Public Participation in Environmental Policy.* Resources for the Future, pp. 99–117.

Luckert, M. K. M. (2006). Has the Myth of the Omnipotent Forester Become the Reality of the Impotent Forester? *Journal of Forestry* 104(6): 299–306.

MacCleery, D. (1992). *American Forests: A History of Resiliency and Recovery.* USDA/ Forest Service, FS–540 in cooperation with the Forest History Society, Durham, North Carolina.

MacCleery, D. (2001). *Pathway to Sustainability: Defining the Bounds on Forest Management.* Durham, North Carolina, Forest History Society.

MacCleery, D. (2008). Re-inventing the United States Forest Service: Evolution from Custodial Management, to Production Forestry, to Ecosystem Management. In C. B. P. Durst, J. Broadhead, R. Suzuki, R. Leslie, and A. Inoguchi (eds), *Re-inventing Forestry Agencies.* Rome, Italy, Food and Agriculture Organization, Regional Office for Asia and the Pacific.

Mann, C. (2009). Statement for the Pew Environment Group. Hearing on H.R. 21 before the Subcomm. on Insular Affairs, Oceans, and Wildlife of the H. Comm. on Natural Resources, 111th Congress, June 18, 2009.

Manring, N. J. (2005). The Politics of Accountability in National Forest Planning. *Administration & Society* 37(1): 57–88.

Marcot, B. G., and Thomas, J. W. (1997). Of Spotted Owls, Old Growth, and New Policies: A History Since the Interagency Scientific Committee Report. Gen. Tech. Rep. PNW-GTR-408. Portland, OR, U.S. Department of Agriculture, Forest Service, Pacific Northwest Research Station.

Marshall, G. R. (2005). *Economics for Collaborative Environmental Management: Renegotiating the Commons.* London and Sterling, VA, Earthscan.

Marshall, G. R. (2007). Nesting, Subsidiarity, and Community-based Environmental Governance beyond the Local Scale. *International Journal of the Commons* 2(1): 75–97.

Marshall, R. (1933). *The People's Forests.* New York, H. Smith and R. Haas.

Martin, P. L. (1969). Conflict Resolution through the Multiple-use Concept in Forest Service Decision-making. *Natural Resources Journal* 9: 228–236.

Martin, S. (1993). Ten Good Reasons Why Zoning is [a] Bad Idea. *Houston Chronicle* Op-Ed, Sept. 12, 1993.

McCay, B. (1996). Common and Private Concerns. In S. Hanna, C. Folke, and K-G. Mäler (eds), *Rights to Nature: Ecological, Economic, Cultural, and Political Principles of Institutions for the Environment.* Washington, D.C., Island Press.

McCloskey, M. (1999). Local Communities and the Management of Public Forests. *Ecology Law Quarterly* 25(4): 624–629.

McGinnis, M. D. (2011). Networks of Adjacent Action Situations in Polycentric Governance. *Policy Studies Journal* 39(1): 51–78.

McKinney, M., and Harmon, W. (2004). *The Western Confluence: A Guide to Governing Natural Resources.* Washington, D.C., Island Press.

McLeod, K. L., and Leslie, H. M. (2009). *Ecosystem-based Management for the Oceans.* Washington, D.C., Island Press.

Means, D. B. (1996). Longleaf Pine Forest, Going, Going... In M. Davis (ed.), *Eastern Old-growth Forests: Prospects for Rediscovery and Recovery.* Washington, D.C., Island Press.

Merriam-Webster (2014). Dictionary, Electronic version. Accessed August 1, 2014 at www.merriam-webster.com.

Merrie, A., and Olsson, P. (2014). An Innovation and Agency Perspective on the Emergence and Spread of Marine Spatial Planning. *Marine Policy* 44: 366–374.

Meyer, J. M. (1997). Gifford Pinchot, John Muir, and the Boundaries of Politics in American Thought. *Polity* 30(2): 267–284.

Millennium Ecosystem Assessment (2005). *Ecosystems and Human Well-being: Current State and Trends.* Findings of the Condition and Trends Working Group of the Millennium Ecosystem Assessment. Washington, D.C., Island Press.

Mohai, P. (1987). Rational Decision Making in the Planning Process: Some Empirical Evidence from RARE II. *Environmental Law* 17(3): 507–556.
Monmonier, M. S. (1996). *How to Lie with Maps*. Chicago, University of Chicago Press.
Mortimer, M. J. (2002). Delegation of Law-making Authority to the United States Forest Service: Implications in the Struggle for National Forest Management. *The Administrative Law Review* 54: 907.
Muir, J. (1917). *Our National Parks*. Boston, MA, Houghton-Mifflin.
Muir, J. (1979). *John of the Mountains: The Unpublished Journals of John Muir*. Madison, WI, University of Wisconsin Press.
Munro, G. D., and Ditto, P. H. (1997). Biased Assimilation, Attitude Polarization, and Affect in Reactions to Stereotype-relevant Scientific Information. *Personality and Social Psychology Bulletin* 23(6): 636–653.
NAPA (2002). *Courts, Congress, and Constituencies: Managing Fisheries by Default*. Report by a Panel of the National Academy of Public Administration for the Congress and the U.S. Department of Commerce. Washington, D.C., National Marine Fisheries Service.
National Park Service Organic Act (1916). 16 U.S. Code Sec. 1.
NCWRC (2010). Coastal Plain Habitats: Pocosin. North Carolina Wildlife Resources Commission Fact Sheet. Accessed August 1, 2014 at http://www.ncwildlife.org/Conserving/Habitats/Coast.aspx.
Nelson, R. H. (1995). *Public lands and private rights: The failure of scientific management*. Lanham, MD, Rowman & Littlefield.
Nelson, R. (2012, December 23). Want to Restore Ocean Ecosystems? Involve People Making Living from the Sea. *Bangor Daily News*. Accessed August 1, 2014 at https://bangordailynews.com/2012/12/23/opinion/want-to-restore-ocean-ecosystems-involve-people-making-living-from-the-sea/?ref=relatedBox.
Nickerson, C., Ebel, R., Borchers, A., and Carriazo, F. (2011). *Major Uses of Land in the United States, 2007*. EIB-89. Washington, D.C., U.S.D.A., Economic Research Service.
Nie, M. A. (2008). *The Governance of Western Public Lands: Mapping its Present and Future*. Lawrence, KS, University Press of Kansas.
NOC (2011). *Legal Authorities Relating to the Implementation of Coastal and Marine Spatial Planning*. Washington, D.C., Council on Environmental Quality, National Ocean Council. Accessed August 1, 2014 at http://www.whitehouse.gov/sites/default/files/microsites/ceq/cmsp_legal_compendium_2-14-11.pdf.
NOC (2013a). *National Ocean Policy Implementation Plan*. Washington, D.C., National Ocean Council.
NOC (2013b). *Marine Planning Handbook*. Washington, D.C., National Ocean Council.
NOPC (2012). *National Ocean Policy Coalition Responds To Draft Ocean Action Plan*. Press release from the National Ocean Policy Coalition, January 12, 2012. Accessed August 1, 2014 at http://oceanpolicy.com/2012/01/12/national-ocean-policy-coalition-responds-to-draft-ocean-action-plan.
Norse, E.A. (2005). Ending the range wars on the last frontier: zoning the sea. In E. A. Norse and L. B. Crowder (eds), *Marine Conservation Biology: The Science of Maintaining the Sea's Biodiversity*. Washington, D.C., Island Press.
NRC (1990). *Managing Troubled Waters*. Washington, D.C., National Academy Press.

NRC (1992). *Oceanography in the Next Decade: Building New Partnerships.* Washington, D.C., National Academy Press.

NRC (1994). *Improving the Management of U.S. Marine Fisheries.* Washington, D.C., National Academy Press.

NRC (1998). *Review of Northeast Fishery Stock Assessments.* Washington, D.C., National Academy Press.

NRC (1999). *Improving Fish Stock Assessments.* Washington, D.C., National Academy Press.

NRC (2000). *Improving the Collection, Management, and Use of Marine Fisheries Data.* Washington, D.C., National Academy Press.

NRC (2001). *Marine Protected Areas: Tools for Sustaining Ocean Ecosystems.* Washington, D.C., National Academy Press.

NRC (2002a). *Science and Its Role in the National Marine Fisheries Service.* Washington, D.C., National Academy Press.

NRC (2002b). *Effects of Trawling and Dredging on Seafloor Habitat.* Washington, D.C., National Academy Press.

NRC (2004). *Improving the Use of the "Best Scientific Information Available" Standard in Fisheries Management.* Washington, D.C., National Academy Press.

O'Leary, R., and Bingham, L. (2003). *The Promise and Performance of Environmental Conflict Resolution.* Washington, D.C., Resources for the Future.

Oakerson, R. J., and Parks, R. B. (2011). The Study of Local Public Economies: Multi-organizational, Multi-level Institutional Analysis and Development. *Policy Studies Journal* 39(1): 147–167.

Orbach, M. (2003). Beyond the Freedom of the Seas: Ocean Policy for the Third Millennium. *Oceanography* 16(1): 20.

Ostrom, E. (2005). *Understanding Institutional Diversity.* Princeton, Princeton University Press.

Ostrom, E. (2007). A Diagnostic Approach for Going Beyond Panaceas. *Proceedings of the National Academy of Sciences* 104(39): 15181–15187.

Ostrom, E., Gardner, R., and Walker, J. (1994). *Rules, Games, and Common-pool Resources.* Ann Arbor, MI, University of Michigan Press.

O'Toole, R. (1997). *Should Congress Transfer Federal Lands to the States?* Policy Analysis No. 276. Washington, D.C., Cato Institute.

Page, S. (2006). Path Dependence. *Quarterly Journal of Political Science* 1: 87–115.

Pauly, D., Christensen, V., Dalsgaard, J., Froese, R., and Torres, F. (1998). Fishing down Marine Food Webs. *Science* 279(5352): 860–863.

Payne, E. (2007). Old Growth, New Ideas. Flux Magazine, Issue 15, Spring 2007. Accessed August 1, 2014 at http://www.fluxstories.com/archive/2007.php.

Pew Oceans Commission (2003). *America's Living Oceans: Charting a Course for Sea Change. A Report to the Nation: Recommendations for a New Ocean Policy.* Arlington, VA, Pew Oceans Commission.

Pierson, P. (2000). Increasing Returns, Path Dependence, and the Study of Politics. *American Political Science Review* 94(2): 251–267.

Pinchot, G. (1905). *A Primer of Forestry.* Bulletin 24, Bureau of Forestry, USDA.

Pinchot, G. (1907). *The Use of the National Forests.* Washington, D.C., Govt. Printing Office.

Pinchot, G. (1947). *Breaking New Ground.* New York, Harcourt, Brace, and Co.

Qiu, W., and Jones, P. J. (2013). The Emerging Policy Landscape for Marine Spatial Planning in Europe. *Marine Policy* 39: 182–190.

Quattrone, G. A., and Tversky, A. (1988). Contrasting Rational and Psychological Analyses of Political Choice. *The American Political Science Review* 82(3): 719–736.

Rabalais, N., and Turner, R. (eds) (2013). *Coastal Hypoxia: Consequences for Living Resources and Ecosystems.* Washington, D.C., American Geophysical Union.

Rakestraw, L. (1991). *History of the Willamette National Forest.* Willamette National Forest, Eugene, OR, U.S. Dept. of Agriculture.

Rapp, V. (2008). *Northwest Forest Plan—The First 10 Years (1994–2003): First-decade Results of the Northwest Forest Plan.* Gen. Tech. Rep. PNW-GTR-720. Portland, OR: USDA, Forest Service, Pacific Northwest Research Station.

Reich, C. A. (1962). The Public and the Nation's Forests. *California Law Review* 50(3): 381–407.

RFA (2009). Recreational Fishing Alliance comments on the Interim Report of the Interagency Ocean Policy Task Force. Oct. 17, 2009 letter to CEQ. Accessed August 1, 2014 at http://joinrfa.org/wp-content/uploads/2013/03/CEQComments_101909.pdf.

Ritchie, H. (2014). Understanding Emerging Discourses of Marine Spatial Planning in the U.K. *Land Use Policy* 38: 666–675.

Rose, R. (1991). What is Lesson-drawing? *Journal of Public Policy* 11(1): 1–22.

Rose, R. (1993). *Lesson-drawing in Public Policy: A Guide to Learning Across Time and Space.* Chatham, NJ, Chatham House Publishers.

Rothwell, D., and VanderZwaag, D. (2006). *Towards Principled Oceans Governance: Australian and Canadian Approaches and Challenges.* New York, Routledge.

Ruhl, J. (2012). Panarchy and the Law. *Ecology and Society* 17(3): 31.

Russ, G. R., and Zeller, D. (2003). From Mare Liberum to Mare Reservarum. *Marine Policy* 27(1): 75–78.

Sabatier, P. A. (2007a). *Theories of the Policy Process, Second Edition.* Boulder, CO, Westview Press.

Sabatier, P. A. (2007b). Fostering the Development of Policy Theory. In P. Sabatier (ed.), *Theories of the Policy Process, Second Edition.* Boulder, CO, Westview Press.

Sabatier, P. A., and Jenkins-Smith, H. (1999). The Advocacy Coalition Framework: An Assessment. In P. Sabatier (ed.), *Theories of the Policy Process.* Boulder, CO, Westview Press.

Sabatier, P. A., and Weible, C. M. (2005). *Innovations in the Advocacy Coalition Framework.* Paper presented at the American Society for Public Administration meeting, Milwaukee, WI.

Sabatier, P. A., and Weible, C. M. (2007). The Advocacy Coalition Framework: Innovations and Clarification. In P. Sabatier (ed.), *Theories of the Policy Process, Second Edition.* Boulder, CO, Westview Press.

Sabatier, P. A., Loomis, J., and McCarthy, C. (1995). Hierarchical Controls, Professional Norms, Local Constituencies, and Budget Maximization—An Analysis of United-States-Forest-Service Planning Decisions. *American Journal of Political Science* 39(1): 204–242.

Salcido, R. E. (2007). Offshore Federalism and Ocean Industrialization. *Tulane Law Review* 82: 1355.

Sanchirico, J. M., Eagle, J., Palumbi, S., and Thompson, Jr, B. (2010). Comprehensive Planning, Dominant-use Zones, and User Rights: A New Era in Ocean Governance. *Bulletin of Marine Science* 86: 273–285.

Sax, J. L. (1970). The Public Trust Doctrine in Natural Resource Law: Effective Judicial Intervention. *Michigan Law Review* 68(3): 471–566.

Schlager, E. (1995). Policy Making and Collective Action: Defining Coalitions Within the Advocacy Coalition Framework. *Policy Sciences* 28(3): 243–270.

Schlager, E. (2007). A Comparison of Frameworks, Theories, and Models of Policy Processes. In P. Sabatier (ed.), *Theories of the Policy Process, Second Edition.* Boulder, CO, Westview Press.

Schlager, E., and Ostrom, E. (1992). Property-rights Regimes and Natural-resources: A Conceptual Analysis. *Land Economics* 68(3): 249–262.

Scott, J. C. (1998). *Seeing like a State: How Certain Schemes to Improve the Human Condition Have Failed.* New Haven, CT, Yale University Press.

Scott, D. (2001). *A Wilderness-forever Future: A Short History of the National Wilderness Preservation System.* Seattle, WA, Pew Wilderness Center.

Shackeroff, J. M., Hazen, E. L., and Crowder, L. B. (2009). The Oceans as Peopled Seascapes. In K. L. McLeod and H. M. Leslie (eds), *Ecosystem-based Management for the Oceans.* Washington, D.C., Island Press.

Sherman, K., and Alexander, L. (1986). *Variability and Management of Large Marine Ecosystems.* AAAS Selected Symposium 99, Boulder, CO, Westview Press.

Smith, P. D., and McDonough, M. H. (2001). Beyond Public Participation: Fairness in Natural Resource Decision Making. *Society & Natural Resources* 14(3): 239–249.

Smith, W. B., Miles, P. D., Vissage, J. S., and Pugh, S. A. (2004). *Forest Resources of the United States, 2002.* General Technical Report NC–241. St. Paul, MN, U.S. Dept. of Agriculture, Forest Service, North Central Research Station.

Spalding, M. (2011). Making Lemonade. *The Environmental Forum* 28(1): 30–33.

St. Martin, K. (2009). Toward a Cartography of the Commons: Constituting the Political and Economic Possibilities of Place. *The Professional Geographer* 61(4): 493–507.

St. Martin, K., and Hall-Arber, M. (2008). The Missing Layer: Geo-technologies, Communities, and Implications for Marine Spatial Planning. *Marine Policy* 32(5): 779–786.

Stankey, G. M., Bormann, B. T., Ryan, C., Shindler, B., Sturtevant, V., Clark, R. N., and Philpot, C. (2003). Adaptive Management and the Northwest Forest Plan: Rhetoric and Reality. *Journal of Forestry* 101(1): 40–46.

Steele, J. H. (1985). A Comparison of Terrestrial and Marine Ecological Systems. *Nature* 313(6001): 355–358.

Steelman, T. A. (2001). Elite and Participatory Policymaking: Finding Balance in a Case of National Forest Planning. *Policy Studies Journal* 29(1): 71–89.

Steelman, T. A., and DuMond, M. E. (2009). Serving the Common Interest in U.S. Forest Policy: A Case Study of the Healthy Forests Restoration Act. *Environmental Management* 43(3): 396–410.

Steinberg, P. E. (1999). Lines of Division, Lines of Connection: Stewardship in the World Ocean. *Geographical Review* 89(2): 254–264.

Steinberg, P. E. (2001). *The Social Construction of the Ocean.* Cambridge, Cambridge University Press.

Steins, N. A., and Edwards, V. M. (1999). Collective Action in Common-pool Resource Management: The Contribution of a Social Constructivist Perspective to Existing Theory. *Society & Natural Resources* 12(6): 539–557.

Sun, H. (2011). Toward a New Social-political Theory of the Public Trust Doctrine. *Vermont Law Review* 35: 563–622.

Susskind, L., McKearnen, S., and Thomas-Larmer, J. (eds) (1999). *The Consensus Building Handbook*. Thousand Oaks, CA, Sage.

Teeguarden, D. E. (1986). Benefit-cost Analysis in National Forest System Planning: Policy, Uses, and Limitations. *Environmental Law* 17: 393.

Thomas, C. W. (2003). *Bureaucratic Landscapes: Interagency Cooperation and the Preservation of Biodiversity*. Cambridge, MA, MIT Press.

Thomas, J. C., and Mohai, P. (1995). Racial, Gender, and Professional Diversification in the Forest Service from 1983 to 1992. *Policy Studies Journal* 23(2): 296–309.

Thomas, J. W., Forsman, E. D., Lint, J. B., Meslow, E. C., Noon, B. B., and Verner, J. (1990). *A Conservation Strategy for the Northern Spotted Owl: Report of the Interagency Science Committee*. Portland, Oregon, USDA Forest Service, Bureau of Land Management, U.S. Fish and Wildlife Service, and National Park Service.

Thomas, J. W., Raphael, M. G., Anthony, R. G., and Grant, G. (1993). *Viability Assessments and Management Considerations for Species Associated with Late-successional and Old-growth Forests of the Pacific Northwest*. Portland, Oregon, U.S. Department of Agriculture, Forest Service.

Tonsfeldt, W. (2010). *Celebrating the Siuslaw: A Century of Growth*. Siuslaw National Forest. USDA Forest Service.

Torfing, J. (2009). Rethinking Path Dependence in Public Policy Research. *Critical Policy Studies* 3(1): 70–83.

True, J., Jones, B., and Baumgartner, F. (2007). Punctuated Equilibrium Theory. In P. Sabatier (ed.), *Theories of the Policy Process, Second Edition*. Boulder, CO, Westview Press.

Turnipseed, M., Sagarin, R., Barnes, P., Blumm, M. C., Parenteau, P., and Sand, P. H. (2010). Reinvigorating the Public Trust Doctrine: Expert Opinion on the Potential of a Public Trust Mandate in U.S. and International Environmental Law. *Environment* 52(5): 6.

Tyldesley, D., and Hunt, B. (2003). Review of How the Land Use Planning System Could Influence the Development of a Marine Spatial Planning System for England. *English Nature Research Reports, Number 566*.

USCOP (2004a). *An Ocean Blueprint for the 21st Century: Final Report*. U.S. Commission on Ocean Policy, Washington, D.C., Govt. Printing Office.

USCOP (2004b). *Appendix 6: Review of U.S. Ocean and Coastal Law. The Evolution of Ocean Governance Over Three Decades*. U.S. Commission on Ocean Policy, Washington, D.C., Govt. Printing Office.

USFS (1969). *Douglas Fir Supply Study*. Portland, OR, USDA Forest Service, Pacific Northwest Forest and Range Experiment Station.

USFS (1990). *Critique of Land Management Planning*. FS-452. Washington, D.C., USDA Forest Service, Policy Analysis Staff.

USFS (1994). *A National Framework: Ecosystem Management*. Program Aid 1502. Washington, D.C., USDA Forest Service.

USFS (2002). *Revised Land and Resource Management Plan for the Croatan National Forest*. Management Bulletin R8-MB-108A. Atlanta, GA, USDA Forest Service Southern Region.

USFS (2004). *Land Acquisition Handbook*. FSH 5409.13, Ch. 30. Eff. 2/27/2004. Washington, D.C., USDA Forest Service.

USFS (2010). National Forests in North Carolina: FY2009 Monitoring and Evaluation Report. Asheville, NC, USDA Forest Service, NC Forest Supervisor's Office.

USFWS (2008). Red-cockaded Woodpecker: *Picoides borealis.* Fact sheet. U.S. Fish and Wildlife Service, January 2008. Accessed August 1, 2014 at http://www.fws.gov/rcwrecovery/files/rcwoodpecker.pdf.

USPLLRC (U.S. Public Land Law Review Commission) (1970). *One Third of the Nation's Land: A Report to the President and to the Congress.* Washington, D.C.

Wallace, W. J. (2014). *Blue Mind: The Surprising Science That Shows How Being Near, In, On, or Under Water Can Make You Happier, Healthier, More Connected, and Better at What You Do.* New York, Little, Brown & Company.

Weber, E. P. (2000). A New Vanguard for the Environment: Grass-roots Ecosystem Management as a New Environmental Movement. *Society & Natural Resources* 13(3): 237–259.

Weible, C. M. (2007). An Advocacy Coalition Framework Approach to Stakeholder Analysis: Understanding the Political Context of California Marine Protected Area Policy. *Journal of Public Administration Research and Theory* 17(1): 95–117.

Weinberg, A. (2012). *Retaining Working Forests: Eastern North Carolina.* New York, Open Space Institute.

Wenk, E. (1972). *The Politics of the Ocean.* Seattle, University of Washington Press.

White House (2009). Memorandum to The Heads of Executive Departments and Agencies, concerning A National Policy for the Oceans, Our Coasts, and the Great Lakes, June 12, 2009.

Wilen, J. E. (2000). Renewable Resource Economists and Policy: What Differences Have we Made? *Journal of Environmental Economics and Management* 39(3): 306–327.

Wilkinson, C. F. (1980). The Public Trust Doctrine in Public Land Law. *University of California Davis Law Review* 14: 269–316.

Wilkinson, C. F. (1997). The National Forest Management Act: The Twenty Years Behind, the Twenty Years Ahead. *University of Colorado Law Review* 68: 659.

Wilkinson, C. F., and Anderson, H. M. (1987). *Land and Resource Planning in the National Forests.* Washington, D.C., Island Press.

Wondolleck, J. M., and Yaffee, S. L. (2000). *Making Collaboration Work: Lessons from Innovation in Natural Resource Management.* Washington, D.C., Island Press.

Yaffee, S. L., and Wondolleck, J. M. (2003). Collaborative Ecosystem Planning Processes in the United States: Evolution and Challenges. *Environments* 31(2): 59–72.

Young, E., and Fricke, P. (eds) (1975). *Sea Use Planning: Fabian Tract 437.* London, UK Fabian Society.

Young, O. (2006). Vertical Interplay Among Scale-dependent Environmental and Resource Regimes. *Ecology and Society* 11(1): 27.

Zahariadis, N. and Allen, C. (1995). Ideas, Networks, and Policy Streams: Privatization in Britain and Germany. *Policy Studies Review* 14: 71–98.

Zahniser, H. (1961). Wilderness Forever. In D. Brower (ed.), *Wilderness: America's Living Heritage.* San Francisco, Sierra Club.

Zivnuska, J. A. (1961). The Multiple Problems of Multiple Use. *Journal of Forestry* 59(8): 555–560.

Zivnuska, J. A. (1963). Guest Editorial. Forestry: A Profession or a Field of Work? *Journal of Forestry* 61(5): 339–340.

INDEX

For Product Safety Concerns and Information please contact our EU representative GPSR@taylorandfrancis.com
Taylor & Francis Verlag GmbH, Kaufingerstraße 24, 80331 München, Germany

www.ingramcontent.com/pod-product-compliance
Ingram Content Group UK Ltd.
Pitfield, Milton Keynes, MK11 3LW, UK
UKHW022130190926
475702UK00013B/1724

* 9 7 8 0 8 1 5 3 9 5 3 4 8 *